Witness for Freedom

C. PETER RIPLEY,

editor

COEDITORS

Roy E. Finkenbine

Michael F. Hembree

Donald Yacovone

Witness for

AFRICAN

AMERICAN

VOICES

ON RACE,

SLAVERY, AND

EMANCIPATION

Freedom

The University of

North Carolina Press

Chapel Hill & London

The publication of this work was made possible in part through a grant from the Division of Research Programs of the National Endowment for the Humanities, an independent federal agency whose mission is to award grants to support education, scholarship, media programming, libraries, and museums, in order to bring the results of cultural activities to a broad, general public.

Library of Congress Cataloging-in-Publication Data

Witness for freedom : African American voices on race, slavery, and emancipation / C. Peter Ripley, editor; coeditors, Roy E. Finkenbine, Michael F. Hembree, Donald Yacovone.

    p.   cm.

Includes bibliographical references (p.   ) and index.

ISBN-13: 978-0-8078-2072-8 (cloth : alk. paper).

ISBN-10: 0-8078-2072-5 (cloth : alk. paper).

ISBN-13: 978-0-8078-4404-5 (pbk. : alk. paper)

ISBN-10: 0-8078-4404-7 (pbk. : alk. paper)

1. Slavery—United States—Anti-slavery movements—Sources.   2. Abolitionists—United States—History—19th century—Sources.   3. Afro-Americans—History—To 1863—Sources.   I. Ripley, C. Peter, 1941–

E449.W84   1993

973.7′114—dc20   92-21591

                    CIP

THIS BOOK WAS DIGITALLY MANUFACTURED.

For the gang at the B A P *Café*

CONTENTS

ILLUSTRATIONS

ACKNOWLEDGMENTS

Witness for Freedom is a cooperative effort with Roy E. Finkenbine, Michael F. Hembree, and Donald Yacovone, who worked their way through the five-volume series, *The Black Abolitionist Papers*, to compile a body of documents that tells the black abolitionists' story. The National Historical Publications and Records Commission, the National Endowment for the Humanities, the L. J. and Mary Skaggs Foundation, and The Florida State University provided support, for which we are grateful.

We wish to acknowledge the manuscript curators, repository directors, and librarians who allowed us to publish documents from their collections. Joe M. Richardson, Philip Morgan, Larry Powell, Clarence Mohr, R. Hal Williams, and Jerome Stern helped us refine the idea for *Witness for Freedom*.

As always, John, Mary Ann, Jerry, Joe, Phil, Barbara, Hal, Bob, and Catfish did their part. Thanks.

C. P. R.
Tallahassee, Florida
February 1992

EDITORIAL STATEMENT

The Black Abolitionist Papers Project began in 1976 with the mission to collect and publish the documentary record of African Americans involved in the movement to end slavery in the United States. The project originated from an understanding that broad spans of African American history have eluded scholarly attention because the necessary research materials are not readily available. Except for several small manuscript collections of better-known black leaders (usually those who continued their careers after emancipation), the personal papers, business records, speeches, essays, letters, and other documentary sources of black abolitionists have not survived or been systematically identified and made available to scholars. The same holds true for antebellum black newspapers.

During its first phase, the Black Abolitionist Papers Project conducted an international search for documents. A four-year collection process took the project to thousands of manuscript collections and newspapers in England, Scotland, Ireland, and Canada as well as in the United States. This effort netted nearly 14,000 letters, speeches, essays, pamphlets, and newspaper editorials from over 200 libraries and 110 newspapers. What resulted is the documentary record of hundreds of black men and women and their efforts to end American slavery.

The Black Abolitionist Papers were microfilmed during the second phase of the project. The microfilmed edition includes all the primary documents gathered during the collection phase on seventeen reels of film with a published guide and index (New York, N.Y.: Microfilming Corporation of America, 1981–83; Ann Arbor, Mich.: University Microfilms International, 1984–   ). The guide contains a detailed description of the collection procedures.

The third and final phase of the project was the publication of a five-volume series of edited and annotated representative documents in *The Black Abolitionist Papers* (Chapel Hill, N.C., 1985–92). The five volumes treat the history of African American involvement in an international reform movement that spanned thirty-five years in the United States, the British

Isles, and Canada. But they also reveal the full sweep of African American life and culture in antebellum America.

The selection of documents for the published series was guided by a thorough reading of the entire collection. The African American voices in those documents expressed the major themes and elements of black abolitionism—the events, ideas, individuals, goals, and organizations that made up the movement and the life and times of those who participated in it. We chose documents that best represented African American thought and action during the years of antislavery struggle.

The documents led us to another principle that governed the selection process. Antislavery was a commanding force in the antebellum black community, but it cannot be separated from the remainder of African American life and culture during those years—race relations in the free states, black churches and schools in northern cities, black family life, Caribbean immigration, African missionary work, fugitive slave settlements in Canada, and a host of other personal, public, and national matters. Ending slavery was the most urgent force in a vigorous African American society, informing and shaping every part of the black community, and we selected documents that reflected this crowded agenda.

Several additional considerations influenced the selection of documents. The guiding principle was to publish documents that fairly represent the goals, ideas, and actions of black abolitionists and, to a lesser extent, that reveal their personal concerns. We included documents by as many black abolitionists as possible and avoided the temptation to rely on the eloquent statements of a few polished professionals. We sought to document immediate antislavery objectives (often dictated by local needs and issues) as well as broad, international goals. The published volumes fairly reflect the variety of document types—letters (both public and private), essays, autobiographical narratives, impromptu remarks, formal speeches, circulars, resolutions, and debates—found in the microfilmed collection.

The documents chosen for publication in *The Black Abolitionist Papers* represent less than a tenth of the entire collection. Given their limited number, the documents alone could only hint at the full dimensions of this complex story. The written history in the volumes—the introductions and annotations—highlight the documents' key elements and themes. In the five-volume collection, each document is introduced by a headnote, which provides a historical context that enhances the reader's understanding of the document and related black abolitionist activities. Notes identify a variety of items that appear within the documents, such as people, places, events, organizations, institutions, laws, and legal decisions. We devoted more space to subjects on which there was little or no readily available information, particularly black individuals and significant events and institutions in the black community.

The axiom that "less is better" governed the project's transcription of published documents. Our goal was to present the documents in a form as close to the original as possible while making them serviceable for the reader. In letters, the following items were uniformly and silently located regardless of where they appear in the original: place and date, recipient's name and address, salutation, closing, signature, marginal notes, and post-scripts. In manuscript documents, idiosyncratic spelling, underlining, and quotation marks were retained. Words that were crossed through in the original were also retained.

The project adopted the following principles for transcribing documents found in published sources (newspapers, pamphlets, annual reports, and other nineteenth-century printed material): redundant punctuation was eliminated; quotation marks were converted to modern usage; obvious mis-spellings and printer's errors were corrected; printer's brackets were con-verted to parentheses; and audience reaction within a speech was treated as a separate sentence with parentheses, for example, (Hear, hear.). We let stand certain nineteenth-century printing conventions such as setting names or addresses in capital or italic letters in order to maintain the visual character of the document. The insertion of three asterisks into the text of a document signals that material was deleted from the document. The intru-sive *sic* was rarely used. Brackets were used in their traditional fashion: to enclose information that we added and to indicate our inability to transcribe words or phrases with certainty.

Our transcription guidelines for manuscript documents differed slightly from those used for printed sources. We took greater editorial liberties with documents from printed sources because they seldom came to us directly from a black abolitionist's hand. Speeches and letters sent to newspapers were apt to pass through the hands of an editor, a publisher, and a typesetter, all of whom might make errors. These guidelines were influenced by the availability of all the documents in their original form in the microfilmed edition.

WITNESS FOR FREEDOM

With the exception of documents 1, 3, 4, 38, 60, 65, and 75, all the documents in *Witness for Freedom* are drawn from *The Black Abolitionist Papers* volumes, where they appear with introductory essays and full annotation. Readers who seek additional information should consult *The Black Abolitionist Papers* volumes. Following each document in this work, the original source is given, as well as a citation to the volume and page numbers where the document appears in *The Black Abolitionist Papers* (abbreviated as *BAP*). A brief chronology of major events follows the Editorial Statement. A longer, footnoted treatment of the introduction to *Witness for Freedom* appears in volume 3 of *BAP*. The glossary has brief descriptions of the people, events, organizations, laws, and legal decisions mentioned in these documents. Our debts to scholars whose work contributed to this volume are acknowledged in the bibliographical essay, as well as in the appropriate volumes of *BAP*.

CHRONOLOGY

1619   First African slaves brought to North America.

1780s Slavery abolished in most northern states; slave manumissions in the South increase; free black communities emerge.

1808   Importation of slaves banned by Congress.

1816   American Colonization Society founded.

1820   Missouri Compromise limits expansion of slavery.

1822   Denmark Vesey conspiracy in South Carolina.

1826   Massachusetts General Colored Association founded by David Walker.

1827   Slavery abolished in New York State.

Freedom's Journal (New York, N.Y.), the first African American newspaper, founded by John B. Russwurm and Samuel E. Cornish.

1829   Appeal published by David Walker.

Antiblack riots in Cincinnati prompt African American immigration to Upper Canada.

1830   African American population surpasses 2.3 million (300,000 free, 2,000,000 slave), about 18 percent of the total population.

The black national convention movement begins with meeting in Philadelphia.

1831   Liberator (Boston, Mass.) founded by William Lloyd Garrison.

Nat Turner slave insurrection in Virginia prompts southern states to enact stricter slave codes and antiabolition laws.

1832   New England Anti-Slavery Society founded.

Thoughts on African Colonization published by William Lloyd Garrison.

1833   American Anti-Slavery Society founded.

1834   Slavery abolished in the British Empire; African Americans commemorate the Emancipation Act with annual First of August celebrations.

1835   American Moral Reform Society founded at the black national convention in Philadelphia.

1836   New York Committee of Vigilance founded.

"Gag rule," restricting congressional discussion of the slavery issue, passed by Congress.

1837 Elijah Lovejoy, abolitionist newspaper editor, murdered in Alton, Illinois.

Colored American (New York, N.Y.) founded by Samuel E. Cornish.

New York Political Association founded to promote black suffrage.

1838 Campaign begins for African American voting rights in Pennsylvania.

1839 *Amistad* slave ship mutiny.

Liberty party, the first antislavery political party, founded.

1840 African American population increases to more than 2.8 million (385,000 free, 2,480,000 slave), about 16 percent of the total population.

American Anti-Slavery Society schism over strategy, tactics, and principles.

American and Foreign Anti-Slavery Society founded.

Black state convention movement begins with meeting in Albany, New York.

1841 Union Missionary Society, forerunner of the American Missionary Association, founded by African American clergymen.

Creole slave ship incident.

1842 White mob violence against northern African American communities in the 1830s and 1840s culminates with antiblack riots in Philadelphia.

Prigg v. *Pennsylvania* overturns personal liberty laws and threatens fugitive slaves.

Northern Star and Freeman's Advocate (Albany, N.Y.) founded by Stephen A. Myers.

Palladium of Liberty (Cincinnati, Ohio) founded by David Jenkins.

1843 Henry Highland Garnet calls for slave violence at the black national convention in Buffalo, New York.

Mystery (Pittsburgh, Pa.) founded by Martin R. Delany.

1844 Boston school integration campaign begins.

1845 "Gag rule" rescinded by Congress.

Narrative of the Life of Frederick Douglass, the first of three autobiographies, published by Frederick Douglass.

Texas admitted to the Union as a slave state.

1846 Mexican War begins.

1847 *Ram's Horn* (New York, N.Y.) founded by Willis A. Hodges and Thomas Van Rensellaer.

North Star (Rochester, N.Y.) founded by Frederick Douglass.

1848 Treaty of Guadalupe Hidalgo ends Mexican War; western territories opened to slavery.

1849 *Impartial Citizen* (Syracuse, N.Y.) founded by Samuel Ringgold Ward.

1850 The African American population exceeds 3.6 million (400,000 free, 3,200,000 slave), about 15.7 percent of the total population.

Compromise of 1850, including enactment of the Fugitive Slave Law, prompts protest and mass immigration to Canada.

1851 *Voice of the Fugitive* (Windsor, Canada West) founded by Henry Bibb.

Christiana (Pa.) slave riot.

Shadrach rescue in Boston.

Jerry rescue in Syracuse, New York.

1852 *Uncle Tom's Cabin* published by Harriet Beecher Stowe.

Condition, Elevation, Emigration and Destiny of the Colored People of the United States published by Martin R. Delany.

1853 *Clotel*, the first African American novel, published by William Wells Brown.

National Council of the Colored People, the first national black organization, founded at the black national convention in Rochester, New York.

Provincial Freeman (Toronto, Canada West) founded by Samuel Ringgold Ward.

Aliened American (Cleveland, Ohio) founded by William H. Day.

1854 First of three biannual national emigration conventions held in Cleveland, Ohio.

Kansas-Nebraska Act, passed by Congress, prompts emergence of Republican party.

Anthony Burns rescue attempt in Boston.

1855 *My Bondage and My Freedom* published by Frederick Douglass.

Colored Patriots of the American Revolution published by
William C. Nell.

Legal Rights Association founded in New York City to challenge
discrimination.

1857   *Dred Scott* v. *Sanford* denies African American citizenship.

1858   Wellington-Oberlin (Ohio) rescue.

Niger Valley Exploring Party organized by Martin R. Delany.

African Civilization Society founded by Henry Highland Garnet.

1859   Harpers Ferry raid.

Weekly Anglo-African and *Anglo-African Magazine* (New York,
N.Y.) founded by Thomas Hamilton.

1860   The African American population surpasses 4.4 million (488,000
free, 3,950,000 slave), about 14.1 percent of the total
population.

Abraham Lincoln elected president.

1861   Civil War begins with attack on Fort Sumter.

Lincoln administration rejects enlistment of African American
soldiers.

1862   *Pacific Appeal* (San Francisco, Calif.) founded by Peter Anderson
and Philip A. Bell.

Confiscation Acts passed by Congress.

First unofficial black Union regiments organized in Kansas,
Louisiana, and South Carolina.

1863   Emancipation Proclamation issued.

Federal government authorizes formation of black Union
regiments; Massachusetts Fifty-fourth Regiment organized;
African American regiments involved in battles at Port Hudson,
Milliken's Bend, and Fort Wagner.

Draft riots in New York City result in mob violence against the
city's African American community.

1864   National Equal Rights League founded at black national
convention in Syracuse, New York.

1865   *Elevator* (San Francisco, Calif.) founded by Philip A. Bell.

Bureau of Refugees, Freedmen, and Abandoned Lands founded.

Civil War ends with Confederate surrender at Appomattox Court
House; Lincoln assassinated.

Thirteenth Amendment abolishing slavery ratified.

Witness for Freedom

INTRODUCTION

THE RISE OF BLACK ABOLITIONISM

On a brisk December morning in 1833, sixty-two reformers from eleven northern states gathered in Philadelphia to transform the American antislavery movement. Ignoring threats of violence, they opened their proceedings at Adelphi Hall to a skeptical public and an unfriendly press. The founding convention of the American Anti-Slavery Society (AASS) brought together Quakers, Protestant clergymen, and distinguished reformers, including three blacks: Robert Purvis, a handsome, urbane young Philadelphian who, despite his light complexion, proudly identified himself as an African American; James G. Barbadoes, a Boston clothier and barber; and James McCrummill, a barber and dentist, who provided accommodations for the tempestuous young editor of the Boston *Liberator*, William Lloyd Garrison. After the first day-long session, Garrison retired to McCrummill's comfortable Philadelphia home a few blocks away on Third Street. With an oil lamp burning through the night, he worked intently on a draft of the society's Declaration of Sentiments. The delegates debated the draft during the following sessions, and on 6 December, the final day of the convention, they came forward to sign the document, just as the Founding Fathers had signed the Declaration of Independence in Philadelphia fifty-seven years before.

The AASS Declaration of Sentiments represented an interracial consensus on goals and methods of the antislavery movement. It called for an immediate end to slavery without compensation for slave owners and rejected violence and the use of force, trusting instead in "the overthrow of prejudice by the power of love—and the abolition of slavery by the spirit of repentance." The declaration repudiated the colonization movement's plan to remove all free blacks to Africa as "delusive, cruel and dangerous."

By addressing the issues of prejudice, slavery, and colonization, the Declaration of Sentiments gave voice to the primary concerns of African Americans. Freeing the two million slaves and ending the racism that contaminated American society were long-sought goals, but colonization had been the most pressing concern of free blacks throughout the decade preceding the Philadelphia convocation.

The colonization movement was a mix of diverse interests that came together to settle free blacks and newly emancipated slaves in Africa. Most colonizationists believed that free blacks endangered American society. They accepted the popular myth that blacks lacked the moral character and ability to become useful citizens. Even whites who considered slavery evil reasoned that sending blacks to a colony in Africa would ease white anxieties and thereby encourage manumissions, and at the same time provide free blacks with a refuge from American oppression. Most white abolitionists and antislavery organizations at the time supported colonization. These gradual abolitionists theorized that emancipation would be achieved, gradually and peacefully, through the courts, individual manumissions, and the political system. Removing freed blacks would hasten that process, they believed. Some southern slaveholders shared these sentiments, but most supported colonization for very different reasons. They feared that the presence of emancipated slaves would threaten slavery and hoped to purge the nation of free blacks before they "whisper[ed] liberty in the ears of the oppressed."

The movement emerged after the American Colonization Society (ACS) —the leading proponent of free black repatriation to the African continent— was established in 1816. Before long the ACS boasted of support from several Protestant denominations, reform clergy, gradualist antislavery societies, fourteen state legislatures, and a host of prominent political figures, including Henry Clay, James Madison, James Monroe, and Daniel Webster. The ACS hoped its considerable political influence would persuade the federal government to finance its newly created Liberian colony on the West African coast. Within a decade, the ACS had acquired robust leadership, broad support, and a full treasury devoted to recruiting black settlers and chartering ships to transport them to Liberia.

Free blacks—particularly in the northern states—rejected colonization as a threat to their future on the American continent. "Here we were born, and here we will die," promised a defiant New York City group. Philadelphia blacks took the lead, holding four mass meetings between 1817 and 1819 to condemn colonization. Their angry protests set the tone for the struggle that followed.

By the late 1820s, the colonization question preoccupied northern black leaders. *Freedom's Journal*, the nation's first black newspaper, opened its columns to critics of colonization. David Walker—Boston's aggressive black abolitionist whose call for slave resistance shocked northern anti-slavery moderates and southern slaveholders alike—proclaimed that "Our Wretchedness [is] in Consequence of the Colonizing Plan." During the early 1830s, several black national conventions denounced the ACS, claiming that its delegates were "aggrieved by its very existence." Baltimore blacks, led by William Watkins, published anticolonization essays, confronted colonizationist speakers at public meetings, and intimidated potential emigrants so successfully that the colonizationists abandoned the Chesapeake area as a field of labor.

From Baltimore to Boston, free black communities rallied against what William C. Nell described as "the hydra-headed monster." In meeting halls and churches across the North, angry blacks gathered to state their case against an African return by affirming their American identity. Resentful that their many contributions to the new Republic were so easily forgotten, they reminded whites that blacks had helped push back the wilderness and had fought for the revolutionary cause. Claiming their rights as "countrymen and fellow-citizens," they resolved not to be removed.

But despite patriotic statements and a vigorous public campaign against colonization, many African Americans feared that emigration might be forced on them. Watching the federal government remove southern Native Americans to new lands in the West, they feared the worst for themselves each time the ACS pushed for federal funds to finance the Liberian settlement. An elderly black woman spoke for the rising black abolitionist movement: "It was a very wicked thing for them to bring us here in the way they did, but it would be more wicked to send us back."

In their critique of the colonization movement, African American leaders stripped away the facade of philanthropy, revealing that the movement had no antislavery goals or genuine concern for free blacks. They focused on colonization's role in bolstering slavery and intensifying racial prejudice. For them, the colonizationists' incessant references to black inferiority tended "to justify the slaveholder in his crime, and increase already existing oppression," and the restrictive black laws combined with the colonization appeal to intimidate free blacks into seeking sanctuary in Africa. Black leaders considered colonization to be a "direct road to perpetuate slavery" and regarded leaving the country as nothing less than abandoning the slave. They insisted that remaining at home and demonstrating African American capacity for social and economic improvement would discredit charges of racial inferiority and undermine slavery. For free blacks, affirming their citizenship, opposing colonization, and creating a place for themselves in American society were antislavery acts.

An organized black abolitionist movement grew out of the battle against colonization. Anticolonization efforts showed what careful organization and continued protest could accomplish. During the mid-1820s, leaders in the struggle against the ACS in Boston, New Haven, Philadelphia, Baltimore, and other free black communities banded together in local abolitionist groups to advance broad and ambitious reform goals, including emancipation and equality.

Newly organized and growing in confidence, African Americans set out to discredit colonization among white abolitionists and to convince them that an immediate end to slavery was the only true antislavery course. African American protests against colonization and calls for immediate emancipation came at an opportune moment. During the 1820s, the American antislavery movement was transformed by a complex set of intellectual, social, and economic forces. By 1830, black abolitionism joined with these forces to prepare the ground for the rise of immediate abolition.

The conversion of William Lloyd Garrison proved to be enormously important in the shift of the American antislavery movement to the black abolitionist viewpoint. Garrison, who would become America's best-known and most influential white abolitionist, began his career committed to colonization and the gradual demise of slavery, but as he worked with blacks in Baltimore and Philadelphia during the 1820s, he abandoned colonization, embraced racial equality, and advocated immediate emancipation.

Grateful for their new ally, African Americans did all they could for the energetic and irascible Garrison. Without their support, his *Liberator* would not have survived its crucial early years; blacks underwrote the printing costs for the first issue in 1830, enlisted subscribers, served as agents in most northern cities, purchased the bulk of its advertising, organized the Colored Liberator Aiding Association to coordinate the paper's fund-raising efforts, and contributed hundreds of essays and letters to its columns. A grateful Garrison acknowledged their efforts in 1834 when he wrote that the *Liberator* "belongs especially to the people of color—it is their organ."

Together with Garrison and a small but earnest band of white reformers, black abolitionists redirected the American antislavery movement. Encouraged by Garrison's example, and informed about colonization by blacks, a growing number of white abolitionists adopted immediatist beliefs, reject-

ANTI-COLONIZATION

AND

Woman's Rights Ticket.

Members to State Council.

Robert Purvis,
Wm. Whipper, Columbia, Pa.
Samuel Van Brakle,
Benjamin Clark, York, Pa.
Alphonso M. Sumner,
James McCrummill.
J. J. Gould Bias,
Francis A. Duterte,
Edward Bennet, Harrisburg, Pa.
David B. Bowser,
Rev. Lewis Woodson, Pittsburg, Pa.
Rev. A. R. Green, Pittsburg, Pa.
John C. Vashon, Pittsburg, Pa.
Samuel Williams,
James C. Wilson, M. D.
Benjamin D. Moore,
Joseph Gardner, Reading, Pa.
Rev. William Jackson, West Phila.
Prof. Charles L. Reason,
Rev. Joseph Clinton.

Anti-Colonization and Woman's Rights ticket. From Langston Hughes,
Milton Meltzer, and C. Eric Lincoln, eds., A Pictorial History of Blackamericans,
5th rev. ed. (New York, 1973).

ing what Garrison now called the "pernicious doctrine of *gradual* emancipation." They demanded a quick end to slavery, supported racial equality, and repudiated colonization. Blacks and whites came together in 1833 to organize the American Anti-Slavery Society and within three years established five hundred auxiliaries across the North.

By the mid-1830s, black abolitionists could look to the recent past with satisfaction and to the future with optimism. They had infused immediate abolition—the most important reform movement in American history—with thoughtful analysis and new ambitions. By discrediting the ACS, converting Garrison and other key American abolitionists to immediatism, and insuring the success of the *Liberator*, they had played a major role in the antislavery movement. Years later, while reflecting on the antislavery crusade, James McCune Smith, the Scottish-trained physician whose sharp insights influenced black abolitionism for three decades, explained that white enthusiasm for immediatism had been "nurtured into warmth, clothed with lustre and shot up into mid air by the hot sympathies of colored men's bosoms."

At the same time, African Americans were influenced by their collaboration with Garrison and other white reformers. Black leaders were drawn closer to the theories of moral reform, a body of ideas and principles usually associated with the broader antebellum reform movement and Garrisonian abolitionism. Moral reformers believed in human progress and the possibility of perfecting society by correcting individual behavior. They promoted honest labor, self-discipline, piety, and sobriety. Many reformers, as pacifists, advocated nonviolence and nonresistance; some repudiated all forms of force—even the power wielded by government institutions—and refused to participate in the political process. They adopted moral suasion, a belief that moral example and rational argument would persuade the public to abandon vice and corruption and create a more virtuous society.

Lofty ideas about improving man and society provided black leaders with the philosophical framework for promoting uplift within the African American community. They reasoned that moral reform would elevate the race, and racial improvement would, in time, satisfy white Americans that blacks were worthy of freedom and equality. Caught up in the optimism of the early days of the antislavery movement, black and white abolitionists shared a vision: as reform progressed, all evils attendant to the human condition would vanish—including slavery and prejudice.

Black abolitionists understood that the moral reform message placed an enormous antislavery obligation on the free black community. The burden of proof, wrote Samuel E. Cornish, the editor of the *Colored American*, rested on free blacks: "It is for us to convince the world by uniform propriety of conduct, industry, and economy, that we are worthy of esteem and patronage." Cornish argued that the fate of every slave rested upon the actions of free blacks—"On our conduct in a great measure, their salvation depends."

The moral reform movement animated African American communities throughout the North and sparked an unprecedented level of organizational activity. Blacks established hundreds of organizations and institutions dedicated to self-improvement and cultural enrichment: mutual aid societies, churches, schools, literary societies, library companies, debating clubs, and temperance organizations. These new institutions drew large numbers of African Americans into civic activities, helped define leadership, created a sense of unity and purpose in the black community, and prepared African Americans for the continuing struggle for racial equality.

Moral reform relied upon sincere arguments and the power of persuasion to achieve its goals. Delegates at the 1832 black national convention concluded that racial elevation was best achieved "by *moral suasion alone.*" Black leaders set aside more aggressive and confrontational tactics during the 1830s. Guided by the principle of moral suasion and anxious to cooperate with white reformers, they used public meetings, speeches, published tracts and pamphlets, correspondence to sympathetic individuals, and appeals in the reform press to advance their goals.

But when black abolitionists began to examine the results of moral reform and moral suasion in the late 1830s and early 1840s, they concluded that the battle for emancipation and equality needed new strategies and tactics. Their situation was worsening, not improving, and hard evidence in black life supported that claim. Slavery continued to thrive, race relations had not improved, race riots had not abated, blacks had lost voting rights instead of gaining them, and the few occupations open to them were rapidly being given over to new immigrants. More threatening yet, the kidnapping of fugitive slaves, free blacks, children, and especially the poor dramatically increased in black communities after Texas independence opened up a new market for slaves.

Escalating racial violence in the 1830s mocked moral reform and underscored its limitations. Rioting whites beat and abused African Americans and destroyed their property, especially symbols of black success such as churches, businesses, the homes of the elite, and meeting places for moral reform organizations. After the vicious Philadelphia race riot of August 1842, the elegant and respected Robert Purvis wrote that the "wantonness, brutality and murderous spirit" of the mob had convinced him of his race's "utter and complete nothingness in public estimation."

Disillusioned African Americans rethought the efficacy of moral reform during the early 1840s. There was less talk about hard work, thrift, temperance, cultivation of the mind, and proper decorum and more calls for action—"We need more radicalism among us," insisted the discouraged black Garrisonian Charles L. Remond. He warned African Americans that they were "too indefinite in views and sentiments—too slow in movements"; he urged them to fight for their rights, regardless of the cost. More and more, African American leaders came to share the view that "physical and political efforts are the only methods left for us to adopt."

BLACK ABOLITIONISTS AND THE ANTISLAVERY MOVEMENT

Abolitionists regarded northern public opinion as the key to a successful campaign against slavery. In this forum, abolitionists competed with proslavery apologists who cast African bondage in the soft light of paternalism. Slavery's defenders offered soothing assurances that the institution civilized and Christianized Africans, who were contented, well cared for, kindly treated, and best left to southern control. Such comforting thoughts gained wide acceptance in the North during the 1830s.

In the debate over slavery, African American voices established the credibility of the antislavery argument. Black abolitionists, particularly fugitive slaves, challenged proslavery claims with an authority hard-earned through personal experience. White antislavery leaders soon discovered that black lecturers were more convincing than white ones, and that fugitive slaves were the most convincing of all. An agent for the Massachusetts Anti-Slavery Society informed Garrison in 1841 that "the public have itching ears to hear a colored man speak, and particularly a *slave*." Nothing moved antislavery audiences like a "true narrative fallen from the lips of a veritable fugitive." When the American Anti-Slavery Society hired Charles L. Remond as its first black lecturing agent in 1838, his "singular eloquence" established a place for black abolitionists at the antislavery podium.

Antislavery societies rushed African American speakers into the field, preferring "one who has felt in his own person the evils of Slavery, and with the strong voice of experience can tell of its horrors." By the mid-1840s, Frederick Douglass, Samuel R. Ward, and dozens of other former slaves were lecturing throughout the North. Henry Bibb, a spirited lecturer with a dramatic slave past, was so swamped with requests to speak that he reported, "If I had a thousand tongues, I could find useful employment for them all." Not all blacks had the eloquence of Bibb, Douglass, or Remond, but a fugitive's halting, emotional account of slavery could just as effectively sway northern public opinion.

African American lecturers took their message wherever they could find an audience—from local antislavery gatherings to national reform conventions; from frontier villages to European capitals. When recounting their personal experiences, former slaves used a rich and emotion-laden variety of methods to convince their listeners of slavery's inhumanity. They displayed instruments of domination—branding irons and bullwhips. Some reenacted scenes from their escapes. Henry "Box" Brown exhibited the crate he used to ship himself out of Virginia slavery, and William Wells Brown toured with a panoramic series of paintings depicting his years in bondage.

Published slave autobiographies took the antislavery message from the lecture halls into the homes of white Americans. Subjects too delicate or too complex for public discussion were fully explored in the narratives. The slaves' own poignant, written stories so discredited proslavery arguments that the antislavery movement considered the narratives to be the "infallible means of abolitionizing the free states." By articulating "the *victim's account*" of slavery, the narratives proved, as J. W. C. Pennington asserted, that even "the mildest form of slavery . . . is comparatively the worst form." Slave narratives reached thousands of readers in the United States and abroad. Solomon Northup's compelling *Twelve Years a Slave* (1853) sold twenty-seven thousand copies in two years. Douglass's immensely popular *Narrative* (1845), published in the United States and Europe, eventually sold over thirty thousand copies.

Through lecture tours and slave narratives, black abolitionists challenged proslavery propaganda, undermined notions of racial inferiority, and established their central role in the antislavery movement. Their passion and militancy refuted the myth of the contented slave, and their stories of slavery's brutal conditions—the toil, deprivation, and physical violence—disabused white audiences of the image of the kind master. A shocked northern public heard accounts of torture, rape, forced separation of slave families, and the moral depravity that corrupted everyone associated with slavery.

While black abolitionism shaped the antislavery movement and influenced public opinion, it also touched every aspect of free black life and culture. Abolitionism strengthened the bond between free black and slave, infused the African American community with a new sense of purpose, drew participants from across social and economic lines, and shaped a new group of community leaders—the men and women, many of them former slaves, who became professional abolitionists.

Abolitionism gave rise to new organizations and institutions and transformed existing ones. No institution reflected this change more clearly than the black church. At the national level, black denominations were often circumspect on the slavery issue, especially those with churches in the South. But individual northern congregations were the hub of community reform activity. Churches served as assembly halls for antislavery and reform organizations, classrooms for black students, shelters for fugitive slaves, and gathering places for public protests. Black clergymen brought their abolitionism to the pulpit; ignoring threats of white mob violence and warnings against "preaching politics on the Sabbath," they made antislavery a central part of their gospel mandate.

For black abolitionists, ending slavery was only one component of the larger struggle to reform America. African Americans regarded prejudice as the most formidable obstacle to racial progress and worried that white abolitionists did not bring the same urgency to the problem of racism in the North as they did to slavery in the South. James McCune Smith saw it clearly: "While abolitionists have preached immediate Emancipation for the slave States, they have tolerated gradual Emancipation in the free States." Too many white allies appeared hesitant to acknowledge the inseparable, mutually reinforcing relationship between slavery and prejudice, causing black clergyman Theodore S. Wright to remark that his white colleagues "overlooked the giant sin of prejudice . . . at once the parent and the offspring of slavery."

The divergence of antislavery goals that separated black and white abolitionists was not the only sign of trouble within the movement. Throughout the 1830s, black abolitionists grew more aware of racism within the antislavery ranks and criticized white abolitionists for their behavior and attitudes. Samuel Ringgold Ward, whose commanding physical presence riveted audiences, chided abolitionists "who love the colored man at a distance." Pittsburgh black nationalist Martin R. Delany chafed at the patronizing attitude of white reformers who "presumed to *think* for, dictate to, and *know* better what suited colored people, than they know for themselves." Frederick Douglass detested the arrogance of his white associates when they advised him to retain "a little of the plantation speech" in his lectures and avoid any analysis of slavery; "Give us the facts," they instructed, "we will take care of the philosophy." Perhaps most galling of all, blacks concluded that white prejudice, paternalism, and presumptuousness kept blacks from leadership positions within the antislavery movement. African Americans were seldom in charge, despite conspicuous involvement in the AASS and its auxiliaries as fund-raisers, lecturers, and organizers. For one reader of the *Colored American*, white abolitionist attitudes stifled free blacks: "OUR FRIENDS," he lamented, "HINDER OUR IMPROVEMENT."

When the antislavery crusade began to divide in the late 1830s, blacks grew alarmed that an internal struggle over doctrine and tactics would wreck the movement. Some white abolitionists, uneasy with Garrison's radicalism, left the AASS to form the American and Foreign Anti-Slavery Society (AFASS) in 1840. Others seeking to address the issue of slavery through the political process founded the Liberty party. Black abolitionists, impatient with the schism, criticized their colleagues for fighting over irrelevant issues, for weakening the movement with their squabbling, and for having "forgotten the poor, down-trodden slave." One black abolitionist reminded the competing factions that such issues as pacifism, women's rights, and theological disagreements were *"neither parts, nor parcel of that great and holy cause"* and insisted that white abolitionists again make slavery "the paramount question."

When the irreparable schism forced blacks to choose sides, a majority found the Garrisonian armor "too cumbersome to buckle on." They left their oldest ally in favor of a more practical abolitionism—one that called for political action, voting rights, and direct involvement in antislavery political parties. Uncertain if white abolitionists still shared their commitment to racial equality and their concern for the slave, black leaders sought greater autonomy and the independence to redirect the movement toward black abolitionist goals.

BLACK ABOLITIONIST INDEPENDENCE IN
THE ANTISLAVERY MOVEMENT

Independence was the dominant theme of black abolitionism in the 1840s. Many blacks concluded that their deference to white reform leadership in the 1830s had been costly to racial pride and identity. "To be dependent is to be degraded," Frederick Douglass explained; "men may pity us, but they cannot respect us." For Douglass, independence created an "essential condition of respectability" that white patronage, however sympathetic, could not provide.

The call for independence in the 1840s signaled the emergence of two abolitionisms. Black and white abolitionists shared some common assumptions about slavery and freedom; both drew on evangelical theology, the idea of universal reform, and an unshakable belief in human progress. But white abolitionism was based mainly on abstract moral principles, while blacks tended to define slavery and freedom in more concrete experiential terms. Black abolitionism was shaped by daily experiences in a racist society. While most white reformers equated abolitionism primarily with freedom for those held in bondage in the South, northern blacks conceived of antislavery as a broader struggle against racial oppression. They sought independence to depart from the narrower focus of white abolitionists and to pursue the entire range of issues that they considered integral to abolitionism, encompassing all of the political, economic, and social injustices that emanated from racism. Black abolitionism, in James McCune Smith's words, extended "from the mere act of riding in public conveyances to the liberation of every slave."

Black abolitionism possessed a seamless quality, fusing a variety of concerns, which gave the movement a practical and intellectual continuity that few white reformers appreciated. A black temperance gathering could adjourn and immediately reconvene as an antislavery meeting with no change in tenor or participants. A black lecturer could use an antislavery tour to solicit donations for a fledgling black newspaper, a church building fund, or an African mission. A black vigilance committee, while aiding fugitive slaves, could also organize a petition campaign for black voting rights. The range and continuity of these activities helped broaden the meaning of black abolitionism to include much of northern black life, institutions, and culture.

A new generation of African American leaders came forward during the 1840s to arouse the aspirations for independence. Frederick Douglass, William Wells Brown, Martin R. Delany, Henry Highland Garnet, Samuel Ringgold Ward, Jermain W. Loguen, James McCune Smith, and others filled the void created by the death or weariness of older black abolitionists. More than years separated the generations. Early leaders tended to be members of the freeborn elite who were educated and well situated in trades or professions, with homes and businesses in Boston, Philadelphia, New York City, and other established communities. Many of the younger black abolitionists came to the movement by way of the plantation. Douglass, Brown, Garnet, Ward, Loguen, Pennington, Henry Bibb, Lewis and Milton Clarke, and other well-known antislavery advocates of the 1840s had experienced slavery and knew its costs.

The antislavery movement became a path to community leadership. During the early 1830s, black abolitionists were community leaders by virtue of their status as social elites. Later in the decade, a different measure applied—men like David Ruggles and Lewis Hayden earned community standing through their antislavery efforts alone. Such skilled practitioners as Douglass, William Still, and Charles L. Remond became professional abolitionists, supporting themselves through their antislavery activities—lecturing, editing black journals, writing and selling their slave narratives, and working in antislavery offices. A large number of professionals were former slaves, whose grim past gave them a distinctive place in the movement and a special influence in the community. Abolitionism also offered expanded roles for black women. Sojourner Truth, Barbara Steward, Sarah Parker Remond, Frances Ellen Watkins Harper, and Mary Ann Shadd Cary became influential authors, journalists, and antislavery lecturers during the 1850s.

In calling for independence, blacks acknowledged that the struggle against slavery and prejudice was primarily their responsibility. "It is emphatically our battle," Smith declared; "no one else can fight it for us." But independence did not necessarily imply racial separatism or forsaking cooperation with white abolitionists. Douglass carefully balanced the need for independence with his integrationist philosophy: "We must be our own representatives and advocates, not exclusively, but peculiarly—not distinct from, but in connection with our white friends." Most blacks agreed. They tempered their desire for autonomy with an understanding of the resources and influence whites brought to the antislavery movement. They maintained close relations with Gerrit Smith, Lewis and Arthur Tappan, Charles Sumner, and other prominent antislavery politicians and businessmen. They looked to the antislavery political parties to give their concerns a national political forum. Black and white reformers continued to cooperate in every important antislavery venture—traveling and working together, opening their homes to each other to share their hospitality as they shared a common sense of purpose. Black leaders might chastise their white allies and call for autonomy, then respectfully solicit white assistance. This alternating criticism and approval, defiance and deference, reflected the ongoing tension that existed between black aspirations for independence and the realities of a white-controlled antislavery movement.

Even as they maintained a commitment to interracial collaboration within the antislavery movement, blacks in the 1840s increasingly emphasized the practical and symbolic value of racially separate organizations and initiatives. Telltale signs were everywhere. They established their own reform organizations, developed a vibrant press, labored to recover their African and American past, created networks to assist fugitive slaves, organized to protect and expand their voting rights, and increased their involvement in the political process. In their quest for independence and empowerment, blacks shaped an abolitionism more racially exclusive and far more aggressive than that of the 1830s.

The African American press served as a touchstone for independence. "Too long others have spoken for us," wrote John B. Russwurm, editor of the first black newspaper, *Freedom's Journal*, in 1827. But throughout the 1830s, inadequate resources and the presence of such white antislavery journals as the *Liberator* and *Emancipator* curbed black ambitions for a press of their own. Samuel E. Cornish set the standard for the antebellum black press in 1837 with his *Colored American*. Adopting a spirited, independent editorial stance, Cornish's paper provided a forum for blacks to debate questions of racial identity, the origins and nature of racism, and the character and goals of their institutions. The *Colored American* also broached subjects too sensitive or controversial for the white reform press—discussions of racial prejudice, incompetent leadership, and disunity within the black community.

No African American editor better demonstrated the talent, initiative, and resolve required for success than Frederick Douglass. The *North Star*, founded in 1847, marked an unprecedented achievement in black journalism for its intellectual rigor, sophistication, and remarkable longevity—thirteen years as a weekly. Aware of the antislavery symbolism of his editorship, Douglass initialed his writings in the *North Star* and in 1851 renamed it

Frederick Douglass' Paper to remove doubts among skeptical whites that a fugitive slave with no formal education could become such a skilled writer. Despite editorial controversies and a long-running battle with the Garrisonians, he earned widespread recognition for his acumen and journalistic skills. Douglass's achievement represented what black abolitionists sought—an independent and influential role in shaping the antislavery movement.

African American communities affirmed their antislavery commitment and growing independence by establishing permanent vigilance committees to assist the ever-increasing number of fugitives and to combat the increased threat of kidnapping by slave traders. The New York Committee of Vigilance, founded in 1835 and led by David Ruggles, was one of the most skilled and aggressive of these groups. Blacks in Philadelphia, Boston, Detroit, and other northern cities established similar organizations in the following years. Committees disseminated information about kidnappers and slave catchers; dispensed food, clothing, money, and medicine to fugitives; provided legal services and temporary shelter; and resettled fleeing slaves in the North or provided safe passage to Canada. As vigilance committees developed, their activities expanded to include the broader goals of black abolitionism. While assisting fugitives, they also organized petition campaigns for black suffrage, opposed Jim Crow restrictions, and fought for passage of personal liberty laws.

Vigilance committees were part of a skillfully orchestrated, black-directed underground railroad network that operated across the North and the upper South. This loosely linked web of northern vigilance committees, groups of southern blacks, and a few whites (notably Quaker abolitionists) liberated some slaves and aided countless others in their escape to freedom. The underground railroad's organization and success varied according to time and place. During the 1820s and 1830s, Ohio blacks liberated slaves in Kentucky and aided runaway slaves who passed through their state. In Washington, D.C., a major slave-trading center, blacks organized an underground network of uncommon courage and design. Beginning in the mid-1830s, and continuing for over a decade, they helped free thousands of slaves from plantations in Virginia and Maryland. Working in a variety of trades and professions, these daring men and women used their good standing in white society to visit plantations and encourage slaves to escape.

As black abolitionists shaped a bolder and more autonomous movement in the 1840s and 1850s, they developed new measures to combat racism and force the issue of slavery to the center of American political life. They challenged discrimination and oppression with petition campaigns, legal action, legislative appeals, and economic pressure; when those tactics failed, they adopted more confrontational methods, including violence. The struggle for voting rights and acceptance of politics as a primary antislavery weapon embodied the new spirit of independence.

The battle for the franchise that began during the late 1830s drew African Americans away from passive Garrisonian measures and into antislavery politics. Their efforts kept voting rights before the public and forced state legislatures across the North to consider the issue. Equally important, blacks gained leadership and organizational experience that they later employed in the struggle for enfranchisement during Reconstruction.

Most African American leaders accepted the principle of political action but disagreed over which party—Whig, Liberty, Free Soil, or Republican— could best fight slavery and racial prejudice. Antislavery purists clashed with political pragmatists. Purists argued that no one in good conscience could support the Whig party, which tolerated slavery and opposed racial equality. More practical-minded abolitionists accepted compromise to achieve modest but important civil rights gains. African American allegiances shifted along the unstable ground of antebellum politics and varied from state to state but never included the Democratic party, the political symbol of slavery and racial hatred. Black votes were too few in number to affect national policy, but at the local level, where they represented a swing vote between Democrats and Whigs, they won occasional civil rights victories.

The rise of an antislavery political party, the growing influence of antislavery in national politics, and the election of abolitionists to Congress persuaded African Americans that a profound change was taking place in American political life. The Liberty party's nomination of Samuel Ringgold Ward as its vice-presidential candidate confirmed their faith in political action. The presence of black leaders at the founding meeting of the Free Soil party in 1848 represented, as Douglass remarked, "one of the most powerful blows ever dealt upon the skull of American prejudice." Black office seekers garnered few successes, but the symbolism of their candidacies fostered racial pride and sustained the independent course they had taken.

African American leaders in the 1840s called for more militant tactics to bring down the Jim Crow barriers in American society. This call to militancy permeated black abolitionism, renewing the movement and opening the way for more assertive action. Blacks organized mass protests, conducted petition campaigns, and testified before state legislative committees on behalf of civil rights. They challenged segregation on railroad cars and streetcars in nearly every northern state by sitting in seats reserved for whites, acts that sometimes brought violence and bloodshed. The transit protests were organized over the objections of Garrisonians, who opposed confrontational tactics; yet the results, earned at great personal risk, validated the new direction of black abolitionism.

Segregated schools became special targets of African American militancy during the 1840s. For many blacks, separate schools symbolized racism and its crushing effects on black aspirations. Organized boycotts yielded mixed results in New York, but they ended Jim Crow education in Massachusetts when the legislature succumbed to continued pressure in 1855 and mandated integrated education throughout the state.

As black abolitionists explored an ever-widening range of tactics, they debated the value of violence. A white Garrisonian might counsel abolitionists to return "a kiss for every blow," but blacks were inclined to justify self-defense, even armed violence, in response to racist mobs, kidnappers, and slave catchers. For African Americans, the use of force was not simply a philosophical or moral question, but a practical concern. The U.S. Supreme Court left few alternatives when *Prigg* v. *Pennsylvania* (1842) struck down state personal liberty laws, thus removing the little legal protection available to blacks accused of being runaway slaves. By the end of the 1840s, even such committed black Garrisonians as Charles L. Remond and William Wells Brown had conceded the right of force in self-defense.

Traditionally black abolitionists were cautious about the issue of slave violence. But in the 1840s, they began to sympathize openly with slave revolts and to celebrate slave rebels as cultural heroes comparable to the patriots of the American Revolution. Henry Highland Garnet's "Address to the Slaves," given at the 1843 black national convention, marked a turning point in the black antislavery appeal. It advocated massive civil disobedience and proclaimed that it was the slaves' "SOLEMN AND IMPERATIVE DUTY TO USE EVERY MEANS, BOTH MORAL, INTELLECTUAL, AND PHYSICAL, THAT PROMISES SUCCESS." At first, some black abolitionists distanced themselves from Garnet's open endorsement of slave violence, but by the 1850s, few of them denied the slaves' right to fight for their freedom.

BLACK ABOLITIONISTS, THE SLAVE POWER, AND THE FEDERAL GOVERNMENT

Northern blacks learned from their daily encounters with racism the many and subtle effects of slavery; in John Mercer Langston's words, its influence had "pervaded every crevice and cranny of society." But events of the 1840s and 1850s prompted black abolitionists to focus more closely on the relationship between slaveholding interests—the "slave power"—and the federal government. With the Mexican War and the expansion of slavery into western territories, the government appeared to assume a more active proslavery role. The federal government's complicity with the slave power became dramatically evident with the Fugitive Slave Law (1850), the Kansas-Nebraska Act (1854), and the Dred Scott decision (1857). These concessions to slaveholding interests compelled African Americans to rethink fundamental questions about abolitionism, citizenship, and racial identity. Working through the crosscurrents of hope and despair, protest and resignation, blacks debated their future as American citizens.

The enactment of the Fugitive Slave Law of 1850 provoked a widespread, emotionally charged response. Not since the threat of colonization in the 1820s had the reaction been so forceful. Free blacks recognized immediately that the law subjected all African Americans—not just fugitive slaves—to arbitrary arrest and enslavement. Anger and defiance were keynotes at scores of mass meetings held across the North in the fall of 1850. Protesters embraced a threefold strategy of resistance, rescue, and repeal. Black orators brushed aside pleas for nonviolence and invoked the right of self-defense—the "bowie knife and the revolver," not moral suasion, carried the day. Several gatherings claimed the right of collective defense, threatened to shoot slave catchers, and resolved to rescue anyone arrested as a fugitive slave. Vigilance committees and protection societies were hastily formed in many northern cities, underground railroad operations were revived and expanded, blacks organized petition campaigns for the repeal of the "bloodhound bill," and the call went out in New York City for a black militia.

Northern response to the Fugitive Slave Law and the Kansas-Nebraska Act instilled a new feeling of optimism among black abolitionists. Northern whites, once indifferent to African American calls for support, expressed concern over the "slave power conspiracy"—the apparent growing control by slaveholders and their allies over the federal government and the nation's democratic institutions. Whites who were once apathetic became convinced that the South was threatening constitutional liberties with the Fugitive Slave Law and increasing sectional tensions by expanding slavery into the territories. African Americans had argued for years that their struggle was one for universal freedom and democratic principles, that to restrict the rights of a minority was to jeopardize the rights of all. Now they eagerly welcomed large numbers of northern advocates of freedom into the abolitionist ranks.

Yet the confidence that many black abolitionists projected could not mask completely the disheartening effects of federal policy. "We are slaves in the midst of freedom," Martin R. Delany wrote in 1852. Early expressions of optimism faded by the mid-1850s as each new proslavery imposition deepened the alienation felt by African Americans. The westward expansion of slavery, the threatened annexation of Cuba as a slave state, and efforts to reopen the African slave trade appeared to reverse twenty years of antislavery progress. Delegates at the 1855 black national convention sadly concluded that "there is no foot of American Territory over which slavery is not already triumphant."

The Dred Scott decision all but destroyed black hopes. In *Dred Scott* v. *Sanford* (1857), the U.S. Supreme Court upheld the constitutionality of slavery and denied all blacks any claim to American citizenship. Decades of state and local discrimination now had federal constitutional sanction. William Still, a Philadelphia underground railroad agent, concluded that the decision was "more discouraging and more prostrating to the hopes of the colored man than any preceding act of tyranny." The bitterness was palpable. In denouncing the decision, black leaders referred repeatedly to Chief Justice Roger B. Taney's devastating pronouncement that blacks "had no rights which the white man was bound to respect."

The federal government's acquiescence to proslavery forces in the 1850s compelled African American leaders to rethink fundamental assumptions about abolitionism and racial identity. Charles L. Remond, surveying twenty-five years of antislavery efforts, judged them "complete failures." H. Ford Douglas, Robert Purvis, and others disavowed the U.S. Constitution as a document that sanctioned slavery. In the wake of the Dred Scott decision, Remond bitterly questioned black devotion to the American nation: "The time has gone by for colored people to talk of patriotism," he declared; "we owe no allegiance to a country which grinds us under its iron heel and treats us like dogs."

The crisis of the 1850s revived interest in emigration. Proposals for black settlement beyond the United States had appeared intermittently for decades. Haiti, Jamaica, Trinidad, and West Africa were among the locations that attracted black leaders. However, a strong sense of American identity had kept most blacks at home, and years of struggle against the colonization movement had made most blacks suspicious of proposals for an organized exodus. Only Canada, the most accessible sanctuary for fugitive slaves, had attracted significant numbers of black settlers.

The Fugitive Slave Law clarified the emigration issue for many African Americans—they could either flee the country or live in perpetual fear of the slave catcher. Threatened with reenslavement and despairing of any hope for racial progress, thousands crossed into Canada, while others left for Britain, Africa, and the Caribbean. Underground railroad stations along the Canadian border reported thousands crossing in the fall of 1850, reaching as many as forty thousand by the eve of the Civil War.

Emigration advocates placed the departure in a positive light. Martin R. Delany set the tone in *The Condition, Elevation, Emigration and Destiny of the Colored People of the United States* (1852). Delany recognized the antislavery value of free black progress but concluded that since prejudice made advancement impossible in the United States, blacks should immigrate to Africa, Latin America, or the Caribbean. Delany, the most important theorist of black nationalism and emigration, called for the creation of an independent black nation. James T. Holly shared the vision of a black, Christian nationality but favored Haiti as the best location for black progress. The idea of creating a model black republic in Haiti appealed to individuals such as Holly because its national independence had been achieved through a successful slave insurrection. Holly believed that the task for African Americans was "raising a Nationality in Haiti—*to prove that in America, there Shall Be No Geography in Liberty! No Distinctions in Race or Nationality.*"

The concept of black nationhood gave emigration an antislavery character. Some emigrationists anticipated that racial prejudice would end only when Africa became "a great, powerful, Christian, commercial and industrial nation." Others believed that slaveholders would fear a black nation in the Caribbean. Still others hoped that a black nation could strike an economic blow to American slavery by exporting cotton produced by free labor.

Many black abolitionists questioned the antislavery value of emigration. For Frederick Douglass, James McCune Smith, and their allies, to leave the country was to forsake the antislavery struggle, abandon the slave, and forfeit any claim to American citizenship. Throughout the North, African American communities gathered to oppose emigration programs. New Bedford blacks denounced emigration as "abandoning homes and enslaved brethren, gratifying negro-haters at the North and slavery propagandists at the South." Others warned that leaving the country served "only to embolden our oppressors to renew efforts to pass those *hellish black laws.*"

Most African Americans resolved to continue the struggle in the United States. William Still spoke for the majority when he wrote to friends in Canada West that "the duty to *stay here and fight it out* seems paramount." But like many antiemigrationists of the late 1850s, he stayed with scant hope that circumstances would soon improve. A few prominent antiemigrationists, including Frederick Douglass, seemed prepared to reconsider the emigration appeal and leave the country when John Brown's raid and the coming of the Civil War interrupted their plans. After a decade of frustration and defeat, violence brought new hope.

On 16 October 1859, John Brown led twenty-one men in an unsuccessful attempt to seize the federal arsenal at Harpers Ferry in western Virginia. Five blacks—Shields Green, Osborne P. Anderson, Dangerfield Newby, John Copeland, Jr., and Lewis S. Leary—fought with him. Although Brown obtained some support from black abolitionists, most African American leaders hesitated to join Brown's campaign. The uncertainty of his plans worried many potential enlistees, and others feared the retribution whites would unleash upon their families and their communities.

Even though Brown failed, the raid riveted the nation's attention on the issue of slavery. In the wake of Brown's trial and execution, blacks elevated him to the status of hero and martyr. He represented a fusion of militant abolitionism with America's revolutionary heritage. The Harpers Ferry raid prompted a display of interracial unity not seen in the antislavery movement since the early days of William Lloyd Garrison. The memorial ceremonies that followed Brown's execution brought thousands of whites and blacks together, united in their veneration of Brown and his actions.

For African Americans, the Harpers Ferry raid signaled slavery's imminent demise. Buoyed by the raid, black abolitionists renewed their calls for slave rebellion and armed revolt against the South. They saw in Brown the "merciless whirlwinds of God's indignation"—he died for white sins and had sacrificed himself for black freedom.

BLACK ABOLITIONISTS AND THE CIVIL WAR

With the eruption of the Civil War in April 1861, most northern whites rallied to defend the Constitution and preserve the Union. Southerners fought for independence to guarantee states' rights, preserve a way of life, and make slavery secure. Blacks understood the war very differently from either northern or southern whites—for them it was the beginning of the end of slavery. But it took nearly two years of horrifying fighting against a determined Confederacy for the North and President Abraham Lincoln to grasp what Frederick Douglass wrote at the start: the "Negro is the . . . pivot upon which the whole rebellion turns."

Blacks rushed to enlist in the army after the attack on Fort Sumter, believing that national war aims would certainly include emancipation. But the more than eighty-five hundred men who had joined black volunteer militia units by the fall of 1861 were rejected for military service by the federal government. President Lincoln, sensitive to volatile public opinion on racial matters and fearful of losing the border states to the Confederacy, concluded that the North was not ready to enlist blacks, much less to fight a war against slavery.

Their patriotism spurned by the Lincoln administration, African Americans reconsidered their initial support for the Union cause. Some believed they should endorse the war in the hope that to do so would ease racial tensions and move the nation toward emancipation. Perhaps as many as a third of all northern blacks felt that duty and reason compelled them to stand with the government. The majority, however, remained critical, arguing that Lincoln would never emancipate the slaves or grant blacks their full rights.

By the close of 1861, most African Americans had decided to withhold their approval of the war until the destruction of slavery became its principal aim. Religious leaders declared that blacks had no business fighting for a country that oppressed them, and the African American press reminded its readers that their first responsibility was to the slave. The New York *Weekly Anglo-African*, the most influential black paper of the era, counseled blacks to denounce the government but to organize, drill, and stand ready "as Minute Men, to *respond when the slave calls*." Wounded by the rejection and angered by official indifference to their patriotism and aspirations, most blacks resolved to save their "labors for the slave, and the slave alone" and left the government to care for itself.

Nearly two years of bloody and inconclusive fighting changed northern opinion on the issues of emancipation and black recruitment. Facing the prospect of a prolonged war with appalling Union casualties, by mid-1862 northern leaders began to reexamine the use of black troops. More important, Lincoln concluded that a Union victory depended upon eliminating one of the South's most valuable assets—its slave labor population—through emancipation.

With the January 1863 Emancipation Proclamation, and the subsequent call for black troops, Union war aims and black goals converged. Once African Americans could simultaneously fight for the Union and the slave, black leaders across the North hailed the change as the opportunity they had been seeking—a patriotic and courageous call to arms would validate decades of antislavery claims. Black military service, they believed, would help destroy slavery and undermine claims of racial inferiority, the first step in ending prejudice and establishing claims to equal citizenship in the postwar nation. Participation in the war became an abolitionist act, an opportunity to obtain "indemnity for the past, and security for the future."

Although black volunteers from Louisiana and South Carolina had fought gallantly by the spring of 1863, the North remained doubtful that substantial numbers of African Americans would prove battleworthy. Whites questioned whether blacks could or would fight, and even white antislavery leaders anxiously awaited news of black conduct under fire. Amid such speculation, black units like the Fifty-fourth Massachusetts Regiment—the first regular black army unit organized in the free states—represented a daring experiment and assumed enormous importance. The *Weekly Anglo-African* reported that "the whole world . . . [waits] to see if you will prove yourselves." Black leaders understood that "if, by any means, the 54th should fail, . . . it will be a blow from which we northern men would never recover."

From across the North, African Americans flocked to Massachusetts to join up, some the sons of eminent black leaders like Frederick Douglass. By war's end, over 70 percent of all northern black males of military age served in the army or navy. Nearly 180,000 from North and South enlisted in the Fifty-fourth and other Union regiments, 10 percent of all Union forces. Northern blacks watched with pride as these units fought bravely at Port Hudson, Milliken's Bend, Fort Wagner, and other battles that demonstrated to skeptics—including the Lincoln administration and the Union military command—that African Americans would be good soldiers.

*Black troops at the battle of Milliken's Bend. From Langston Hughes,
Milton Meltzer, and C. Eric Lincoln, eds.,* A Pictorial History
of Blackamericans, *5th rev. ed. (New York, 1973).*

The opportunity to bear arms generated a wave of optimism among black
abolitionists that slavery would end and equal rights would certainly follow.
But such feelings were quickly tempered by the Union army's treatment
of black recruits. African American soldiers were issued inferior weapons
and inadequate rations, paid at less than half the rate of white soldiers,
often led by incompetent and racist white officers, relegated to fatigue duty,
brutalized for minor breaches of discipline, and executed for infractions of
the military code. They lived, said one black spokesman, "under a tyranny
inexorable as slavery itself, more absolute and fearful than the inquisition."

The issue of equal pay symbolized the government's mistreatment of
black troops. African Americans had volunteered with the understanding
that they would receive the same pay and treatment as whites. But once
they were in the service, the government determined that all blacks, regardless of rank, would receive less pay than white privates. Black soldiers, led
by the Fifty-fourth Massachusetts, placed enormous burdens on themselves
and their families by refusing pay. Near-mutinous conditions occurred in
some regiments, sometimes quelled by swift executions. After eighteen
months of protests, blacks gained the cooperation of prominent Republican

politicians who enacted legislation granting equal pay. Blacks celebrated this victory as an affirmation of their claims to equal treatment as Americans.

Despite their achievement, African Americans fought the same abolitionist battles with the Lincoln administration that had preoccupied them for over thirty-five years. They had to force emancipation on a president who would reunite the nation without reforming the South, if he could do that. Once again they had to combat plans to compensate slaveholders for the loss of their slave property—"It is the slave who ought to be compensated," one black abolitionist explained. Lincoln's shocking revival of colonization as a solution to the nation's racial problems outraged blacks, reminding the African American poet Frances Ellen Watkins Harper "of a man almost dying with a loathsome cancer, and busying himself about having his hair trimmed according to the latest fashion." To many black leaders, Lincoln came to represent "the godless will of a criminal nation."

Lincoln's Emancipation Proclamation confirmed the black judgment that racial progress came too slowly and would not be granted in full. Northern blacks understood the measure to be a dramatic change in policy and hailed it as the beginning of black freedom. Yet the proclamation left most black abolitionists anxious and disappointed. It was, as Lincoln admitted, a military necessity, not a humanitarian measure; it struck at the Confederacy, not on behalf of the slave. The proclamation came two years after the start of the war, freed only some slaves, and exempted slaves in the border states or those owned by "loyal" masters, thus reinforcing slavery in parts of the South. Well-attuned to the halfhearted efforts of professed friends, African Americans saw that Lincoln had done the least, rather than the most, against slavery. The Emancipation Proclamation was an unavoidable war measure and "is *per se*," the *Weekly Anglo-African* announced, "no more humanitarian than a hundred pounder rifled cannon."

Lincoln's wartime Reconstruction program offered additional evidence of the chasm that separated black abolitionist goals from the national purpose. His December 1863 "Proclamation of Amnesty and Reconstruction" began the process of bringing the South back into the Union. Mild in its punishment of former rebels and inviting to the defeated Confederate states, it promised a pardon and the return of all rights to southerners who took an oath of loyalty to the United States. State governments had merely to write new state constitutions that abolished slavery to qualify for readmission. Lincoln only briefly considered enfranchising some African Americans based on their wealth, education, military service, and prewar status; he offered freed slaves few rights and little protection from their former owners. His disregard for the abolitionists' long-held goals of political rights, economic security, and social justice, one black leader lamented, had "pronounced a death-knell to our peaceful hopes."

Four months after Appomattox, William Wells Brown announced that "the government has broken faith with the black man," leaving him to "the tyrants of the South." The government's apparent unwillingness to control the South convinced African American leaders that they must advance bold programs. Blacks understood that without political power and social and economic security their freedom was not secure. Viewing the war and Reconstruction as part of a continuing struggle dating from the beginning of the antislavery movement, they made it their primary responsibility to press public officials for racial equality, civil rights, the vote, and a just Reconstruction of the southern states. Henry Highland Garnet argued that "the battle has just begun in which the fate of the black race in this country is to be decided."

African American leaders worked hard to impart to the nation the wisdom they had gained through decades of battling prejudice and racism in the North: anything less than full rights and privileges as American citizens would doom all blacks to the second-class status that free blacks in the North had endured since the Revolution. Experience had convinced black abolitionists that emancipation and the vote were not enough. For freedom to have substance, blacks required judicial and economic equality as well as political power. They fought to secure their rights in the North, to reconstruct southern society, and to prepare the freedmen for the trials ahead.

Black abolitionists streamed South throughout the war and after, bringing relief supplies, assisting the former slaves in the transition to freedom, and establishing their political power. The old underground railroad system reversed direction and brought money and supplies into the South from scores of black churches and freedmen's aid societies. Black teachers and missionaries sought to direct the North's educational and religious work among the freedmen, and prominent black abolitionists helped found organizations to win the vote and protect black civil rights.

Blacks understood that a true reconstruction of the South and their political enfranchisement rested upon the federal government's willingness to advance their interests. But wartime Reconstruction set the course the government would follow. Before the close of 1865, blacks saw firsthand that Washington intended to abandon them in order to make peace with the

South. Their final guarantee of freedom and independence depended upon the government's determination to support black rights with a vigilant occupying force, an unbiased implementation of the law, and a fair opportunity to gain economic security. No such commitment existed.

BLACK ABOLITIONIST LEGACY

The devotion of many white abolitionists to ending slavery in the United States is a familiar story of genuine conviction and sacrifice. But in no other slaveholding country was the free black population so intensely abolitionist. The role of free blacks in developing and nurturing the antislavery movement made American abolitionism unique and, at the same time, transformed African American life and culture.

African Americans labored in large and small ways to advance the most important reform movement in American history. They informed and animated the struggle—infused it with philosophy, tactics, and practitioners whose authority and creditability could not be denied or refuted. From Frederick Douglass, whose ironic humor and thoughtful analysis stimulated antislavery sentiment throughout the North, to anonymous black families, who courageously opened their homes to fugitive slaves on the run, African Americans guided the drive for emancipation along a steady path.

Black abolitionists sought to recast the antislavery crusade from a fixed battle to end chattel slavery in the South to a broad, national campaign against all forms of racial injustice. By insisting that the issue of racial prejudice was inseparable from the slavery question, African Americans became the most persistent voice for racial equality in American society. In advancing that position, they also defined the central element of black abolitionism, giving it qualities that set it apart from the mainstream movement.

Blacks worked mightily to familiarize white reformers and the northern public with the terrible reality of racism in the North, to convince them that prejudice was as toxic to the nation as slavery and as worthy of condemnation. The failure of most white abolitionists to appreciate the intimate relationship between northern racism and southern slavery discouraged black abolitionists and created tensions within the antislavery ranks. During nearly thirty years of common struggle, this persistent strain among would-be allies influenced African American leaders, causing them to clarify their attitudes on matters of race, class, culture, politics, and American society and identity. Antislavery tension in the North—as well as a bitter struggle against the slaveholding South—defined black abolitionism.

Black abolitionism left a permanent imprint on African American society. During the antebellum years, while black communities grew and matured, abolitionism inspired and shaped institutions, informed intellectual life, and rallied citizens to the task of transforming the nation. The rise of abolitionism instilled northern black communities with confidence and purpose. Men and women from diverse backgrounds came together with a shared optimism and common objectives to create antislavery and reform organizations, establish their own press, write and publish their own literature, and assemble at state and national conventions. Black abolitionists instilled community institutions such as churches, schools, reading rooms, and mutual aid societies with abolitionist sentiment and racial purpose. Black abolitionism redefined leadership in the African American community, calling forward new leaders with antislavery experience—fugitive slaves, vigilance committee organizers, and antislavery professionals—to join the established black elite—the clergy, professionals, and businessmen. Black abolitionism touched nearly every facet of African American society, from the naming of schools to the claiming of America as a homeland. Debates over moral reform, colonization, emigration, separate institutions, color and caste, war and peace, and reform tactics and goals enriched black intellectual life and helped define the character of African American society in a racist nation.

Black abolitionism left the United States a benevolent heritage through its vigorous role in the antislavery crusade, its enormous influence on African American culture and institutions, and its generous contribution to the nation's understanding of the meaning of freedom and justice.

Chapter 1

The Rise of Black

Abolitionism

THE COLONIZATION
CONTROVERSY

The African American struggle to claim the United States as a
homeland gave rise to the black abolitionist movement. With the
creation of the American Colonization Society (ACS) in 1816, free
blacks confronted a program to resettle them in Africa. More than
a few black leaders supported the drive for an African repatriation.
They were drawn to the ACS's plan for a Liberian colony because it
promised blacks self-government and the rights denied them in the
United States. But most African Americans rejected colonization,
embraced the United States as their true home, and refused to abandon it or the slave. Recognizing the ACS as a threat to their claims
as American citizens, blacks organized to challenge the society's
program point by point.

1 OUR PRESENT HOMES

*Philadelphia blacks took the lead by organizing a series of mass meet-
ings to condemn colonization. At one gathering held in 1817, just
a few months after the founding of the ACS, participants carefully
spelled out their objections to Liberian settlement.*

To the humane and benevolent Inhabitants of the city and county of Philadelphia.

The free people of color, assembled together, under circumstances of deep interest to their happiness and welfare, humbly and respectfully lay before you this expression of their feelings and apprehensions.

Relieved from the miseries of slavery, many of us by your aid, possessing the benefits which industry and integrity in this prosperous country assure to all its inhabitants, enjoying the rich blessings of religion, by opportunities of worshipping the only true God, under the light of Christianity, each of us according to his understanding; and having afforded to us and to our children the means of education and improvement; we have no wish to separate from our present homes, for any purpose whatever. Contented with our present situation and condition, we are not desirous of increasing their prosperity but by honest efforts, and by the use of those opportunities for their improvement, which the constitution and laws allow to all. It is therefore with painful solicitude, and sorrowing regret, we have seen a plan for colonizing the free people of color of the United States on the coast of Africa, brought forward under the auspices and sanction of gentlemen whose names give value to all they recommend, and who certainly are among the wisest, the best, and the most benevolent of men, in this great nation.

If the plan of colonizing is intended for our benefit, and those who now promote it will never seek our injury, we humbly and respectfully urge, that it is not asked for by us: nor will it be required by any circumstances, in our present or future condition, as long as we shall be permitted to share the protection of the excellent laws and just government which we now enjoy, in common with every individual of the community.

We, therefore, a portion of those who are the objects of this plan, and among those whose happiness, with that of others of our color, it is intended to promote, with humble and grateful acknowledgments to those who have devised it, renounce and disclaim every connection with it; and respectfully but firmly declare our determination not to participate in any part of it.

If this plan of colonization now proposed, is intended to provide a refuge and a dwelling for a portion of our brethren who are now held in slavery in the south, we have other and stronger objections to it, and we entreat your consideration of them.

The ultimate and final abolition of slavery in the United States, by the operation of various causes, is, under the guidance and protection of a just

God, progressing. Every year witnesses the release of numbers of the victims of oppression, and affords new and safe assurances that the freedom
of all will be in the end accomplished. As they are thus by degrees relieved
from bondage, our brothers have opportunities for instruction and improvement; and thus they become in some measure fitted for their liberty. Every
year, many of us have restored to us by the gradual, but certain march of
the cause of abolition—parents, from whom we have been long separated—
wives and children whom we had left in servitude—and brothers, in blood
as well as in early sufferings, from whom we had been long parted.

But if the emancipation of our kindred shall, when the plan of colonization shall go into effect, be attended with transportation to a distant land,
and shall be granted on no other condition; the consolation for our past
sufferings and of those of our color who are in slavery, which have hitherto
been, and under the present situation of things would continue to be, afforded to us and to them, will cease for ever. The cords, which now connect
them with us, will be stretched by the distance to which their ends will be
carried, until they break; and all the sources of happiness, which affection
and connection and blood bestow, will be ours and theirs no more.

Nor do we view the colonization of those who may become emancipated
by its operation among our southern brethren, as capable of producing their
happiness. Unprepared by education and a knowledge of the truths of our
blessed religion for their new situation, those who will thus become colonists will themselves be surrounded by every suffering which can afflict the
members of the human family.

Without arts, without habits of industry, and unaccustomed to provide by
their own exertions and foresight for their wants, the colony will soon become the abode of every vice, and the home of every misery. Soon will the
light of Christianity, which now dawns among that portion of our species,
be shut out by the clouds of ignorance, and their day of life be closed,
without the illuminations of the gospel.

To those of our brothers who shall be left behind, there will be assured
perpetual slavery and augmented sufferings. Diminished in numbers, the
slave population of the southern states, which by its magnitude alarms its
proprietors, will be easily secured. Those among their bondmen who feel
that they should be free, by rights which all mankind have from God and
from nature, and who thus may become dangerous to the quiet of their
masters, will be sent to the colony; and the tame and submissive will be
retained, and subjected to increased rigor. Year after year will witness these
means to assure safety and submission among their slaves, and the southern

masters will colonize only those whom it may be dangerous to keep among them. The bondage of a large portion of our brothers will thus be rendered perpetual.

Should the anticipations of misery and want among the colonists, which with great deference we have submitted to your better judgment, be realized, to emancipate and transport to Africa will be held forth by slaveholders as the worst and heaviest of punishments; and they will be threatened and successfully used to enforce increased submission to their wishes, and subjection to their commands.

Nor ought the sufferings and sorrows which must be produced by an exercise of the right to transport and colonize such only of their slaves as may be selected by the slaveholders, escape the attention and consideration of those whom with all humility we now address. Parents will be torn from their children—husbands from their wives—brothers from brothers—and all the heart-rending agonies which were endured by our forefathers when they were dragged into bondage from Africa will be again renewed, and with increased anguish. The shores of America will, like the sands of Africa, be watered by the tears of those who will be left behind. Those who shall be carried away will roam childless, widowed, and alone, over the burning plains of Guinea.

Disclaiming, as we emphatically do, a wish or desire to interpose our opinions and feelings between all plans of colonization, and the judgment of those whose wisdom as far exceeds ours as their situations are exalted above ours; *we humbly*, respectfully, and fervently intreat and beseech your disapprobation of the plan of colonization now offered by "the American Society for colonizing the free people of color of the United States." Here, in the city of Philadelphia, where the voice of the suffering sons of Africa was first heard; where was first commenced the work of abolition, on which heaven has smiled, for it could have had success only from the Great Maker; let not a purpose be assisted which will stay the cause of the entire abolition of slavery in the United States, and which may defeat it altogether; which proffers to those who do not ask for them what it calls benefits, but which they consider injuries; and which must insure to the multitudes whose prayers can only reach you through us, *misery, sufferings, and perpetual slavery.*

JAMES FORTEN, Chairman.

RUSSELL PARROTT, Secretary.

Resolutions and Remonstrances of the People of Colour Against Colonization to the Coast of Africa (Philadelphia, Pa., 1818), 5–8.

2   JUSTICE AND HUMANITY

African American protests against the colonization movement expanded in size and grew angrier in tone during the 1820s. In early 1831, black leaders in Wilmington, Delaware, accused the ACS of fostering racism among whites to force blacks to emigrate, and they counseled the society's well-intentioned white supporters that ACS programs were "inimical to the best interests of the people of color."

We the undersigned, in conformity to the wishes of our brethren, beg leave to present to the public in a calm and unprejudiced manner, our decided and unequivocal disapprobation of the American Colonization Society, and its auxiliaries, in relation to the free people of color in the United States. Convinced as we are, that the operations of this Society have been unchristian and anti-republican in principle, and at variance with our best interests as a people, we had reason to believe that the precepts of religion, the dictates of justice and humanity, would have prevented any considerable portion of the community from lending their aid to a plan which we fear was designed to deprive us of rights that the Declaration of Independence declares are the "unalienable rights" of all men. We were content to remain silent, believing that the justice and patriotism of a magnanimous people would prevent the annals of our native and beloved country from receiving so deep a stain. But observing the growing strength and influence of that institution, and being well aware that the generality of the public are unacquainted with our views on this important subject, we feel it a duty we owe to ourselves, our children and posterity, to enter our protest against a device so fraught with evil to us. That many sincere friends to our race are engaged in what they conceive to be a philanthropic and benevolent enterprise, we do not hesitate to admit; but that they are deceived, and are acting in a manner calculated most seriously to injure the free people of color, we are equally sensible.

We are natives of the United States; our ancestors were brought to this country by means over which they had no control; we have our attachments to the soil, and we feel that we have rights in common with other Americans; and although deprived through prejudice from entering into the full enjoyment of those rights, we anticipate a period, when in despite of the more than ordinary prejudice which has been the result of this unchristian scheme, "Ethiopia shall stretch forth her hands to God." But that this formidable Society has become a barrier to our improvement, must be apparent to every individual who will but reflect on the course to be pursued by the emissaries of this unhallowed project, many of whom, under the name of ministers of the gospel, use their influence to turn public sentiment to our disadvantage by stigmatizing our morals, misrepresenting our characters, and endeavouring to show what they are pleased to call the sound policy of perpetuating our civil and political disabilities for the avowed purpose of indirectly forcing us to emigrate to the western coast of Africa. That Africa is neither our nation nor home, a due respect to the good sense of the community forbids us to attempt to prove; that our language, habits, manners, morals and religion are all different from those of Africans, is a fact too notorious to admit of controversy. Why then are we called upon to go and settle in a country where we must necessarily be and remain a distinct people, having no common interest with the numerous inhabitants of that vast and extensive country? Experience has proved beyond a doubt, that the climate is such as not to suit the constitutions of the inhabitants of this country; the fevers and various diseases incident to that tropical clime, are such as in most cases to bid defiance to the force of medicine.

The very numerous instances of mortality amongst the emigrants who have been induced to leave this their native, for their adopted country, clearly demonstrate the fallacy of those statements so frequently made by the advocates of colonization in regard to the healthiness of Liberia.

With the deepest regret we have witnessed such an immense sacrifice of life, in advancing a cause which cannot promise the least advantage to the free people of color, who, it was said, were the primary objects to be benefitted by this "heaven-born enterprise." But we beg leave most respectfully to ask the friends of African colonization, whether their christian benevolence cannot in this country be equally as advantageously applied, if they are actuated by that disinterested spirit of love and friendship for us, which they profess? Have not they in the United States a field sufficiently extensive to show it in? There is embosomed within this republic, rising one million free people of color, the greater part of whom are unable to read even the sacred scriptures. Is not their ignorant and degraded situation worthy of the consideration of those enlightened and christian individuals, whose zeal for the cause of the African race has induced them to attempt the establishment of a republican form of government amid the burning sands of Liberia, and the evangelizing of the millions of the Mahometans and pagans that inhabit the interior of that extensive country?

We are constrained to believe that the welfare of the people of color, to say the least, is but a secondary consideration with those engaged in the colonization project. Or why should we be requested to move to Africa, and thus separated from all we hold dear in a moral point of view, before their christian benevolence can be exercised in our behalf? Surely there is no country of which we have any knowledge, that offers greater facilities for the improvement of the unlearned; or where benevolent and philanthropic individuals can find a people, whose situation has greater claims on their christian sympathies, than the people of color. But whilst we behold a settled determination on the part of the American Colonization Society to remove us to Liberia, without using any means to better our condition at home, we are compelled to look with fearful diffidence on every measure of that institution. At a meeting held on the 7th inst. in this borough, the people of color were politely invited to attend, the object of which was to induce the most respectable part of them to emigrate. The meeting was addressed by several reverend gentlemen, and very flattering accounts given on the authority of letters and statements said to have been received from individuals of unquestionable veracity. But we beg leave to say, that those statements differ so widely from letters that we have seen of recent date from the colony, in regard to the condition and circumstances of the colonists, that we are compelled in truth to say that we cannot reconcile such contradictory statements, and are therefore inclined to doubt the former, as they appear to have been prepared to present to the public, for the purpose of enlisting the feelings of our white friends into the measure, and of inducing the enterprising part of the colored community to emigrate at their own expense. That we are in this country a degraded people, we are truly sensible; that our forlorn situation is not attributable to ourselves is admitted by the most ardent friends of colonization; and that our condition cannot be bettered by removing the most exemplary individuals of color from amongst us, we are well convinced, from the consideration that in the same ratio that the industrious part would emigrate, in the same proportion those who would remain would become more degraded, wretched and miserable, and consequently less capable of appreciating the many opportunities which are now offering for the moral and intellectual improvement of our brethren. We, therefore, a portion of those who are the objects of this plan, and amongst those whose happiness, with that of others of our color, it is intended to promote, respectfully but firmly disclaim every connection with it, and declare our settled determination not to participate in any part of it.

But if this plan is intended to facilitate the emancipation of those who are held in slavery in the South, and the melioration of their condition, by sending them to Liberia; we question very much whether it is calculated to do either. That the emancipation of slaves has been measurably impeded through its influence, except where they have been given up to the Board of Managers, to be colonized in Africa, to us is manifest. And when we contemplate their uneducated and vitiated state, destitute of the arts and unaccustomed to provide even for themselves, we are inevitably led to the conclusion that their situation in that pestilential country will be miserable in the extreme.

The present period is one of deep and increasing interest to the free people of color, relieved from the miseries of slavery and its concomitant evils, with the vast and (to us) unexplored field of literature and science before us, surrounded by many friends whose sympathies and charities need not the Atlantic between us and them, before they can consent to assist in elevating our brethren to the standing of men. We therefore particularly invite their attention to the subject of education and improvement; sensible that it is much better calculated to remove prejudice, and exalt our moral character, than any system of colonization that has been or can be introduced; and in which we believe we shall have the cooperation of the wisest and most philanthropic individuals of which the nation can boast. The utility of learning and its salutary effects on the minds and morals of a people, cannot have escaped the notice of any rational individual situated in a country like this, where in order successfully to prosecute any mechanical or other business, education is indispensable. Our highest moral ambition, at present, should be to acquire for our children a liberal education, give them mechanical trades, and thus fit and prepare them for useful and respectable citizens; and leave the evangelizing of Africa, and the establishing of a republic at Liberia, to those who conceive themselves able to demonstrate the practicability of its accomplishment by means of a people, numbers of whom are more ignorant than even the natives of that country themselves.

In conclusion, we feel it a pleasing duty ever to cherish a grateful respect for those benevolent and truly philanthropic individuals, who have advocated, and still are advocating our rights in our native country. Their indefatigable zeal in the cause of the oppressed will never be forgotten by us, and unborn millions will bless their names in the day when the all-wise Creator, in whom we trust, shall have bidden oppression to cease.

ABRAHAM D. SHADD
PETER SPENCER } Committee to prepare an Address
WM. S. THOMAS

William Lloyd Garrison, *Thoughts on African Colonization* (Boston, Mass., 1832), part 2, 36–40; *BAP*, 3:102–6.

THE GROWTH OF BLACK ABOLITIONISM

Throughout the 1820s, opponents of colonization formed local abolitionist societies with ambitious reform goals. Under the determined leadership of David Walker, Boston blacks organized the Massachusetts General Colored Association (MGCA) in 1826. Over the next few years, the MGCA led local protests, corresponded with northern black leaders, supported the emerging black press, and petitioned the U.S. Congress for an end to slavery in the nation's capital. The MGCA and similar organizations mobilized free black communities and brought unity and structure to the black abolitionist fight for immediate emancipation and racial equality.

3   AN ADDRESS TO THE MASSACHUSETTS GENERAL COLORED ASSOCIATION

In a speech before the MGCA in 1828, David Walker outlined the purposes of the society and called on free blacks to unite in a vigorous struggle for freedom.

Mr. President,—I cannot but congratulate you, together with my brethren on this highly interesting occasion, the first semi-annual meeting of this Society. When I reflect upon the many impediments through which we have had to conduct its affairs, and see, with emotions of delight, the present degree of eminence to which it has arisen, I cannot, sir, but be of the opinion, that an invisible arm must have been stretched out in our behalf. From the very second conference, which was by us convened, to agitate the proposition respecting this society, to its final consolidation, we were by some, opposed, with an avidity and zeal, which, had it been on the opposite side, would have done great honor to themselves. And, sir, but for the undeviating, and truly patriotic exertions of those who were favorable to the formation of this institution, it might have been this day, in a yet unorganized condition. Did I say in an unorganized condition? Yea, had our opponents their way, the very notion of such an institution might have been obliterated from our minds. How strange it is, to see men of sound sense, and of tolerably good judgment, act so diametrically in opposition to their interest; but I forbear making any further comments on this subject, and return to that for which we are convened.

First then, Mr. President, it is necessary to remark here, at once, that the primary object of this institution, is, to unite the colored population, so far, through the United States of America, as may be practicable and expedient; forming societies, opening, extending, and keeping up correspondences, and not withholding anything which may have the least tendency to ameliorate *our* miserable condition—with the restrictions, however, of not infringing on the articles of its constitution, or that of the United States of America. Now, that we are disunited, is a fact, that no one of common sense will deny; and, that the cause of which, is a powerful auxiliary in keeping us from rising to the scale of reasonable and thinking beings, none but those who delight in our degradation will attempt to contradict. Did I say those who delight in our degradation? Yea, sir, glory in keeping us ignorant and miserable, that we might be the better and the longer slaves. I was credibly informed by a gentleman of unquestionable veracity, that a slaveholder upon finding one of his young slaves with a small spelling book in his hand (not opened) fell upon and beat him almost to death, exclaiming, at the same time, to the child, you will acquire better learning than I or any of my family.

I appeal to every candid and unprejudiced mind, do not all such men glory in our miseries and degradations; and are there not millions whose chief glory centres in this horrid wickedness? Now, Mr. President, those are the very humane, philanthropic, and charitable men who proclaim to the world, that the blacks are such a poor, ignorant and degraded species of beings, that, were they set at liberty, they would die for the want of something to subsist upon, and in consequence of which, they are compelled to keep them in bondage, to do them good.

O Heaven! what will not avarice and the love of despotic sway cause men to do with their fellow creatures, when actually in their power? But, to return whence I digressed; it has been asked, in what way will the *General Colored Association* (or the Institution) unite the colored population, so far, in the United States, as may be practicable and expedient? to which enquiry

I answer, by asking the following: Do not two hundred and eight years [of] very intolerable sufferings teach us the actual necessity of a general union among us? Do we not know indeed, the horrid dilemma into which we are, and from which, we must exert ourselves, to be extricated? Shall we keep slumbering on, with our arms completely folded up, exclaiming every now and then, against our miseries, yet never do the least thing to ameliorate our condition, or that of posterity? Shall we not, by such inactivity, leave, or rather entail a hereditary degradation on our children, but a little, if at all, inferior to that which our fathers, under all their comparative disadvantages and privations, left on us? In fine, shall we, while almost every other people under Heaven, are making such mighty efforts to better their condition, go around from house to house, enquiring what good associations and societies are going to do us? Ought we not to form ourselves into a general body, to protect, aid, and assist each other to the utmost of our power, with the beforementioned restrictions?

Yes, Mr. President, it is indispensably our duty to try every scheme that we think will have a tendency to facilitate our salvation, and leave the final result to that God, who holds the destinies of people in the hollow of his hand, and who ever has, and will, repay every nation according to its works.

Will any be so hardy as to say, or even to imagine, that we are incapable of effecting any object which may have a tendency to hasten our emancipation, in consequence of the prevalence of ignorance and poverty among us? That the major part of us are ignorant and poor, I am at this time unprepared to deny. But shall this deter us from all lawful attempts to bring about the desired object? Nay, sir, it should rouse us to greater exertions; there ought to be a spirit of emulation and inquiry among us, a hungering and thirsting after religion; these are requisitions, which, if we ever be so happy as to acquire, will fit us for all the departments of life; and, in my humble opinion, ultimately result in rescuing us from an oppression, unparalleled, I had almost said, in the annals of the world.

But some may even think that our white brethren and friends are making such mighty efforts, for the amelioration of our condition, that we may stand as neutral spectators of the work. That we have many good friends, yea, very good, among that body, perhaps none but a few of those who have ever read at all will deny; and that many of them have gone, and will go, [to] all lengths for our good, is evident from the very works of the great, the good, and the godlike Granville Sharp, Wilberforce, Lundy, and the truly patriotic and lamented Mr. Ashmun, late Colonial Agent of Liberia, who, with a zeal which was only equalled by the goodness of his heart, has lost his life in our cause; and a host of others too numerous to mention: a number of private gentlemen too, who, though they say but little, are nevertheless, busily engaged for good. Now, all of those great, and indeed, good friends whom God has given us, I do humbly, and very gratefully acknowledge. But that we should cooperate with them, as far as we are able by uniting and cultivating a spirit of friendship and of love among us, is obvious, from the very exhibition of our miseries, under which we groan.

Two millions and a half of colored people in these United States, more than five hundred thousand of whom are about two thirds of the way free. Now, I ask, if no more than these last were united (which they must be, or always live as enemies) and resolved to aid and assist each other to the utmost of their power, what mighty deeds could be done by them for the good of our cause?

But, Mr. President, instead of a general compliance with these requisitions, which have a natural tendency to raise us in the estimation of the world, we see, to our sorrow, in the very midst of us, a gang of villains, who, for the paltry sum of fifty or a hundred dollars, will kidnap and sell into perpetual slavery, their fellow creatures! and, too, if one of their fellow sufferers, whose miseries are a little more enhanced by the scourges of a tyrant, should abscond from his pretended owner, to take a little recreation, and unfortunately fall in their way, he is gone! for they will sell him for a glass of whiskey! Brethren and fellow sufferers, I ask you, in the name of God, and of Jesus Christ, shall we suffer such notorious villains to rest peaceably among us? Will they not take our wives and our little ones, more particularly our *little ones*, when a convenient opportunity will admit, and sell them for money, to slaveholders, who will doom them to *chains, handcuffs*, and even unto death? May God open our eyes on these children of the devil and enemies of all good!

But, sir, this wickedness is scarcely more infernal than that which was attempted a few months since, against the government of our brethren, the Haytiens, by a consummate rogue, who ought to have, long since, been *haltered*, but who, I was recently informed, is nevertheless, received into company among some of our most respectable men, with a kind of brotherly affection which ought to be shown only to a gentleman of honor.

Now, Mr. President, all such mean, and more than disgraceful actions as these, are powerful auxiliaries, which work for our destruction, and which are abhorred in the sight of God and of good men.

But, sir, I cannot but bless God for the glorious anticipation of a not very distant period, when these things which now help to degrade us will no more be practised among the sons of Africa—for, though this, and perhaps another, generation may not experience the promised blessings of Heaven, yet, the dejected, degraded, and now enslaved children of Africa will have, in spite of all their enemies, to take their stand among the nations of the earth. And, sir, I verily believe that God has something in reserve for us, which, when he shall have poured it out upon us, will repay us for all our suffering and miseries.

Freedom's Journal (New York, N.Y.), 19 December 1828.

4 DAVID WALKER'S APPEAL

David Walker's Appeal . . . to the Coloured Citizens of the World *(1829)—the most militant African American document of its time— shocked the nation with its fierce analysis of white oppression. The* Appeal *alarmed southern whites, who saw in it a call for slave revolts, and it focused white reformers on the need for immediate emancipation.*

* * * I am fully aware, in making this appeal to my much afflicted and suffering brethren, that I shall not only be assailed by those whose greatest earthly desires are, to keep us in abject ignorance and wretchedness, and who are of the firm conviction that Heaven has designed us and our children to be slaves and *beasts of burden* to them and their children. I say, I do not only expect to be held up to the public as an ignorant, impudent and restless disturber of the public peace, by such avaricious creatures, as well as a mover of insubordination—and perhaps put in prison or to death, for giving a superficial exposition of our miseries, and exposing tyrants. But I am persuaded, that many of my brethren, particularly those who are ignorantly in league with slave-holders or tyrants, who acquire their daily bread by the blood and sweat of their more ignorant brethren—and not a few of those too, who are too ignorant to see an inch beyond their noses, will rise up and call me cursed—Yea, the jealous ones among us will perhaps use more abject subtlety, by affirming that this work is not worth perusing, that we are well situated, and there is no use in trying to better our condition, for we cannot. I will ask one question here,—Can our condition be any worse?—Can it be more mean and abject? If there are any changes, will they not be for the better, though they may appear for the worst at first? Can they get us any lower? Where can they get us? They are afraid to treat us worse, for they know well, the day they do it they are gone. * * *

Fear not the number and education of our *enemies*, against whom we shall have to contend for our lawful right; guaranteed to us by our Maker; for why should we be afraid, when God is, and will continue, (if we continue humble) to be on our side?

The man who would not fight under our Lord and Master Jesus Christ, in the glorious and heavenly cause of freedom and of God—to be delivered from the most wretched, abject and servile slavery, that ever a people was afflicted with since the foundation of the world, to the present day—ought to be kept with all of his children or family, in slavery, or in chains, to be butchered by his *cruel enemies*. * * *

I know well that there are some talents and learning among the coloured people of this country, which we have not a chance to develop, in consequence of oppression; but our oppression ought not to hinder us from acquiring all we can. For we will have a chance to develop them by and by. God will not suffer us always to be oppressed. Our sufferings will come to an *end*, in spite of all the Americans this side of *eternity*. Then we will want all the learning and talents among ourselves. "Every dog must have its day," the American's is coming to an end. * * *

The whites want slaves, and want us for their slaves, but some of them will curse the day they ever saw us. As true as the sun ever shone in its meridian splendor, my colour will root some of them out of the very face of the earth. They shall have enough of making slaves of, and butchering, and murdering us in the manner which they have. No doubt some may say that I write with a bad spirit and that I, being a black, wish these things to occur. Whether I write with a bad or a good spirit, I say if these things do not occur in their proper time, it is because the world in which we live does not exist, and we are deceived with regard to its existence. It is immaterial however to me, who believe or who refuse—though I should like to see the whites repent peradventure God may have mercy on them, some however, have gone so far that their cup must be filled. * * *

Ignorance and treachery one against the other—a grovelling, servile and abject submission to the lash of tyrants, we see plainly, my brethren, are not the natural elements of the blacks, as the Americans try to make us believe; but these are misfortunes which God has suffered our fathers to be enveloped in for many ages, no doubt in consequence of their disobedience to their Maker, and which do, indeed, reign at this time among us, almost to the destruction of all other principles: for I must truly say, that ignorance, the mother of treachery and deceit, !! gnaws into our very vitals. Ignorance, as it now exists among us, produces a state of things, Oh my Lord! too horrible to present to the world. Any man who is curious to see the full force of ignorance developed among the coloured people of the United States of America, has only to go into the southern and western states of this confederacy, where, if he is not a tyrant, but has the feelings of a human being, who can feel for a fellow creature, he may see enough to make his very heart bleed! He may see there, a son take his mother, who bore almost the pains of death to give him birth, and by the command of a tyrant, strip her as naked as she came into the world, and apply the cowhide to her, until she falls a victim to death in the road! He may see a husband take his dear wife, not infrequently in a pregnant state, and perhaps far advanced, and beat her for an unmerciful wretch, until his infant falls a lifeless lump at his feet! * * *

The whites have had us under them for more than three centuries, murdering us and treating us like brutes. * * * They do not know, indeed, that there is an unconquerable disposition in the breasts of the blacks, which, when it is fully awakened and put in motion, will be subdued, only with the destruction of the animal existence. Get the blacks started, and if you do not have a gang of tigers and lions to deal with, I am a deceiver of the blacks and of the whites. * * *

If you commence, make sure work—do not trifle, for they will not trifle with you—they want us for their slaves, and think nothing of murdering us in order to subject us to that wretched condition—therefore, if there is an *attempt* made by us, kill or be killed. Now, I ask you, had you not rather be killed than to be a slave to a tyrant, who takes the life of your mother, wife, and dear little children? Look upon your mother, wife and children, and answer God Almighty; and believe this, that it is no more harm for you to kill a man, who is trying to kill you, than it is for you to take a drink of water when thirsty; in fact, the man who will stand still and let another murder him, is worse than an infidel, and, if he has common sense, ought not to be pitied. * * *

Oh! coloured people of these United States, I ask you, in the name of that God who made us, have we, in consequence of oppression, nearly lost the spirit of man, and, in no very trifling degree, adopted that of brutes? Do you answer, no?—I ask you, then, what set of men can you point me to, in all the world, who are so abjectly employed by their oppressors, as we are by our *natural enemies*?

How can, Oh! how can those enemies but say that we and our children are not of the HUMAN FAMILY, but were made by our Creator to be an inheritance to them and theirs forever? How can the slaveholders but say that they can bribe the best coloured person in the country, to sell his brethren for a trifling sum of money, and take that atrocity to confirm them in their avaricious opinion, that we were made to be slaves to them and their children? * * *

Men of colour, who are also of sense, for you particularly is my APPEAL designed. Our more ignorant brethren are not able to penetrate its value. I call upon you therefore to cast your eyes upon the wretchedness of your brethren, and to do your utmost to enlighten them—*go to work and enlighten your brethren*! Let the Lord see you doing what you can to rescue them and yourselves from degradation. Do any of you say that you and your family are free and happy, and what have you to do with the wretched slaves and other people? So can I say, for I enjoy as much freedom as any of you, if I am not quite as well off as the best of you. Look into our freedom and happiness, and see of what kind they are composed!! They are of the very lowest kind—they are the very *dregs*!—they are the most servile and abject kind, that ever a people was in possession of! If any of you wish to know how FREE you are, let one of you start and go through the southern and western States of this country, and unless you travel as a slave to a white man (a servant is a *slave* to the man he serves) or have your free papers (which if you are not careful they will get from you), if they do not take you up and put you in jail, and if you cannot give good evidence of your freedom, sell you into eternal slavery, I am not a living man. * * * And yet some of you have the hardihood to say that you are free and happy! May God have mercy on your freedom and happiness!! * * *

I advanced it therefore to you, not as a *problematical*, but as an unshaken and forever immovable *fact*, that your full glory and happiness, as well as all other coloured people under Heaven, shall never be fully consummated, but with the *entire emancipation of your enslaved brethren all over the world.* * * *

There is a great work for you to do, as trifling as some of you may think of it. You have to prove to the Americans and the world, that we are MEN, and not *brutes*, as we have been represented, and by millions treated. Remember, to let the aim of your labours among our brethren, and particularly the youths, be the dissemination of education and religion. It is lamentable, that many of our children go to school, from four until they are eight or ten, and sometimes fifteen years of age, and leave school knowing but a little more about the grammar of their language than a horse does about handling a musket. * * *

I would crawl on my hands and knees through mud and mire, to the feet of a learned man, where I would sit and humbly supplicate him to instil into me, that which neither devils nor tyrants could remove, only with my life— for coloured people to acquire learning in this country, make tyrants quake and tremble on their sandy foundation. Why, what is the matter? Why, they know that their infernal deeds of cruelty will be made known to the world. Do you suppose one man of good sense and learning would submit himself, his father, mother, wife and children, to be slaves to a wretched man like himself, who, instead of compensating him for his labours, chains, hand-cuffs and beats him and family almost to death, leaving life enough in them, however, to work for, and call him master? No! no! he would cut his devilish throat from ear to ear, and well do slave-holders know it. The bare name of educating the coloured people, scares our cruel oppressors almost to death.

It is a notorious fact, that the major part of the white Americans, have, ever since we have been among them, tried to keep us ignorant, and make us believe that God made us and our children to be slaves to them and theirs. *Oh! my God, have mercy on Christian Americans!!!*

David Walker's Appeal in Four Articles; Together with a Preamble, to the Coloured Citizens of the World, 3d ed. (Boston, Mass., 1830), 64–98.

THE RISE OF IMMEDIATISM

By 1830 African American leaders had forged a three-part program—fighting colonization, ending slavery, and gaining equal rights—and for the first time, they found white reformers willing to support their cause. More than anyone else, William Lloyd Garrison symbolized black hopes for change. Once a supporter of gradual emancipation and black resettlement in Africa, Garrison, by 1830, had joined blacks in opposing racism, slavery, and colonization. African Americans welcomed the appearance of Garrison's antislavery newspaper the *Liberator*, hailing it as "the uncompromising advocate of our indefeasible rights." The timely and generous backing of black abolitionists, particularly Joseph R. Cassey and James Forten, Sr., of Philadelphia, carried the *Liberator* through its first year.

5 BLACK LEADERS AND WILLIAM LLOYD GARRISON

James Forten's letter to William Lloyd Garrison reveals the close relationship between Garrison and black leaders, the importance they placed on his antislavery efforts, and the black role in the rise of an immediatist antislavery movement.

Philad[elphi]a., [Pennsylvania]
December 31st, 1830

Dear Sir:

I am extremely happy to hear by your letter of the 15 inst. that you are about establishing a Paper in Boston. I hope your efforts may not be in vain; and may the "Liberator" be the means of exposing, more and more, the odious system of Slavery, and of raising up friends to the oppressed and degraded People of Colour, throughout the Union. Whilst so much is doing in the world, to ameliorate the condition of Mankind, and the spirit of Freedom is marching with rapid Strides, and causing Tyrants to tremble; may America awake from the apathy in which she has long slumbered. She must, sooner or later, fall in with the irresistible current. Great efforts are now making in the cause of Liberty: The People are becoming more interested and determined on the subject.

Although the Southern States have enacted severe laws, against the Free People of Colour, they will find it impossible to go in opposition to the Spirit of the Times. We have only to hope, that many such Philanthropists, as Mr. Lundy and yourself, will come forward, to plead our cause; we can never feel sufficiently grateful to ~~that~~ our long tried, faithful and zealous friend Mr. Lundy. He has indeed laboured for us, through evil and good report, and under many disadvantages & hardships; may he hereafter receive his reward.

I learn with the greatest regret, that so much prejudice exists in the Eastern States; but may the "Standard you are about to erect in the Eyes of the Nation" be the means of dispersing those clouds of Error, and of bringing many Advocates to our Cause.

I would have answered your Letter earlier, had it not been owing in the first place, to a multiplicity of business, which prevented me from soliciting Subscribers to your Paper. I herewith enclose you the Money for twenty ~~five~~ seven Subscribers, and their names and places of abode, you will also herewith receive. I would request you to send on a few Extra Papers that I may hand them to my friends.

Wishing you every success, and that the Liberator may have an extensive Patronage. I remain with the greatest Respect. Your's,

JAMES FORTEN

P.S. I think if Mr. Joseph Cassey will act as your Agent that he will obtain many Subscribers to your Paper.

Anti-Slavery Collection, Boston Public Library, Boston, Massachusetts; published by courtesy of the Trustees of the Boston Public Library; *BAP*, 3:85–86.

MORAL REFORM

Black abolitionists believed that the moral progress of free black society would shatter racist stereotypes and dramatically alter American race relations. They wrote and lectured on the value of reform principles—education, temperance, religion, and economy—while cautioning against gambling, dancing, ostentatious public displays, and extravagant living. They promoted practical expressions of moral reform by establishing hundreds of organizations and institutions dedicated to self-improvement. "All eyes are upon us," the editor of the *Colored American* cautioned his readers. Infused with antislavery worth, moral reform became the cornerstone of black abolitionism in the 1830s.

6   BY MORAL SUASION ALONE

Moral reform and moral suasion were dominant themes in the black national convention movement of the 1830s. Delegates to the 1832 convention affirmed these principles in an address to their constituents.

To the Free Colored Inhabitants of these United States.

FELLOW CITIZENS:

We have again been permitted to associate in our representative character, from the different sections of this Union, to pour into one common stream, the afflictions, the prayers, and sympathies of our oppressed people; the axis of time has brought around this glorious, annual event. And we are again brought to rejoice that the wisdom of Divine Providence has protected us during a year, whose autumnal harvest, has been a reign of terror and persecution, and whose winter has almost frozen the streams of humanity, by its frigid legislation. It is under the influence of times and feelings like these, that we now address you. Of a people situated as we are, little can be said, except that it becomes our duty, strictly to watch those causes that operate against our interests and privileges; and to guard against whatever measures that will either lower us in the scale of being, or perpetuate our degradation in the eyes of the civilized world. * * *

We yet anticipate in the moral strength of this nation, a final redemption from those evils that have been illegitimately entailed on us as a people. We yet expect by due exertions on our part, together with the aid of the benevolent philanthropists of our country, to acquire a moral and intellectual strength, that will unshaft the calumnious darts of our adversaries, and present to the world a general character, that they will feel bound to respect and admire. * * *

You there see that your country expects much from you, and that you have much to call you into action, morally, religiously, and scientifically. Prepare yourselves to occupy the several stations to which the wisdom of your country may promote you. We have been told in this Convention, by the Secretary of the American Colonization Society, that there are causes which forbid our advancement in this country, which no humanity, no legislation and no religion can control. Believe it not. Is not humanity susceptible of all the tender feelings of benevolence? Is not legislation supreme—and is not religion virtuous? Our oppressed situation arises from their opposite causes. There is an awakening spirit in our people to promote their elevation, which speaks volumes in their behalf. We anticipated at the close of the last Convention, a larger representation and an increased number of delegates; we were not deceived, the number has been tenfold. And we have a right to expect that future Conventions will be increased by a geometrical ratio, until we shall present a body, not inferior in numbers to our state legislatures, and the *phenomena* of an *oppressed people*, deprived of the rights of citizenship, in the midst of an enlightened nation, devising plans and measures, for their personal and mental elevation, by *moral suasion alone*. * * *

Finally, before taking our leave, we would admonish you, by all that you hold dear, beware of that bewitching evil, that bane of society, that curse of the world, that fell destroyer of the best prospects, and the last hope of civilized man, INTEMPERANCE.

Be righteous, be honest, be just, be economical, be prudent, offend not the laws of your country—in a word, live in that purity of life, by both precept and example—live in the constant pursuit of that moral and intellectual strength, which will invigorate your understandings, and render you illustrious in the eyes of civilized nations, when they will assert, that all that illustrious worth, which was once possessed by the Egyptians, and slept for ages, has now arisen in their descendants, the inhabitants of the new world.

Minutes and Proceedings of the Second Annual Convention for the Improvement of the Free People of Colour in these United States, Held by Adjournments in the City of Philadelphia, From the 4th to the 13th of June, inclusive, 1832 (Philadelphia, Pa., 1832), 32–36; *BAP*, 3:109–13.

7   RESPONSIBILITY OF COLORED PEOPLE IN THE FREE STATES

African American communities carried an enormous antislavery burden. In a Colored American *editorial, editor Samuel E. Cornish underscored the importance of free black conduct for improving race relations and ending slavery and prejudice.*

Brethren, God hath laid on us great responsibility—we have to act an important part, and fill an important place, in the great cause of humanity and religion—and in the work of emancipation. On *our* conduct and exertions much, very much depends. It is our part, by virtue, prudence and industry, to uphold the hands of our devoted and sacrificing friends—let us not be found wanting. Should we prove unworthy [of] our few privileges, we shall furnish our enemies the strongest arguments, with which to oppose the emancipation of the slave, and to hinder the elevation of the free.

On the other hand, should we establish for ourselves a character—should we as a people, become more religious and moral, more industrious and prudent, than other classes of community, it will be impossible to keep us down. This we should do, we are more oppressed and proscribed than others, therefore we should be more circumspect and more diligent than others.

We live in an age of reform, and if we lay not hold of every means of reformation and improvement, we shall be left in the background, and the contrast between our condition and that of our white brethren will be widened—then let us as a whole people, avail ourselves of every mea-

Samuel E. Cornish.
Courtesy of Moorland-Spingarn Research Center, Howard University.

sure calculated to cultivate the mind and elevate the morals. No oppressed COLORED AMERICAN, who wishes to occupy that elevation in society, which God has designed he should occupy, should be intemperate or even touch, as a beverage, intoxicating drinks, none should be idle or extravagant, none profane the Sabbath nor neglect the sanctuary of God, but all, all should be up and doing, should work while it is day. We owe it to ourselves and we owe it to the poor slaves, who are our brethren.

On *our* conduct, in a great measure, *their* salvation depends. Let us show that we are worthy to be freemen; it will be the strongest appeal to the judgement and conscience of the slave-holder and his abettors, that can be furnished; and it will be a sure means of our elevation in society, and to the possession of all our rights, as men and citizens. But brethren we are encouraged in these matters—we rejoice that there is a redeeming spirit abroad in the land: and merely suggest these things, to stir up your pure minds by way of remembrance.

Colored American (New York, N.Y.), 4 March 1837; *BAP*, 3:219–20.

8   A READING ROOM

Black abolitionists promoted practical expressions of moral reform in the 1830s. Several African American leaders, including Samuel Cornish, championed "reading rooms" as an effective method to spread antislavery literature and encourage literacy among urban citizens.

The Committee of Publication have in contemplation the opening of a *Reading Room*, in connection with this Paper. Our large exchange list, together with the pamphlets and other literary productions, which are presented and furnished us, weekly, will give great facilities to such an enterprise; and there is nothing so much needed by all classes of our people, as a well-furnished and well-selected reading establishment. Such an institution would be productive of the greatest good. Its influence and effects would be two-fold. While it would, *directly*, produce much good to our community, it would also be a preventative of much evil.

The reason why we have so many empty minds and idle hands, is our deficiency of literary and scientific institutions. Where the acquirement of knowledge, mental and moral, is neglected, there the vices grow and luxuriate. As an evidence of this fact, we have only to go into certain parts of our city, which are cursed with tippling and gaming-houses, instead of being blessed with institutions of science and literature, and there we find all sorts and complexions of people, living in ignorance and given up to the practice of EVERY VICE.

But take any portion of our city, or any other city or town, where the institutions of learning, and establishments for the arts are maintained, and there you will find the morals and manners of the people improved and elevated.

Then, brethren, if such be the influence of institutions of knowledge and refinement, of all people, we should avail ourselves of every chance of procuring them. We need all the moral character and the mental resources we can possibly husband. We are barbarously oppressed by a refined and christian people, and need more than *common intelligence and grace*, to sustain us; and we know of no better way of procuring these blessings for ourselves and our posterity, than by establishing and maintaining moral and literary institutions.

In this way we may fill up the years of our oppression, and pass the days of our pilgrimage profitably, and comparatively happily. In this way, we may train up our offspring to virtue and religion, and prepare them to be a blessing to future generations. And in this way, we may prevent worlds of vice, and save thousands of the young and thoughtless from those evil practices, which accumulate miseries, and lead to ruin and death.

The expense of the room will be two dollars a year, to subscribers. This sum will be necessary to meet the rent, and other expenses of the establishment. Subscriptions will be received at this office, in all the next week. Our brethren who intend patronizing the enterprise, and availing themselves of its privileges, will please to call without delay. We hope also that our people in other towns and cities, will adopt the same measure, for mutual improvement and benefit. We shall be glad to send papers, and give other facilities to all such establishments.

Colored American (New York, N.Y.), 10 February 1838; *BAP*, 3:261–62.

9   T E M P E R A N C E

Temperance was an essential component of moral reform. Black abolitionists established dozens of local abstinence societies, temperance grocery stores, and boardinghouses. The following essay by Jacob C. White, Jr., of Philadelphia explains the value of the temperance appeal.

Phil[adelphia], [Pennsylvania]
Mar[ch] 24th, 1854

What Rum is doing for the Colored People

We are all familiar with the effects produced by intoxicating liquors. We hear temperance lectures plainly setting forth the evils of intemperance and admonishing the youth to beware lest they should fall into the net which surrounds them on all sides, and become less than worthless to Society. Notwithstanding the admonitions which are daily given to our young men, we find them frequenting these earthly hells, not only throwing away the time which might be improved with great advantage both to themselves and to the people at large, but also throwing away their money for that which brings unto them nothing but want, misery, death, and eternal torment. A vast amount of good might be accomplished if the money spent by our young men, for liquors[,] was employed for the purpose of elevating our people and promoting the cause of education among them. Aside from this, the Respectable Groggeries are ruining the very class of our people to whom we are to look as warriors who are to fight ~~for us~~ for our liberty, and our rights, when the heads of our Fathers Shall be laid low in the silent tomb, and wrapped in the cold embrace of death (shall be those who are now so earnestly pleading for suffering humanity, and their immortal souls have taken their flight to receive the recompense for the deeds done in the service of their people). If there is any people who have a good reason for advocating the passage of the "Maine Liquor Law," or some other kind of prohibitory liquor law, it is the Colored people of this country: if for nothing but a matter of policy. So that they should have men to fight their battles, and contend with our enemies for our rights, which state of things cannot possibly exist if the grog shops are not Suppressed or some measures taken to reclaim our young men who have been so unfortunate as to become addicted to the habit of drinking rum. Let us then do all that we can to eradicate this evil, and put forth all our energies for the purpose of having the youth trained in such a manner that they will be fitted for usefulness when they grow up to be men & women. When this is accomplished we will see a marked difference in the Colored People of this country, in a political and social point of view.

JACOB C. WHITE

Leon Gardiner Collection, Historical Society of Pennsylvania, Philadelphia, Pennsylvania; published by permission; *BAP*, 4:210–11.

PREJUDICE

Racial oppression shaped the character of black abolitionism. Northern free blacks lived in a state of "quasi-freedom" where they were
denied basic legal and political rights, victimized by racial violence, ridiculed by the popular press, and excluded from church,
school, and marketplace. Through their daily encounters with racial
prejudice, black abolitionists came to realize that true emancipation
extended beyond merely ending slavery. They conceived of the
antislavery movement as a manifold struggle and fought against
prejudice in the North with the same determination that they
challenged slavery in the South.

10 THE EFFECT OF RACIAL PREJUDICE

*Black abolitionists spoke and wrote about racial prejudice with an
authority born of personal experience. Presbyterian clergyman Theodore S. Wright informed the annual meeting of the New York State
Anti-Slavery Society of the impact of prejudice on African Americans.*

* * * This is serious business, sir. The prejudice which exists against
the colored man, the freeman, is like the atmosphere everywhere felt by
him. It is true that in these United States, and in this state, there are men,
like myself, colored with a skin like my own, who are not subjected to the
lash; who are not liable to have their wives and infants torn from them;
from whose hand the Bible is not taken. It is true that we may walk abroad;
we may enjoy our domestic comforts, our families; retire to the closet; visit
the sanctuary, and may be permitted to urge on our children and our neighbors in well doing. But, sir, still we are slaves—everywhere we feel the
chain galling us. It is by that prejudice which the resolution condemns; the
spirit of slavery; the law which has been enacted here, by a corrupt public
sentiment, through the influence of slavery which treats moral agents, different from the rule of God, which treats them irrespective of their morals
or intellectual cultivation. This spirit is withering all our hopes, and oft

times causes the colored parent as he looks upon his child, to wish he had never been born. Often is the heart of the colored mother, as she presses her child to her bosom, filled with sorrow to think that, by reason of this prejudice, it is cut off from all hopes of usefulness in this land. Sir, this prejudice is wicked.

If the nation and church understood this matter, I would not say a word on this question; I would not speak a word about that killing influence that destroys the colored man's reputation. This influence cuts us off from every thing; it follows us up from childhood to manhood; it excludes us from all stations of profit, usefulness and honor; takes away from us all motive for pressing forward in enterprises, useful and important to the world and to ourselves.

In the first place, it cuts us off from the advantages of the mechanic arts, almost entirely. A colored man can hardly learn a trade, and if he does, it is difficult for him to find anyone who will employ him to work at that trade, in any part of the State. In most of our large cities, there are associations of mechanics, who legislate out of their society colored men. And in many cases, where our young men have learned trades, they have had to come down to low employments, for want of encouragement in these trades.

It must be a matter of rejoicing to know that in this place, many colored fathers and mothers have the privileges of education. It must be a matter of rejoicing, that in this vicinity colored parents can have their children trained up in schools. At present, we find the colleges barred against us.

I will say nothing about the inconvenience which I have experienced myself, and which every man of color experiences, though made in the image of God. I will say nothing about the inconvenience we find in traveling; how we are frowned upon and despised. No matter how we may demean ourselves, we find embarrassments everywhere.

But, sir, this prejudice goes farther. It debars men from heaven. While, sir, this slavery cuts off the colored portion of the community from religious privileges, men are made infidels. What, they demand, is your Christianity? How do you regard your brethren? How do you treat them at the Lord's table? Where is your consistency in talking about the heathen; traversing the ocean to circulate the Bible everywhere, while you frown upon them at your door? These things meet us, and weigh down our spirits.

And, sir, the constitution of society, molded by this prejudice, destroys souls. I have known extensively, that in revivals which have been blest and enjoyed, in this part of the country, the colored population were overlooked.

I recollect an instance. The Lord God was pouring out His Spirit. He was entering every house, and sinners were converted. I asked, Where is the colored man? where is my brother? where is my sister? who is feeling for him and her? who is weeping for them? who is endeavouring to pull them out of the fire? No reply was made. I was asked to go around with one of the elders, and visit them. We went, and they humbled themselves. The church commenced efficient efforts, and God blessed them as soon as they began to act for these people, as though they had souls.

And, sir, the manner in which our churches are regulated destroys souls. Whilst the church is thrown open to everybody, and one says, come, come in and share the blessings of the sanctuary, this is the gate to heaven—he says to the colored man, *be careful where you take your stand.* I know an efficient church in this State, where a respectable colored man went to the house of God, and was going to take a seat in the gallery, and one of the officers contended with him, and says—"you can not go there, sir."

In one place the people had come together to the house of the Lord. The Sermon was about to be preached—the emblems were about to be administered—and all at once the persons who managed the church, thought the value of their pews would be diminished, if the colored people sat in them. They objected to their sitting there, and the colored people left and went into the gallery, and that too when they were thinking of soon handling the memorials of the broken body and shed blood of the Savior! And, sir, this prejudice follows the colored man everywhere, and depresses his spirits. * * *

Let me, through you, sir, request this delegation, to take hold of this subject. This will silence the slaveholder, when he says, where is your love for the slave? Where is your love for the colored man who is crushed at your feet? Talking to us about emancipating our slaves when you are enslaving them by your feelings, and doing more violence to them by your prejudice, than we are to the slaves by our treatment! They call on us to evince our love for the slave, by treating man as man, the colored man as a man, according to his worth.

Friend of Man (Utica, N.Y.), 27 October 1836; *BAP*, 3:183–86.

11 SEGREGATED STREETCARS

Northern blacks risked personal safety to defy racist practices. The testimony of New York City teacher Elizabeth Jennings recounts her mistreatment after she refused to leave a streetcar reserved for whites.

Sarah E. Adams and myself walked down to the corner of Pearl and Chatham Sts. to take the Third Ave. cars. I held up my hand to the driver and he stopped the cars, we got on the platform, when the conductor told us to wait for the next car; I told him I could not wait, as I was in a hurry to go to church (the other car was about a block off). He then told me that the other car had my people in it, that it was appropriated for that purpose. I then told him I had no people. It was no particular occasion; I wished to go to church, as I had been going for the last six months, and I did not wish to be detained. He insisted upon my getting off the car; I told him I would wait on the car until the other car came up; he again insisted on my waiting in the street, but I did not get off the car; by this time the other car came up, and I asked the driver if there was any room in his car. He told me very distinctly, "No, that there was more room in my car than there was in his." Yet this did not satisfy the conductor; he still kept driving me out or off of the car; said he had as much time as I had and could wait just as long. I replied, "Very well, we'll see." He waited some few minutes, when the drivers becoming impatient, he said to me, "Well, you may go in, but remember, if the passengers raise any objections you shall go out, whether or no, or I'll put you out." I answered again and told him I was a respectable person, born and raised in New York, did not know where he was born, that I had never been insulted before while going to church, and that he was a good for nothing impudent fellow for insulting decent persons while on their way to church. He then said I should come out and he would put me out. I told him not to lay his hands on me; he took hold of me and I took hold of the window sash and held on; he pulled me until he broke my grasp and I took hold of his coat and held on to that, he also broke my grasp from that (but previously he had dragged my companion out, she all the while screaming for him to let go). He then ordered the driver to fasten his horses, which he did, and come and help him put me out of the car; they then both seized hold of me by the arms and pulled and dragged me flat down on the bottom of the platform, so that my feet hung one way and my head the other, nearly on the ground. I screamed murder with all my voice, and my companion screamed out "you'll kill her; don't kill her." The driver then let go of me and went to his horses; I went again in the car, and the conductor said you shall sweat for this; then told the driver to drive as fast as he could and not to take another passenger in the car; to drive until he saw an officer or a Station House. They got an officer on the corner of Walker and Bowery, whom the conductor told that his orders from the agent were to admit colored persons if the passengers did not object, but if they did, not to let them ride. When the officer took me there were some eight or ten persons in the car. Then the officer, without listening to anything I had to say, thrust me out, and then pushed me, and tauntingly told me to get redress if I could; this the conductor also told me, and gave me some name and number of his car; he wrote his name Moss and the car No. 7, but I looked and saw No. 6 on the back of the car. After dragging me off the car he drove me away like a dog, saying not to be talking there and raising a mob or fight. I came home down Walker St., and a German gentleman followed, who told me he saw the whole transaction in the street as he was passing; his address is Latour, No. 148 Pearl St., bookseller. When I told the conductor I did not know where he was born, he answered, "I was born in Ireland." I made answer it made no difference where a man was born, that he was none the worse or better for that, provided he behaved himself and did not insult genteel persons.

I would have come up myself, but am quite sore and stiff from the treatment I received from those monsters in human form yesterday afternoon. This statement I believe to be correct, and it is respectfully submitted.

ELIZABETH JENNINGS

New York Tribune (N.Y.), 19 July 1854; *BAP*, 4:230–32.

1 2   R A C I A L   V I O L E N C E

Each incident of mob violence against northern black communities shattered illusions of racial progress. Philadelphia African Americans suffered six bloody race riots between 1829 and 1849. After the particularly violent outburst of August 1842, black abolitionist Robert Purvis wrote the following letter to white colleague Henry Clarke Wright to convey his deepening sense of despair about American prejudice.

Phila[delphia], [Pennsylvania]
Aug[ust] 22nd, 1842

My Dear Friend Wright:

I have been absent from this city in all of the past week. This I offer in excuse for not acknowledging the receipt of your letter before this, over date of 12th Inst.

But I am even now, in every way disqualified for making proper answers to your interrogatories in reference to one of the most ferocious and bloody spirited mobs, that ever cursed a <u>Christian</u> (?) Community; I know not where I should begin, nor how, or when to end in a detail of the wantonness, brutality and murderous spirit of the Actors, in the late riots, nor of the Apathy and <u>inhumanity</u> of the <u>Whole</u> community in regard to the matter. Press, Church, Magistrates, Clergymen and Devils are against us. The measure of our sufferings is full. "Mans inhumanity to man, indeed make countless millions mourn." From the most painful and minute investigation, in the feelings, views and acts of this community—in regard <u>to us</u>—I am convinced of our utter and complete nothingness in public estimation. I feel that my life and those tendrils of my heart, dearer than life to me, would find no change in death, but a <u>glorious</u> riddance of a life, weighed down & cursed by a despotism whose sway makes Hell of Earth—<u>We</u> the <u>tormented</u>, our persecutors the <u>tormentors</u>. But I must stop; I am sick— miserably sick—every thing around me is as dark as the grave. Here & there the bright countenance of a true friend is to be seen, <u>save that</u>—nothing redeeming, nothing hopeful, despair black as the pall of Death hangs over us. And the bloody <u>Will</u> is in the heart of the community to destroy us.

Robert Purvis. Courtesy of Sophia Smith Collection, Smith College.

I send you the "[Pennsylvania] Freeman." In it you will find much in answer to yr. enquiry. In a few days perhaps I will write you again. To attempt a reply to your letter now is impossible—I feel "I have no feeling scarce conscious what I wish." Yet never to forget my gratitude to you, and all the dear, true, and faithful friends in the sacred cause of human freedom—Yr. brother,

ROBT. PURVIS

Anti-Slavery Collection, Boston Public Library, Boston, Massachusetts; published by courtesy of the Trustees of the Boston Public Library; *BAP*, 3 : 389–91.

TWO ABOLITIONISMS

Black and white abolitionists shared common assumptions about the evil of slavery, the virtue of moral reform, and the certainty of human progress. This shared understanding provided the basis for the interracial solidarity and cooperation so vital in the crusade against slavery. But blacks also brought a distinct perspective to the antislavery movement. Their abolitionism was shaped profoundly by their personal experience with racial oppression. Unlike most white abolitionists, they conceived of antislavery as an all-encompassing struggle for racial equality, and they took a more pragmatic, less doctrinaire approach to antislavery tactics. The contrast between the two abolitionisms—black and white—became increasingly apparent in the 1840s and 1850s as blacks expressed a growing militancy, asserted greater independence, and called for racially exclusive organizations and initiatives.

13   BLACK ABOLITIONISM DEFINED

James McCune Smith defined the essential character of black abolitionism—the struggle for racial equality—in his May 1855 speech to the National Council of the Colored People: "The recognition of our manhood throughout this land is the Abolition of Slavery throughout the land."

* * * The hundred and seventy thousand souls who compose the free colored people of the free States occupy a position in regard to human progress of greater importance and responsibility than any like number of individuals on the face of the globe. The great question of human brotherhood is brought to a direct test in our persons and position; the practicability of democratic institutions, their ability to overcome the last vestige of tyranny in the human heart, the vincibility of caste by Christianity, the power of the gospel, the disenthrallment of three millions of bleeding and crushed slaves; all these issues lend their weight and rest their decision very greatly, if not entirely, on the free colored people of the free States. This weight of responsibility is enough to make men shrink therefrom; but we cannot avoid it if we would. The influence of our land and its institutions reaches to the uttermost parts of the earth; and go where we may, we will find American prejudice, or at least the odor of it, to contend against. It is easiest, as well as manliest, to meet and contend with it here at the fountain-head; nor can we cease affecting these great issues by inactivity; the case is going on, whether we labor or not; and our inactivity will only help deciding it against us and these, and true principles, which it would seem the Providence of God that we are set apart to uphold. Although we may not readily see it, our position is not a hopeless one; it is full of promise. It sometimes happens in great moral, as in great physical battles, that certain divisions of men, by simply maintaining a fixed position, even without striking an active blow, will conduce to the victory; in like manner, by simply maintaining our numbers, and our senses, and our Christianity under the waves of oppression and practical infidelity that have vainly beaten against us, we have done our appointed service in the land where we dwell. But the hour has come for us to take a direct and forward movement. We feel and know it. Just as in 1817 there was a spontaneous movement among our brethren of that generation, with one voice to oppose the Colonization movement, so in this year 1855, throughout the length of the land, do we feel roused to take an active and energetic part in the great question of Liberty or Slavery. We are awakened, as never before, to the fact that if slavery and caste are to be removed from the land, we must remove them, and move them ourselves; others may aid and assist if they will, but the moving power rests with us. Gentlemen, the direction of this newly-awakened power rests greatly with you. Untrammeled by any of the influences that curb or straiten other benevolent or deliberative organizations, you may bring forward, discuss and adopt such plans of movement as may seem best. One or two primary considerations are all I will venture. First, it is important that you thoroughly organize all the colored people; we cannot spare the aid of a single man, or woman, or minor capable of thinking. Then you should adopt means to lay your plans of organization or cooperation before every individual among our people. This can be done by the agency of lectures and of the Press. We must distinctly keep before the people the fact that our labors consist in something beside the declaration of sentiments. We must act up to what we declare. And so closely does oppression encompass us that we can act constantly in behalf of our cause by simply maintaining for ourselves the rights which the laws of the land guarantee to us in common with all citizens. From the mere act of riding in public conveyances, up to the immediate and entire abolition of Slavery in the slave States, the laws of the land and the Constitution of the country are clearly on our side. And that man is a traitor to Liberty and a foe to our Humanity who maintains or even admits that we or any other human beings may be held in slavery on account of the color of skin, or for any reason short of the committing of crime. And from the mere act of riding in public conveyances, up to the liberation of every slave in the land, do our duties extend—embracing a full and equal participation, politically and socially, in all the rights and immunities of American citizens. If these our duties are weighty, we have the means to perform them. Our cause is inseparably wrapped up with every genial reform moving over the land.

> Freedom, hand in hand with labor,
> Walketh strong and brave;
> On the forehead of his neighbor
> No man writeth slave!

The States which have legislated in behalf of the Temperance reform have also made movements toward recognizing our rights as citizens thereof. But efforts on our own part have helped toward this good result; in Massachusetts, mainly by efforts of some colored citizens, one a member of this Council, the last vestige of caste in Public Schools has been abolished. In Connecticut, on the petition of her colored citizens, led by a member of this Council, both Houses of the Legislature have done their share toward granting us equal suffrage, and the Governor has recently strongly recommended the same. In New York, through the efforts of a member of this Council and the President of our State Council, aided by the moving eloquence of another member of our Council, the Legislature passed a vote of equal suffrage—a vote for which during the past twenty years we have petitioned and struggled in vain. In Pennsylvania, a strong and able effort has been made to obtain the franchise by our colored brethren, and not without some signs of success. Even in Illinois, hitherto covered with deeper infamy in caste than any other State, there are signs that the labors of her intelligent and energetic colored citizens have not been in vain. Gentlemen, these cheering and grand results have followed the almost isolated labors of less than a hundred colored men; I had almost said of five. What may we not do if we secure the hearty, earnest and steady cooperation of ten thousand such men! If a hundred colored men have struck these blows under which Slaveocracy reels and staggers, how easily will ten thousand overthrow that atrocious system. We have the men and the spirit, and a favorable public sentiment; let us address ourselves to the work of organization. The time is come when our people must assume the rank of a first-rate power in the battle against caste and Slavery; it is emphatically our battle; no one else can fight it for us, and with God's help we must fight it ourselves. Our relations to the Anti-Slavery movement must be and are changed. Instead of depending upon it, we must lead it. We must maintain our citizenship and manhood in every relation—civil, religious and social—throughout the land. The recognition of our manhood throughout this land *is* the Abolition of Slavery throughout the land. * * *

New York Tribune (N.Y.), 9 May 1855; *BAP*, 4:290–93.

Chapter 2

African Americans
and the Antislavery
Movement

BLACKS AS ADVOCATES

African Americans were the antislavery movement's most effective advocates. Their speeches and published writings infused the antislavery crusade with a message that was authentic, credible, and emotional. The personal testimony of former slaves repudiated lies about slave life; the public presence of such gifted and dignified men as Samuel Ringgold Ward and Frederick Douglass undermined notions of racial inferiority. Black abolitionists lectured throughout the northern states, Canada, and the British Isles. At times they received a celebrity's reception from enthusiastic audiences; in other instances they found public indifference; and occasionally they confronted angry mobs. Many used creative and dramatic methods to convey their message: they toured with pictorial exhibits of plantation life, reenacted their escape from slavery, debated proslavery apologists, and displayed whips and chains at the podium. By bringing the slavery question to the center of American life, black lecturers and writers played a principal role in the most ambitious reform movement in U.S. history.

14 YOUR OBEDIENT SERVANT

Correspondence by fugitive slaves to their former masters, often published as "open letters" in reform newspapers, provided an effective counterpoint to proslavery propaganda. John Roberts's letter to Richard C. Stockton, a Baltimore planter, appeared in the Toronto Christian Guardian.

Toronto, Upper Canada
July 8, 1837

Sir:

I have seen in the Rochester *Democrat* of the Fourth of July, your publication inviting me again to assume the bonds of a Slave. And can you think, that I would voluntarily relinquish Freedom, fully secured to me by the British Government, to return to American Slavery, the vilest that now crushes man and defies God? Is this the appreciation you have of Liberty? If so, I value it more highly. No, Sir, dear to me as are the thoughts of my wife and child, I cannot again become a Slave, if this be the price at which I must purchase the enjoyment of their Society. For them would I freely expend my life—but to become a Slave again! no, never. To ask it, is an insult to the spirit of Liberty, to the Dignity of human nature, to that Heaven born religion you profess.

You say that with "an excellent character for integrity, stability, and sobriety," I have served you "upwards of twenty years." And does this expenditure of my primest manhood entitle me to no reward in my declining years? Send me, then, my wife, my child. Disproportioned as would be the cost of doing this, to the value of the services I have rendered you, 'tis all I ask; it shall be your full acquittance. From one who feels anything of the power of the religion you profess—or who has any touch of humanity, or any regard for justice, I could not ask less, nor would he think of performing less.

You seem to doubt the *sincerity* of the friend, by whose aid I have been enabled to achieve my liberty. How has the habit of oppression warped your judgment and dulled your sensibilities—that you should suspect the motives of those who strike from the helpless Slave his long worn chains. Take it to yourself: what would you think of the friendship of him who, at the hazard of all things, should deliver you or your child from Moorish or Algerine bondage? Would you be so ungrateful as to suspect his motives, when you were a beggar in all things but in thanks? No: you would not. And you would feel a generous indignation, too, against the frozen-hearted traducer who would persuade you to suspect his sincerity. If you should ever be so unfortunate as to be in Slavery, may you find those who will deliver you as I have been delivered—who will make you, as I am made a FREEMAN. *Then*; you will acknowledge their worth, and know how to honour their friendship. Farewell, Sir, may you enjoy the happiness of those who strive to make others happy,

JOHN ROBERTS

Christian Guardian (Toronto, Canada), 12 July 1837; *BAP*, 2:65–66.

15 BLACK ABOLITIONIST LECTURERS

The American Anti-Slavery Society commissioned Charles L. Remond as its first black lecturing agent in 1838. In a letter to Maine abolitionist Austin Willey, Remond describes the difficulties of his antislavery tour in Maine.

Bangor, [Maine]
Oct. 27th, 1839

My Dear Friend Willey:
Upon the eve of setting out for Washington Co., you will be somewhat surprised to learn that Hampden has disgraced herself, and advanced the abolition cause. On the 16th inst., I lectured in the congregational meeting house in Hampden. On the following evening, I again lectured in the baptist meeting house, to a large and attentive assembly. At the close of my talk, a request was made that all those favorable to the formation of a society should stop after the audience was dismissed. When, in consequence of some little confusion, it was thought advisable to postpone the

meeting until the following thursday evening, to be held at the Academy building; on which evening I agreed to be present. On going to the place on the appointed evening, as I passed towards the house, I noticed three or four individuals near the door, and before I entered the house, was besmeared with eggs. I took no notice of the insult, but went in and sat down; some sensation was discoverable, when the chairman of the meeting rose, saying, the question upon the propriety or impropriety of forming an anti-slavery society was before the audience; when Mr. [Hannibal] Hamlin, the Representative elect, observed, that he believed it to be customary on such occasions, for those, who proposed the formation of a society, to open a discussion in the affirmative, at least, it was agreeable to common sense; upon which Mr. Bartlett, my friend, moved that I be invited to open the discussion, upon which I rose, saying that before I could take a part in the discussion, I wished to have an expression of the audience whether I came within the call for the meeting; being myself a stranger, I did not wish to intrude my opinion, or a single thought upon the hearing of the audience, but simply wished to say, before sitting down, that when entering that house, I was insulted in a manner I had never before been under the painful necessity of relating. At this moment some inhuman fellows aimed a number of stones and eggs at my head—which—thank GOD, missed the mark, and passed with great swiftness through the window behind me. Immediately there was screaming and a simultaneous rush for the door—the ladies were apparently much alarmed. Without moving from my position, I requested the audience to resume their seats, as there was no harm intended to any person but myself; and if in order to put down the cause in which I was engaged, it was necessary I should be pelted with eggs, be it so; that if I must be stoned, be it so; that if they must walk over my prostrate and bleeding body, be it so; for while I lived, and a single slave clanks his chain upon the soil which gave me birth, I will exercise the prerogative of thinking and speaking in his behalf, though slaveholders, mobocrats, eggs and brickbats multiply as fast and as thick as the locusts of Egypt. I then took my seat, and the motion was put and unanimously carried in favor of my speaking. I then endeavored to argue the necessity of forming a society on the ground of its being a question which interested every individual, composing that intelligent assembly; I occupied some twenty five or thirty minutes. On taking my seat, Mr. Hamlin rose and answered me in a speech some one hour, bringing forward every objection which has been stated from the time of William Lloyd Garrison's incarceration in the prison at Baltimore, down to the capture of the noble Cinque; beginning with the charge, that we scruple not at the most gross violation of the Federal Constitution, and ending with his solemn conviction and opinion, that all that was wished by the abolitionists, was to bring about a general amalgamation of the blacks and whites etc. etc. When I again answered the gentleman in a speech of eight or ten minutes, and was again replied to by him, and Mr. Mathews, who also spoke against the formation of an anti-slavery society—attempting to show that the efforts of the abolitionists have put back emancipation fifty years, and that emancipation was about to take place a few years since, when the formation of anti-slavery societies completely defeated the objects and wishes of the friends of emancipation in Kentucky &c. It being now ten o'clock, a motion to adjourn one week prevailed, and Mr. Hamlin, and his party retired, evidently convinced that the opponents to abolition had lost ground, eggs, stones and his eloquent arguments to the contrary notwithstanding.

On the following evening, agreeable to appointment, I went to Orrington and addressed the friends on the duty and necessity of forming an anti-slavery society, in that village; at the close of the lecture, the sense of the audience was taken by the rising of a very large number of friends, who I was informed by Rev. Mr. Young, composed the respectability and piety of the place. A committee was appointed to draft a constitution, and a time appointed for another lecture and the organization of a society. Intending to return to Bangor the same evening, my friends went to the fence for my horse and chaise, when it was discovered that some evil minded persons had cut my harness in pieces, and also the top and lining of the chaise, thus disappointing me in my plans, and subjecting me to $30 or $35 expense.

It was ascertained that these mischievous beings crossed the river from Hampden, with their faces painted black, and were doubtless the same who insulted me the evening before; but for each offence I can forgive them. If the friends of order and truth in Orrington will detect the perpetrators, and thus fix the stigma where it belongs, the cause of the poor slave will be advanced. I shall write you soon again, and give some accounts of my labors prior to the outrage. Yours truly,

C . LENOX REMOND

Advocate of Freedom (Augusta, Maine), 2 November 1839; *BAP*, 3:314–16.

16 WILLIAM WELLS BROWN'S PANORAMA

William Wells Brown toured Britain in 1850 with an antislavery panorama—an exhibit of twenty-four painted canvas panels illustrating slave life in the South. As part of the exhibit, he published a forty-eight-page pamphlet explaining the origins and scenes of the panorama.

PREFACE

During the autumn of 1847 I visited an exhibition of a Panorama of the River Mississippi, which was then exhibited in Boston, United States. I was somewhat amazed at the very mild manner in which the "Peculiar Institution" of the Southern States was there represented, and it occurred to me that a painting, with as fair a representation of American Slavery as could be given upon canvass, would do much to disseminate truth upon this subject, and hasten the downfall of the greatest evil that now stains the character of American people. I, therefore, commenced collecting a number of sketches of plantations in the Slave States, illustrating the life of the Slave, from his birth, to his death in bondage, or his flight from the "Stars and Stripes" to the British possessions of North America. After considerable pains and expense, I succeeded in obtaining a series of sketches of beautiful and interesting American scenery, as well as of many touching incidents in the lives of Slaves. These drawings have been copied by skillful artists in London, and form the subjects of the Panorama now submitted to public inspection. While I have endeavoured to give a correct idea of the "Peculiar Institution," I have refrained from representing those distinguished pictures of vice and cruelty which are inseparable from Slavery; so that whatever may be said of my Views, I am sure that the Slaveowners of America can have nothing to complain of on the score of exaggeration. Many of the scenes I have myself witnessed, and the truthfulness of all of them is well known to those who are familiar with the Anti-slavery literature of America; and if the Exhibition shall be instrumental in aiding the American Abolitionists in their noble efforts to abolish Negro Slavery, the main object for which it was brought forward will have been accomplished. * * *

A DESCRIPTION

OF

WILLIAM WELLS BROWN'S

ORIGINAL

PANORAMIC VIEWS

OF THE

SCENES IN THE LIFE OF AN AMERICAN SLAVE,

FROM HIS BIRTH IN SLAVERY TO HIS DEATH OR HIS ESCAPE TO HIS FIRST HOME OF FREEDOM ON BRITISH SOIL.

FICTION.

"We hold these truths to be self-evident: that all men are created equal; that they are endowed by their Creator with certain inalienable rights, and that among these are LIFE, LIBERTY, and the PURSUIT OF HAPPINESS."—
Declaration of American Independence.

FACT.

"They touch our country, and their shackles fall."—COWPER.

LONDON:

PUBLISHED BY CHARLES GILPIN,

5, BISHOPSGATE STREET WITHOUT;

AND TO BE HAD OF ALL BOOKSELLERS.

Title page from William Wells Brown, A Description of William Wells Brown's
Original Panoramic Views of the Scenes in the Life of an American Slave . . .
(London, [1849]). Courtesy of Boston Athenaeum.

VIEW SECOND

Two Gangs of Slaves Chained and on Their Way to the
Market—Cruel Separation of a Mother from her
Child—White Slaves

We have now before us a gang of Slaves on their way to the City of Washington. You see that they are chained together. The white men in the foreground of the view are the agents of the notorious Franklin and Armfield, of Washington, one of the largest slave-dealing houses in the United States. The house before us is an Inn. The agents have been in different directions purchasing slaves, and have joined their gangs together in this place.

On the right of you, you see a woman who will not go on, and a slave in the act of taking away her young child. She has been separated from it and they are now whipping her to make her proceed without it.

You readily recognise two Slaves as being nearly white.

It is not uncommon to see slaves as white as their masters, and a great deal better-looking, chained and driven as the beasts of the field. * * *

VIEW THIRD

The Capitol of the United States—A Public Meeting
to Sympathise with the French Revolution

We have now arrived at the City of Washington. The large building before us is the Capitol of the United States; and the concourse of people on the right of it, are holding a meeting to sympathise with the French Revolution of 1848.

You will also observe, on the left of the Capitol, a gang of Slaves. These are the same that we saw in the last view.

Although it is very common to see Slaves chained and driven past the Capitol, yet the managers of this meeting are very reasonably disconcerted at having a gang of Slaves driven so near them, at the very time that they are making speeches and passing resolutions in favour of Republicanism in France.

Nothing can more forcibly show the hypocrisy, or the gross inconsistency, of the citizens of the United States than their pretended sympathy for people in foreign countries, while they chain, whip, and sell, their own countrymen. * * *

VIEW NINTH

A Cotton Plantation—Slaves Picking Cotton—
the Whipping-post Punishment

The "picking season," as it is called, is the hardest time for slaves on a cotton plantation. As the cotton must be picked at a certain stage of ripeness, the slaves are usually worked, during this season of the year, from fourteen to sixteen hours out of the twenty-four.

We here have before us a cotton plantation with slaves picking cotton. The usual task for a man is eighty pounds per day; for a woman, seventy pounds; but they often work them far above this task. During the task time, if a slave fails to accomplish his task, he receives five cuts with the cat-o'-nine-tails, or the negro whip, for every pound of cotton that is wanting to make up the requisite number. In the distance you observe a woman being whipped at the whipping-post, near which are the scales for weighing the cotton. It should here be borne in mind, that a large portion of this cotton is consumed by the people of Great Britain and other countries in Europe. * * *

VIEW THIRTEENTH

Tanning a White Boy

* * * The view now before us presents the case of two men in the act of tanning a white boy, that he may more readily be retained in slavery. It is not an uncommon occurrence for a white boy of poor parents to be reduced to a state of chattel slavery, in a Slave State. The writer was personally acquainted with a white boy in St. Louis, Missouri, who was taken to New Orleans and sold into slavery. * * *

VIEW FIFTEENTH

Ride and Tie, a Clever Mode of Escaping from
Slavery—A Witty Reply

In 1846 two Slaves were seen passing an inn on the public road between Lexington, Ky., and Covington, on the banks of the Ohio River. One of them was on horseback, while the other was tied with one end of a rope; the other end of which the man on horseback held in his hand. In this way he was apparently driving the slave before him to his master's home or to a distant market. A white man, at the inn, on seeing them, came out and asked the rider what he was doing with that negro; his reply was, "He is a runaway nigger, massa, and I have got him fast; and if massa ever get him, he will cook his dinner for him nicely." Of course they were permitted to pass without further question. When they reached a forest, or got out of sight of dwellings, the man on horseback would suffer himself to be tied while the other took his place on horseback. In this way they travelled on until they reached the Ohio, when the horse was turned loose and told to "go home," while the Slaves crossed the river and made good their escape to Canada.

We need not inform the reader, that the whole was an ingenious mode of eluding inquiry, and more readily making their escape out of Slavery. Had they been travelling on the highway, as travellers do in Great Britain, they would have been asked for their Free papers, or a pass; and in the event of not producing either, they would have been seized as runaway Slaves. * * *

William Wells Brown, *A Description of William Wells Brown's Original Panoramic Views of the Scenes in the Life of an American Slave* . . . (London, [1849]); *BAP*, 1:191–216.

17 CONTENT WITH FREEDOM

William and Ellen Craft's extraordinary and well-publicized escape from slavery earned them international recognition for their daring. Writing from Britain, Ellen discredited the rumor that she was disillusioned with free life and wished to return to her former master. In proclaiming her preference for freedom, Ellen wrote one of the movement's most poignant statements.

Ockham School
near Ripley, Surrey, [England]
Oct[ober] 26, 1852

Dear Sir:

I feel very much obliged to you for informing me of the erroneous report which has been so extensively circulated in the American newspapers: "That I had placed myself in the hands of an American gentleman in London, on condition that he would take me back to the family who held me as a slave in Georgia." So I write these few lines merely to say that the statement is entirely unfounded, for I have never had the slightest inclination whatever of returning to bondage; and God forbid that I should ever be so false to liberty as to prefer slavery in its stead. In fact, since my escape from slavery, I have got on much better in every respect than I could have possibly anticipated. Though, had it been to the contrary, my feelings in regard to this would have been just the same, for I had much rather starve in England, a free woman, than be a slave for the best man that ever breathed upon the American continent. Yours very truly,

ELLEN CRAFT

Anti-Slavery Advocate (London), December 1852; *BAP*, 1:330.

18 WHAT THE SLAVES THINK

Fugitive slave lecturer J. Sella Martin spoke of slavery with an authority gained from grim experience. He drew on his slave past to inform a Bristol, England, audience about slavery's unmitigated evil.

Men enter into conversation with me in railway carriages, and they say, "We are as much opposed to slavery as you are; but then, after all slavery ought to have been gradually abolished, and not immediately." Well now, suppose it ought, it was not. (Laughter.) It would cost just as much blood and treasure to get the negroes back into slavery as it has cost to get them out, and if these people really meant to criticise where they can remedy, and not to find fault merely in a querulous spirit, they would accept the state of facts as they present themselves and make the best of it. (Hear, hear.) I will tell you what is the fact. The people that find fault with abolition generally do not want it, gradual or immediate. They say that the negroes were very well contented when they were in slavery. "I have seen them," some will say, "and heard them say they were contented." They have told me that frequently, and there was never a greater mistake in the world. Here a white man says that the negroes were contented. Well, I am a negro, and I was not contented. (Loud applause.) The white man was not in slavery; I was, and I know where the shoe pinched; and I say I was not contented. But then, Mr. Chairman, suppose it were the fact that the black man was contented in bondage, suppose he was contented to see his wife sold on the auction-block or his daughter violated or his children separated from him, or having his own manhood crushed out of him, I say that is the heaviest condemnation of the institution, that slavery should blot out a man's manhood so as to make him contented to accept this degradation, and such an institution ought to be swept from the face of the earth. (Loud applause.) While there is an irresponsible power committed to the hands of the slaveholder, and while human nature remains as it is, it is impossible to talk about treating slaves kindly. You cannot do it. I was once on a plantation—I went there accidentally—and I saw a lot of negroes gathered by the side of the water. In the middle of the stream there stood a stalwart negro with an axe on his shoulder. The overseer was trying to urge the negroes on the bank to go in and make him come out, but the boys all knew him, and he said, "Do not approach me, for I will brain the first one that does, and die in this water." The boys knew that he would do it, and they would not approach him. Finally, the overseer had to send for the young master, who came down and said to the negro, "Jim, you must come out of the water." Jim said, "I will come out if you promise that I shall not be flogged. I have done nothing to be flogged for. I do my work faithfully. You sold away my wife. I have made up my mind never to be flogged, and I will not come out of the water." The young master appealed to him by all the feelings connected with their boyhood, all the reminiscences and associations of their early life, but the negro still refused; and at last the young master said to the negro-driver, who was standing by, "You must shoot him down: there is no help for it." The negro-driver then raised his rifle, and in a moment the sharp crack of the rifle sent the poor corpse floating down the stream, his blood staining the water. Now, that I saw. It was not because the man who did it was bloodthirsty, or tyrannical, or ferocious, or more cruel than any of us might be here, but if the negro had been successful in resisting his authority that day, another negro would have attempted it the next, and so on until all discipline would have been at an end in the plantation. When I have talked about the inherent cruelty of the institution, men have said, "Why do you talk so? Don't you know that I would not kill my horse?" Ah, but people do not remember that there is a great difference between a man and a horse: if you beat a horse, the other horses go on; if a horse is punished for rebellion, another horse will eat his oats just as well. But if one negro becomes successful, another negro becomes successful, and if one is shot down, others are deterred. Therefore I say the institution of slavery is so bitter in itself that it sours everything it comes in contact with. It is no use talking about the majority of slaves having been kindly treated or anything like contented. Not one in ten thousand was contented, and the fact is, that where they were well treated the more discontented they were. I was a slave until I was twenty-two years of age, and I know I suffered more acute anguish than most of the slaves around me, just because aspirations had been roused in me that were not aroused in them; because I was associated with gentlemen who were so near to liberty and brought me so near to it that I wanted it all the more.

Nonconformist (London), 8 November 1865; *BAP*, 1:565–67.

SLAVE NARRATIVES

Autobiographies of former slaves offered the reading public compelling firsthand accounts of slave life—the drama of escapes, the heartrending tragedy of slave families separated on the auction block, and the brutality of plantation life. The narratives of J. W. C. Pennington, Frederick Douglass, and William Wells Brown were among the many published in the United States and abroad. Royalties from the autobiographies helped support the careers of such professional abolitionists as Douglass and Brown. Many former slaves financed their antislavery lecture tours in the British Isles by selling copies of their narratives along the way. Slave narratives provided a unique and effective means of spreading the antislavery message, and after more than a century, they retain their place in American literature and remain an invaluable historical record of slave life and culture.

19 SLAVERY IN KENTUCKY

Lewis G. Clarke's description of slave life in Kentucky refuted the popular belief that slavery was milder in the border states than in the deep South.

As a general thing, if a Kentuckian has a little money, he'd a deal rather vest it in slaves than any other property. A horse don't know that he's property, and a man does. There's a sort of satisfaction in thinking "You're a man, but you're *mine*. You're as white as I am but you're *mine*." Many a time I've had 'em say to me, "You're my property. If I tell you to hold your hand in the fire till it burns off, you've got to do it." Not that they *meant* to make me put my hand in the fire, but they liked to let me know they had the *power*. The whiter a man is, the lower down they keep him.

Kentucky is the best of the slave States, in respect to the laws, but the masters manage to fix things pretty much to their own liking. The law don't allow 'em to brand a slave, or cut off his ear; but if they happen to switch it off with a cow-hide, nobody says anything about it. Though the laws are better than in other States, they ain't anyways equal. If a negro breaks open a house, he is hung for it, but if a white man does the same thing, he is put in the penitentiary, unless he has money enough to buy himself off. And there is one crime for which more black men are hung than any other, and if a white man does it, it is no crime at all. The law gives him full swing, and he don't fail to use his privilege, I can tell you. Now, if there was nothing else but this, it would make a slave's life as bad as death, many times. I can't tell these respectable people as much as I would like to, but think for a minute how you would like to have *your* sisters, and *your* wives, and *your* daughters, completely, teetotally, and altogether, in the power of a master. You can picture to yourselves a little how you would feel; but oh, if I could *tell* you! A slave woman ain't allowed to respect herself, if she would. I had a pretty sister; she was whiter than I am, for she took more after her father. When she was sixteen years old, her master sent for her. When he sent for her again, she cried, and did not want to go. She told her mother her troubles and she tried to encourage her to be decent, and hold up her head above such things, if she could. Her master was so mad, to think she complained to her mother, that he sold her right off to Louisiana; and we heard afterward that she died there of hard usage.

Now, who would like to be a slave, even if there was nothing bad about it but such treatment of his sisters and daughters? But there's a worse thing yet about slavery; the worst thing in the whole lot; though it's all bad, from the butt end to *pint*. I mean the *patter rollers* (patrols). I suppose you know that they have patter rollers to go round o'nights, to see that the slaves are all in, and not planning any mischief? Now, these are just about the worst fellows that can be found; as bad as any you could pick up on the wharves. The reason is, you see, that no decent man will undertake the business. Gentlemen in Kentucky are ready enough to hire such jobs done, but if you was to ask any of them to *be* a patter roller, he would look upon it as a right down insult, and likely enough would blow out your brains for an answer. They're mighty handy with pistols down there; and if a man don't resent anything that's put upon them, they call him Poke easy. The slaves catch it, too; and them as won't fight, is called Poke easy. But as I was telling ye, they hire these patter rollers, and they have to take the meanest fellows above ground; and because they are so mortal sure the slaves don't *want* their freedom, they have to put all power into their hands, to do with the niggers jest as they like. If a slave don't open his door to them, at any time of night, they break it down. They steal his money, if they can find it, and act just as they please with his wives and daughters. If a husband dares to say a word, or even look as if he wasn't quite satisfied, they tie him up and give him thirty-nine lashes. If there's any likely young girls in a slave's hut, they're mighty apt to have business there; especially if they think any colored young man takes a fancy to any of 'em. Maybe he'll get a pass from his master, and go to see the young girl for a few hours. [If] the patter rollers break in and find him, they'll abuse the girl as bad as they can, on purpose to provoke him. If he looks cross, they give him a flogging, tear up his pass, turn him out of doors, and then take him up and whip him for being out without a pass. If the slave says they tore it up, they swear he lies, and nine times out of ten the master won't come out agin 'em, for they say it won't *do* to let the niggers suppose they may complain of the patter rollers; they must be taught that it's their business to obey 'em in everything; and the patter roller knows that very well. Oh how often I've seen the poor girls sob and cry, when there's been such goings on! Maybe you think, because they're slaves, they ain't got no feeling and no shame! A woman's being a slave, don't stop her genteel ideas; that is, according to their way, and far as they *can*. They know they must submit to their masters; besides, their masters, maybe, dress 'em up, and make 'em little presents, and give 'em more privileges, while the whim lasts; but that ain't like having a parcel of low, dirty, swearing, drunk patter rollers let loose among 'em, like so many hogs. This breaks down their spirits dreadfully, and makes 'em wish they were dead.

Now, who among you would like to have *your* wives, and daughters, and sisters, in *such* a situation? This is what every slave in all these States is exposed to. Yet folks go from these parts down to Kentucky, and come back, and say the slaves have enough to eat and drink, and they are very happy, and they wouldn't mind it much to be slaves themselves. I'd like to have 'em to try it, it would teach 'em a little more than they know now. I'm not going to deny that Kentucky is better than other slave States, in respect of her laws; and she has the best name, too, about treating her slaves. But one great reason of that is, they are proud about punishing in *public*. If a man ties his slave up in the market place, and flogs him till he can't stand, the neighbors all cry out, "What a shame! The man has no regard to his character. What an abominable thing to have that nigger screaming where *everybody can hear!* Shame on him, to do such things in public!"

But if the same man flogs his slave ten times as bad, up garret or down cellar, with his mouth stopped, that he mayn't make a noise, or off in the woods, out of hearing—it's all well enough. If his neighbor hear of it, they only say, "Well, of course there's no managing niggers without letting 'em know who's master." And there's an end of the business. The law, to be sure, don't allow such cruel floggings; but how's a slave going to get the law of his master? The law won't let him, nor any of his slaves, testify; and if the neighbors know anything about it, they *won't* testify. For it won't *do* to let the slaves think they would be upheld in complaining of master or overseer. I told you in the beginning, that it wouldn't *do* to let the slave think he is a *man*. That would spoil slavery, clean, entirely. No, this is the cruelty of the thing—A SLAVE CAN'T BE A MAN. He *must* be made a brute, but he ain't a brute, neither, if he had a chance to act himself out. Many a one of 'em is right smart, I tell you. But a horse *can't* speak, and a slave *daren't*; and that's the best way I can tell the story.

Signal of Liberty (Ann Arbor, Mich.), 23 January 1843; *BAP*, 3:393–95.

20 A THOUSAND MILES TO FREEDOM

After William and Ellen Craft's remarkable escape from slavery was made known, the British public greeted them as celebrities upon their arrival in England late in 1850. William Craft recounted their dramatic journey to freedom before antislavery groups throughout the British Isles, including a meeting in Edinburgh, Scotland.

* * * My wife and I escaped together from Georgia, and came on to Boston, a distance of 2000 miles. We remained quietly in Boston for about two years, till the passage of the Fugitive Slave Bill. A couple of ruffians, who were hired by the men that claimed us as slaves to come to Boston and arrest us, got out warrants for our apprehension and placed them in the hands of the District Marshal, but, for some reason or other, the Marshal refused to execute them. He knew that we had been slaves, and that, from knowing what Slavery was, I was prepared to protect myself and my wife at all hazards against a United States Marshal or anybody else that attempted to drag us back to bondage. (Loud applause.) * * *

My wife belonged to one family and I to another, and we contrived plans for many years, both before and after our marriage, to escape from Georgia. At last we came to the conclusion that my wife should disguise herself in gentleman's apparel (Mrs. Craft being a white woman) that I should attend her as her servant. I set to work, therefore, and collected the clothes necessary to enable us to accomplish our purpose, buying one article of dress at one time and another at another. When everything was ready my wife told her mistress that her aunt, who lived at a place about twelve miles off, was very ill, and that she was exceedingly anxious to go and see her before she died. Her mistress refused to let her away, but my wife, after a great deal of crying, succeeded in getting her consent. I then told the man for whom I was working, who had hired me from my master, that my wife was going to see her sick aunt, and that I wished to go along with her, and at last I was permitted to go. But my wife, instead of going to see her aunt, went to see her uncle in Philadelphia. (Laughter.) She got herself dressed as a gentleman, and pretending that she was suffering severely from inflammatory rheumatism, told the people that we came in contact with, while travelling northwards, that she was going to consult her uncle, who was an eminent physician in Philadelphia. The morning after we received permission to pay a visit to her aunt, I cut her hair square off, dressed her up in the clothes I had procured, and provided her with a pair of green spectacles. A poultice was applied to her right hand, for not being able to write, we were afraid that she would be discovered when requested to register her name at the hotels, &c. We travelled first to Savannah, and then took the steamboat to Charleston in South Carolina. When we arrived there, our luggage was taken off, and we went to a hotel. When we got to the hotel we had a room to ourselves, and the first thing I did was to purchase two hot poultices, one for the face of my poor master, and the other to bind up her hand. (Laughter.) I then went to the kitchen and blackened my master's boots. My master was asked down to dinner and took it along with a number of gentlemen, who were in the hotel, while I was sent to the kitchen to eat some scraps with a rusty knife and fork. But I did not eat very much; I was not very hungry about that time. (Applause.) After dinner I went to see how master was getting along, and it was soon time for us to go down to the steamboat again. She was so lame on account of the inflammatory rheuma-

Ellen Craft in the disguise used in her 1848 escape from slavery. From William Craft and Ellen Craft, Running a Thousand Miles for Freedom *(London, 1860).*

tism, that as we went down to the steamboat I had to hold her by the arm to prevent her from falling. (Laughter.) When we went to the steamboat office, my master asked for a ticket for herself and servant to Philadelphia. I was asked where we came from, and I said we came from Atlanta, which is distant about a hundred miles from the place we belonged to, so that if they thought of telegraphing back, they might be put on a wrong scent. When we were about to leave the office my wife was asked to register her name. She pointed to her poulticed hand, and requested the clerk to do it for her, but he said it was not in accordance with his duty. The captain of the boat, however, who was in the office, said he would put down the name, and accordingly entered the name "William Johnston" in the clerk's books. We soon arrived at Wilmington, where we took the railway cars, and travelled on through Virginia. At Petersburg an old gentleman with some nice daughters got into the car along with us. The old gentleman commenced a conversation with my master, who told him we were from Georgia, and that she was going to see her uncle in Philadelphia, in order to be cured of her inflammatory rheumatism. The old gentleman said, "Ah! I know what that is: I know how to sympathize with you." And if he did know what inflammatory rheumatism was, he knew more than my master did. After some conversation the old gentleman suggested to my master that she should lie down on the sofa at the end of the car, and asked if she would not suffer him to take off her boots, for the sake of giving her ease. She very willingly consented, so as to be freed from the necessity of talking. After she had lain down for some time, I heard one of the young ladies remarking, "this is a very nice young man, I never felt so much for a young man in my life." (Great laughter.) After lying on the sofa for a considerable time, my master rose, and got some cakes and candies from the young ladies. They enjoyed themselves very finely, till at last the old gentleman and his daughters got out at Richmond, Virginia; before he left us he gave my master his address, and said he and his daughters would be very happy to receive a visit from him, whenever he should find it convenient. My master, of course, thanked him very kindly and promised to give him a call when she went that way again. But I guess that she won't go that way again very soon. (Laughter.) We went on then to Fredericksburg—from Fredericksburg we went to Washington, and thence to Baltimore, where we arrived on the third day from the time we made our escape. At Baltimore officers were appointed to prevent fugitive slaves from escaping to Philadelphia, and as we were stepping into the cars a man accosted me and asked where I was going. I said I belonged to a sick young gentleman who was travelling to Philadelphia. I was then told that it was against the rules to let any slaves pass along without having first been examined in the office. So we went to the railway office, and the clerk asked, "Is this your servant?" She said I was. "Well," said he, "it is against our rules to allow any slaves to go along here, unless security is given that all is right. You must get some gentleman who knows you to certify that you have a right to take this slave along with you." She said she had bought tickets in Charleston to carry herself and her servant through to Philadelphia, and that she was acquainted with several gentlemen, but did not know that it was necessary to bring them along with her to certify that she was master of her own slave. "You must stay here then," said the clerk, "as it is against our rules to let you pass." But in the end, after some minutes' consultation with the other clerks, he said, "Well, I don't know what to do about it; he is a sick young fellow, and I suppose I must tell the conductor to let him and his slave pass along." About five o'clock next morning we arrived in Philadelphia, and went to a hotel for colored people, to which we had been recommended by a fellow passenger. After being in the house for a short time, I told the landlord who we were. He introduced us to Mr. William Wells Brown and other friends; but it was thought the safest plan that we should go on to Boston, where we resided in peace and quiet till the passage of the Fugitive Slave Bill. Mr. Craft concluded by stating that he always felt embarrassed in relating the manner of their escape, on account of the deception that they were obliged to use; but he believed that the greatest portion of the guilt of that deception belonged to the system under which they had formerly groaned.

National Anti-Slavery Standard (New York, N.Y.), 30 January 1851; *BAP*, 1:246–49.

21   SLAVE LIFE—A WOMAN'S STORY

In December 1852 a group of prominent Englishwomen published an antislavery appeal. Julia Tyler of Virginia, wife of former president John Tyler, wrote a lengthy response, in which she defended slavery as a benevolent institution. Fugitive slave Harriet Jacobs responded to Tyler's letter, focusing on the delicate subject of the sexual abuse of slave women. Jacobs later told her personal story in Incidents in the Life of a Slave Girl *(1861).*

Sir:

Having carefully read your paper for some months, I became very much interested in some of the articles and comments written on Mrs. Tyler's Reply to the Ladies of England. Being a slave myself, I could not have felt otherwise. Would that I could write an article worthy of notice in your columns. As I never enjoyed the advantages of an education, therefore I could not study the arts of reading and writing, yet poor as it may be, I had rather give it from my own hand, than have it said that I employed others to do it for me. The truth can never be told so well through the second and third person as from yourself. But I am straying from the question. In that Reply to the Ladies of England, Mrs. Tyler said that slaves were never sold only under very peculiar circumstances. As Mrs. Tyler and her friend Bhains were so far used up, that he could not explain what those peculiar circumstances were, let one whose peculiar sufferings justifies her in explaining it for Mrs. Tyler.

I was born a slave, reared in the Southern hot-bed until I was the mother of two children, sold at the early age of two and four years old. I have been hunted through all of the Northern States, but no, I will not tell you of my own suffering—no, it would harrow up my soul, and defeat the object that I wish to pursue. Enough—the dregs of that bitter cup have been my bounty for many years.

And as this is the first time that I ever took my pen in hand to make such an attempt, you will not say that it is fiction, for had I the inclination, I have neither the brain or talent to write it. But to this very peculiar circumstance under which slaves are sold.

My mother was held as property by a maiden lady; when she married, my younger sister was in her fourteenth year, whom they took into the family. She was as gentle as she was beautiful. Innocent and guileless child, the light of our desolate hearth! But oh, my great heart bleeds to tell you of the misery and degradation she was forced to suffer in slavery. The monster who owned her had no humanity in his soul. The most sincere affection that his heart was capable of could not make him faithful to his beautiful and wealthy bride the short time of three months, but every stratagem was used to seduce my sister. Mortified and tormented beyond endurance, this child came and threw herself on her mother's bosom, the only place where she could seek refuge from her persecutor; and yet she could not protect her child that she had bore into the world. On that bosom with *bitter tears* she told her troubles, and entreated her mother to save her. And oh, Christian mothers! you that have daughters of your own, can you think of your sable sisters without offering a prayer to that God who created all in their behalf? My poor mother, naturally high-spirited, smarting under what she considered as the wrongs and outrages which her child had to bear, sought her master, entreating him to spare her child. Nothing could exceed his rage at this, what he called impertinence. My mother was dragged to jail, there remained twenty-five days, with negro traders to come in as they liked to examine her, as she was offered for sale. My sister was told that she must yield, or never expect to see her mother again. There were three younger children; on no other condition could she be restored to them without the sacrifice of one. That child gave herself up to her master's bidding, to save one that was dearer to her than life itself. And can you, Christian, find it in your heart to despise her? Ah, no! not even Mrs. Tyler; for though we believe that the vanity of a name would lead her to bestow her hand where her heart could never go with it, yet, with all her faults and follies, she is nothing more than a *woman*. For if her domestic hearth is surrounded with slaves, ere long before this she has opened her eyes to the evils of slavery, and that the mistress as well as the slave must submit to the indignities and vices imposed on them by their lords of body and soul. But to one of those peculiar circumstances.

At fifteen, my sister held to her bosom an innocent offspring of her guilt and misery. In this way she dragged a miserable existence of two years, between the fires of her mistress's jealousy and her master's brutal passion. At seventeen, she gave birth to another helpless infant, heir to all the evils of slavery. Thus life and its sufferings were meted out to her until her twenty-first year. Sorrow and suffering had made its ravages upon her—she was less the object to be desired by the fiend who had crushed her to the earth; and as her children grew, they bore too strong a resemblance to him who desired to give them no other inheritance save Chains and Handcuffs, and in the dead hour of the night, when this young, deserted mother lay with her little ones clinging around her, little dreaming of the dark and inhuman plot that would be carried into execution before another dawn, and when the sun rose on God's beautiful earth, that broken-hearted mother was far on her way to the capitol of Virginia. That day should have refused her light to so disgraceful and inhuman an act in your boasted country of Liberty. Yet, reader, it is true, those two helpless children were the *sons* of one of your sainted Members in Congress; that agonized mother, his victim and slave. And where she now is God only knows, who has kept a record on high of all that she has suffered on earth.

And, you would exclaim, Could not the master have been more merciful to his children? God is merciful to all of his children, but it is seldom that a slaveholder has any mercy for his slave child. And you will believe it when I tell you, that mother and her children were sold to make room for another sister, who was now the age of that mother when she entered the family. And this selling appeased the mistress's wrath, and satisfied her desire for *revenge*, and made the path more smooth for her young rival at first. For there is a strong rivalry between a handsome mulatto girl and a jealous and *faded* mistress, and her liege lord sadly neglects those little attentions for a while that once made her happy. For the master will either neglect his wife or double his attentions, to save him from being suspected by his wife. Would you not think that Southern women had cause to despise that Slavery which forces them to bear so much deception practiced by their *husbands*? Yet all this is true, for a slaveholder seldom takes a white mistress, for she is an expensive commodity, not submissive as he would like to have her, but more apt to be tyrannical; and when his passion seeks another object, he must leave her in quiet possession of all the gewgaws that she has sold herself for. But not so with his poor *slave victim*, that he has robbed of everything that could make life desirable; she must be torn from the little that is left to bind her to life, and sold by her *seducer* and *master*, caring not where, so that it puts him in possession of enough to purchase another victim. And such are the peculiar circumstances of American Slavery—of all the evils in God's sight the most to be abhorred.

Perhaps while I am writing this, you too, dear Emily, may be on your way to the Mississippi River, for those peculiar circumstances occur every day in the midst of my poor oppressed fellow-creatures in bondage. And oh ye Christians, while your arms are extended to receive the oppressed of all nations, while you exert every power of your soul to assist them to raise funds, put weapons in their hands, tell them to return to their own country to slay every foe until they break the accursed yoke from off their necks, not buying and selling; this they never do under any circumstances. But while Americans do all this, they forget the millions of slaves they have at home, bought and sold under very peculiar circumstances.

And because one friend of the slave has dared to tell of their wrongs you would annihilate her. But in *Uncle Tom's Cabin* she has not told the half. Would that I had one spark from her storehouse of genius and talent, I would tell you of my own sufferings—I would tell you of wrongs that Hungary has never inflicted, nor England ever dreamed of in this free country where all nations fly for liberty, equal rights and protection under your stripes and stars. It should be stripes and scars, for they go along with Mrs. Tyler's peculiar circumstances, of which I have told you only one.

A FUGITIVE SLAVE

New York Tribune (N.Y.), 21 June 1853; *BAP*, 4:164–67.

22 NARRATIVE OF TOM WILSON

Upon his arrival in England in January 1858, fugitive slave Tom Wilson dictated a brief autobiography, which appeared in several London newspapers.

My name is Tom Wilson. I arrived here in a ship called the *Metropolis*, Captain Foster. I am slave-born. I have been under slave bondage ever since I was born. I am now forty-five years old. I belonged to Mr. Henry Fastman, of New York, cotton-presser. I was under him for the space of seven years. Before then I belonged to Colonel Barr, of Woodford, Mississippi. There I had a wife and three children, besides having had another child, which died. I was sold by auction by Major Baird's auctioneer for 2,500 dollars, and was taken down to New Orleans, away from my wife and children, and I haven't seen them since. Shortly after I got there Mr. Fastman's overseer, Burks, commenced to ill-use me. I didn't understand tying the cotton; it was new to me, and I was awkward; so I was flogged. They used to tie me down across a cotton bale and give me 200 or 300 with a leather strap. I am marked with the whip from the ankle bone to the crown of my head. Some years before I was sold from Mississippi, the overseer there, because I resisted punishment once, cut my right arm across the muscle, and then had it stitched up. He did that, as he said, to weaken me, because I was too strong in the arm. About a year and a half after I had been in New Orleans I ran into the woods. I was followed by Burks and a pack of bloodhounds into the Baddenrush swamp. The dogs soon caught me; they tore my legs and body with their teeth. Here are the marks yet. (As he spoke he turned up his trousers legging and exposed formidable seams extending up the calf and above the knee joint.) Burks (he continued) rode up to me with his gun and shot me in the hip with 14 buck shot, which can be seen and examined at any time. The dogs continued to pin me with their teeth. After that I knew nothing about what they did to me for about a week. When I got a little strong they burned my back with a red hot iron, and legs with spirits of turpentine, to punish me for escaping. The put an iron collar round my neck, which I wore for eight months, besides two irons, one on each leg. After that I was watched very closely, but one night, about a week after Christmas, I ran away and hid myself under the sawdust in a sawmill pit, below New Orleans. I was followed by Burks, the overseer, and the dogs, but they did not find me. I crept out and ran away, for more safety, to the Great salt-water Lake, behind Orleans, secreting myself under the bushes and vines. There are alligators in the lake, and as I waded up to the knees in the water the alligators followed me, grunting and bellowing, and trying to get me. I had several times to climb up trees to escape them; but I felt safer among the alligators than among white men. In the morning, at 4 o'clock, I went down to the wharf. On the road I came across some of the men who were out watching for me with guns and dogs. It was just getting light. I began to whistle and sing, and walked close by them, and they paid no attention to me. When I got down to the wharf some of the coloured crew of the American cotton ship *Metropolis* took me on board, and hid me away among the bales. One of the coloured men split on me, and there was a search for me that day; but they did not find me, though they came very near to me, and I trembled to think that I should be taken back and tortured. I was frightened, too, for the coloured men who had befriended me. I was kept out of sight of the white men, and Captain Foster did not know anything about it until after the men had been paid off at Liverpool. I remained hid from a week after Christmas until about three weeks ago, when the ship came here. During the time I was secreted I was kept alive by the coloured men who had been so good to me. They brought me something to eat and drink every night. When I first landed here I was frightened at every white man I passed, and I hid myself about where I could, and begged at night for bread. I was afraid I should be taken into slavery again. I did not know I could not be a slave here.

Inquirer (London), 28 February 1858; *BAP*, 1:430–31.

BLACK WOMEN ABOLITIONISTS

The antislavery movement brought new responsibilities and new opportunities for African American women. From the rise of immediatism in the 1830s, women were directly involved. Maria W. Stewart and Sarah M. Douglass conducted antislavery lectures at a time when such activity was reserved for men. Mary Ann Shadd Cary became the first black woman editor when she joined the staff of the *Provincial Freeman* in 1854. Harriet Myers and Mary E. Bibb worked as unacknowledged editors of newspapers published by their husbands, Stephen A. Myers and Henry Bibb. Other women supplied the antislavery press with correspondence, poetry, essays, and slave narratives. African American women organized antislavery auxiliaries and assisted fugitive slaves along the underground railroad. By sponsoring fairs and bazaars, they raised thousands of dollars to support the antislavery press and antislavery societies. During the Civil War, women directed their fund-raising efforts to support soldiers' aid and contraband relief. Many went South to carry out mission work among the freedmen. Through these activities, women assumed leadership roles in the black community and made their concerns and goals an integral part of black abolitionism.

23 A WOMAN'S ABOLITIONISM

In the summer of 1832, Sarah M. Douglass discussed personal anti-slavery commitment before the Female Literary Society of Philadelphia, a black reform organization.

My Friends—My Sisters:

How important is the occasion for which we have assembled ourselves together this evening, to hold a feast, to feed our never-dying minds, to excite each other to deeds of mercy, words of peace; to stir up in the bosom of each, gratitude to God for his increasing goodness, and feeling of deep sympathy for our brethren and sisters, who are in this land of christian light and liberty held in bondage the most cruel and degrading—to make their cause our own!

An English writer has said, "We must feel deeply before we can act rightly; from that absorbing, heart-rendering compassion for ourselves springs a deeper sympathy for others, and from a sense of our weakness and our own upbraidings arises a disposition to be indulgent, to forbear, to forgive." This is my experience. One short year ago, how different were my feelings on the subject of slavery! It is true, the wail of the captive sometimes came to my ear in the midst of my happiness, and caused my heart to bleed for his wrongs; but, alas! the impression was as evanescent as the early cloud and morning dew. I had formed a little world of my own, and cared not to move beyond its precincts. But how was the scene changed when I beheld the oppressor lurking on the border of my own peaceful home! I saw his iron hand stretched forth to seize me as his prey, and the cause of the slave became my own. I started up, and with one mighty effort threw from me the lethargy which had covered me as a mantle for years; and determined, by the help of the Almighty, to use every exertion in my power to elevate the character of my wronged and neglected race. One year ago, I detested the slaveholder; now I can pity and pray for him. Has not this been your experience, my sisters? Have you not felt as I have felt upon this thrilling subject? My heart assures me some of you have.

And now, my sisters, I would earnestly and affectionately press upon you the necessity of placing your whole dependence on God; poor, weak, finite creatures as we are, we can do nothing for ourselves. He is all powerful; He is waiting to be gracious to us as a people. Do you feel your inability to do good? Come to Him who giveth liberally and upbraideth not; bring your wrongs and fears to Him, as you would to a tender parent—He will sympathise with you. I know from blessed, heart-cheering experience the excellency of having a God to trust to in seasons of trial and conflict. What but this can support us should the pestilence which has devastated Asia be born to us by the summer breezes? What but this can uphold our fainting footsteps in the swellings of Jordan? It is the only thing worth living for— the only thing that can disarm death of his sting. I am earnestly solicitous that each of us may adopt this language:

"I have no hope in man, but much in God—
Much in the rock of ages."

In conclusion, I would respectfully recommend that our mental feast should commence by reading a portion of the Holy Scriptures. A pause should proceed the reading for supplication. It is my wish that the reading and conversation should be altogether directed to the subject of slavery. The refreshment which may be offered to you for the body, will be of the most simple kind, that you may feel for those who have nothing to refresh body and mind.

Liberator (Boston, Mass.), 21 July 1832; *BAP*, 3:116–17.

2 4   THE ANTISLAVERY FAIR

Sarah L. Forten's letter to Elizabeth H. Whittier, a white Quaker abolitionist, provides a detailed portrait of an antislavery fair organized by an interracial women's group in Philadelphia.

Philadelphia, [Pennsylvania]
Dec[ember] 25th, 1836

My Dear Elizabeth:

I have delayed replying to your kind letter untill now because I wished to give you an account of our Anti Slavery Fair—and I knew you would be gratified by a description of it and of the good success [we] had— I presume I may as well dash into the subject ~~the subject~~ at once for a commencement, as to wait and place it in the middle part—or at the end of my letter. Our Society have been making preparations for the last four months to get up this Sale—and many very beautiful fancy productions did they manafacture for the occasion. The[y] hired the Fire Mens Hall in North St. below arch—and decorated it with evergreens—and flowers—and had it brilliantly lighted—there was six Tables—including a refreshment Table— on which most of the eatables were presented—three large Pound Cakes— Oranges—and Grapes were given to us—so our expenses were not great— and the proceeds amounted to more than three hundred Dollars—we only had the Hall for a day and two evenings—so you may see we done well for

FAIR.

The Ladies (of color) of the town of Frankfort propose giving a **FAIR**, at the house of **Mrs. RILLA HARRIS,** (*alias,* Simpson,) on Thursday evening next, for benevolent purposes, under the superintendence of Mrs. Rilla Harris.

All the delicacies of the season will be served up in the most palatable style----such as *Ice Creams, Cakes, Lemonades, Jellies, Fruits, Nuts, &c. &c.*

It is hoped, as the proceeds are to be applied to benevolent purposes, that the citizens generally will turn out and aid in the enterprise.

JULY 6, 1847.

Advertisement for a black women's fair. Courtesy of William L. Clements Library, University of Michigan.

so short a time. There was twel[ve] Ladies superintending the Tables. We had a Post Office opened—for letters to be distributed at 12½ cts. apiece. A Young Lady and myself were superintending Post Mistresses—and we delivered upwards of one hundred letters—nearly one half of which we were obliged to pen ourselves. We were as busy as we could be all the time—and much amusement was afforded by the dispatch with which the mails arrived. In t[he] course of the evening a few lines addressed to the Ladies presiding—were handed in by a Young Gentleman—they are good—and I'll copy them for you at the end of my letter. I wish you could have been here—to contribute and receive a share of the general satisfaction.

Lines addressed to the Ladies presiding at the fair—

> The AntiSlavery Fair—are fair indeed,
> Their pretty eyes from every table,
> Deep blue—dark hazel—or bright sable;
> Will many [of] us captive lead,
> Sow tis not fair—that those who say
> That Slaves should be emancipated,

Should so forget the word <u>today</u>
(By victory, perhaps elated)
As to reduce to Slavery,
Those gentlemen who call to see
What they can buy with ready cash,
Yet <u>they</u> are made to feel the lash
(The eye lash) which it is quite plain,
Though not perhaps inflicting pain
Soon catches—then proceedes to bind
All that are call'd the Batchelor kind.
Ye <u>fair</u> ones of the <u>Fair</u> today,
May this be called a <u>fair</u> proceeding?
Ye fairly take our hearts away;
Unfairly us to bondage leading

———————————————

"All should be free"—"None should be bound"
This is your boasted theory,
Whilst in the <u>act</u>—y'r fairly found
Depriving <u>us</u> of liberty.

There are—as you will percieve several errors in the lines, but as the writer does not aspire to be call'd a Poet—and the effusion was so appropriate to the occasion, I dare say he will not take offence at my transcribing them. They afforded us considerable merriment and if they win a smile from you—he will no doubt be amply repaid. Our excellent friend and advocate Gerrit Smith has been here and we are more than gratified by an acquaintance with him—he has brought his Wife and Daughter, a girl of fourteen years—to spend the Winter in our City—and we are delighted with them both. Miss Smiths health has not been good and her Parents think a change of air will be of service to her. Mrs. S—— is one of the plainest woman in her dress I ever saw. I learn that she devotes nearly <u>all</u> her income to benevolent purposes—this is so praiseworthy I could not forbear to mention it to you. She is also one of these lovely—good natured looking women who take ones heart on the instant. Mr. Smith has gone home.

I have this instant learned with deep regret and suprise of the Death of one of our valuable friends to the Abolition cause—Dr. Edwin P. Atlee— he was only confined to his bed one week—and we were not at all aware that he was dangerously ill—and I have been more than grieved by his sudden demise. He was a ~~active~~ noble member of the Society—and took an active part in many good works. Your Brother—I presume is acquainted with him and will feel regret that one of our useful men has been called away from his good works here—though I doubt not but that he has gone to receive his reward in Heaven. His Parents and Brothers and Sister have gone to Michigan to live—and as he was ill only one week, they will receive a severe shock—one, which they will not soon recover from.

As this is Christmas and two or three of my Relatives have come in to pass the day with us—I am unable to arrange my letter in better order—for a half dozen voices are holding forth on different subjects—making it rather impossible to write in a collected manner. You will therefore receive my excuses for whatever errors you should find. Please accept from myself and family the usual congratulations of the Season with the hope that you may be spared to see many returns of it. I send you one of my Brother Robert Purvis's addresses—on the demise of Thos Shipley. I will no longer intrude upon your time My Dear Friend—but ask you to write me only when you are at leisure. Your Friend

SARAH L. FORTEN

Whittier Papers, Central Michigan University, Mount Pleasant, Michigan; published by permission; *BAP*, 3:201–4.

25 A WOMAN'S PLACE

The forceful and rough-hewn style of Sojourner Truth earned her public recognition as one the foremost proponents of abolitionism and women's rights. She spoke on gender and equality before a women's rights convention on 29 May 1851 in Akron, Ohio.

May I say a few words? Receiving an affirmative answer, she proceeded; I want to say a few words about this matter. I am a woman's rights. I have as much muscle as any man, and can do as much work as any man. I have plowed and reaped and husked and chopped and mowed, and can any

man do more than that? I have heard much about the sexes being equal;
I can carry as much as any man, and can eat as much too, if I can get it.
I am as strong as any man that is now. As for intellect, all I can say is, if
woman have a pint and man a quart—why can't she have her little pint
full? You need not be afraid to give us our rights for fear we will take too
much, for we can't take more than our pint'll hold. The poor men seem to
be all in confusion, and don't know what to do. Why children, if you have
woman's rights give it to her and you will feel better. You will have your
own rights, and they won't be so much trouble. I can't read, but I can hear.
I have heard the bible and have learned that Eve caused man to sin. Well if
woman upset the world, do give her a chance to set it right side up again.
The Lady has spoken about Jesus, how he never spurned woman from him,
and she was right. When Lazarus died, Mary and Martha came to him with
faith and love and besought him to raise their brother. And Jesus wept—
and Lazarus came forth. And how came Jesus into the world? Through God
who created him and woman who bore him. Man, where is your part? But
the women are coming up, blessed be God, and a few of the men are coming
up with them. But man is in a tight place, the poor slave is on him, woman
is coming on him, and he is surely between a hawk and a buzzard.

Anti-Slavery Bugle (Salem, Ohio), 21 June 1851; *BAP*, 4:81–82.

26 ANTISLAVERY POETRY

Frances Ellen Watkins Harper, who lectured on behalf of the anti-slavery and women's rights movements, often recited poetry on those themes.

BURY ME IN A FREE LAND

You may make my grave wherever you will,
In a lowly vale or a lofty hill;
You may make it among earth's humblest graves,
But not in a land where men are slaves.

I could not sleep if around my grave
I heard the steps of a trembling slave;
His shadow above my silent tomb
Would make it a place of fearful gloom.

I could not rest if I heard the tread
Of a coffle-gang to the shambles led,
And the mother's shriek of wild despair
Rise like a curse on the trembling air.

I could not rest if I heard the lash
Drinking her blood at each fearful gash,
And I saw her babes torn from her breast
Like trembling doves from their parent nest.

I'd shudder and start, if I heard the bay
Of the bloodhounds seizing their human prey;
If I heard the captive plead in vain
As they tightened afresh his galling chain.

If I saw young girls, from their mothers' arms
Bartered and sold for their youthful charms
My eye would flash with a mornful flame,
My death-paled cheek grow red with shame.

I would sleep, dear friends, where bloated might
Can rob no man of his dearest right;
My rest shall be calm in any grave,
Where none calls his brother a slave.

I ask no monument proud and high
To arrest the gaze of passers by;
All that my spirit yearning craves,
Is—bury me not in the land of slaves.

Anti-Slavery Bugle (Salem, Ohio), 20 November 1858; *BAP*, 4:403–5.

Frances Ellen Watkins Harper. Courtesy of Library of Congress.

27   BOUND WITH THEM

The sense of community and purpose shared by African Americans extended beyond national borders. In writing to Vice-President Hannibal Hamlin, black women on the Canadian Pacific coast demonstrated their concern for the freed slaves in South Carolina.

Victoria, [Vancouver Island]
April 13, 1863

Hon. Hannibal Hamlin
Sir:
By order of the Committee of Colored Ladies of the British Colony of Victoria, V.I., please find inclosed a draft for £86 14 9 sterling on London, made payable to your order.

Please send it to Beaufort, S.C., for the benefit of the contrabands. One of the reasons for sending this money to Beaufort is, its being the first place a colored regiment was formed, according to law. This money has been raised by and through the colored people of this place, and who are originally from the United States.

We have also sent $170 to the City of Philadelphia for the same purpose, to be used there. You will please accept our thanks as a people for the great interest you have taken in the cause of humanity; and though many miles divide us from those who have the burden to bear in this great struggle for human liberty, our hearts are with you even unto death. Please acknowledge the receipt of this money through THE N. Y. TRIBUNE. Respectfully,

EMILY ALLEN, President

New York Tribune (N.Y.), 2 June 1863; *BAP*, 2:510–11.

ANTISLAVERY AND THE BLACK COMMUNITY

Abolitionism provided blacks with an opportunity to help reform American society. As they responded to the challenge, they influenced the antislavery crusade and brought profound changes to their own communities. Abolitionism energized black society and opened new avenues to community leadership and development. Through antislavery activity, they transformed and radicalized churches, mutual aid societies, and other existing institutions, and they created new organizations—vigilance committees, missionary societies, political associations, and a vibrant press. These efforts extended black abolitionism to nearly every facet of black life and culture.

28 WHAT HAVE THEY DONE?

Charles B. Ray, editor of the Colored American, *describes how the antislavery movement engendered a new optimism and activism in the black community during the 1830s.*

The question "what have abolitionists done for the colored man?" is often asked, and as often sneeringly answered by the inquisitor, NOTHING.

Having some knowledge on this subject, and being not a little interested in these matters, we beg leave to give our candid, unbiased opinion, and this opinion is the result of close observation and long experience. Abolitionists, apart from what they have done in waking up our guilty nation to its sin and danger, and apart from what they have done towards breaking the shackles of the slave, and towards procuring for him rights, privileges, and the Bible, have carried our population forward, in the scale of *improved humanity*, at least, half a century.

Had there been no Anti-Slavery organization or efficient Anti-Slavery action, similar to the organization and action of the American Anti-Slavery

Society for fifty years to come, our free colored population would not have been as efficient and as capable of taking care of themselves, and acting the part of enlightened men and citizens as they *now are*. The concessions made by abolitionists, *willingly*, and by their opponents, of *necessity*, to principle and to human rights, have almost effected among our colored brethren a *new creation*. Think for a moment what must have been the influence of the proclamation of our Declaration of Independence upon the mind and energies of our oppressed nation, in 76? Why it was like proclaiming LIFE to a valley of dry bones. Just so, did the publication of the first document of the abolitionists, which conceded to colored men *humanity and rights* effect our brethren. It seemed to give a new existence and to call forth energies and powers which they were not aware of possessing.

With increased humility before God and increased love and respect for men, the free population of our people, throughout the country, possess feelings of *manhood, energy, enterprise and virtue* which nothing but principles and measures of liberty could inspire. Without the abolition movement our colored citizens would have dragged out an intolerable existence of, at least, fifty years more, without energy, efficiency or elevation. More than this, slavery and colonization were exerting an influence of deterioration over the free colored population and effecting in them feelings of pusillanimity and discouragement, which we dare prophecy, would have eventually sought relief in universal and perpetual bondage or in banishment. "ABOLITION" has awoke this dispirited people to the dignity of manhood and to the energy and enterprize of freemen. With the same zeal and skill, which they now contend for "inalienable rights" do they also seek affluence and cultivation.

Colored American (New York, N.Y.), 13 July 1839; *BAP*, 3:311–13.

29 THE PITTSBURGH JUVENILE ANTI-SLAVERY SOCIETY

Black abolitionism was a community venture that involved men and women of all ages and social stations. David J. Peck and George B.

Vashon described the activities of their antislavery youth group in a report to the Colored American *in 1839. As adults, both men became prominent reform leaders.*

Pittsburgh, [Pennsylvania]
Nov. 14, 1839

Gentlemen:

At a meeting of the Juvenile Anti-Slavery Society, held November 11, it was unanimously resolved that five dollars should be given to the support of the *Colored American*, a paper, which, of all others we ought to support. We hope that this small donation may be the means of doing good, and we pray you in the name of the members of the Juvenile Anti-Slavery Society, to accept it as a small token of the esteem we have for your paper. The Juvenile Anti-Slavery Society (of which we have the honor of being members) was formed on the seventh of July, 1838. It is a "cent a week" society, and is the first and only of the kind formed this side of the mountains. The Society now consists of about forty members: several of whom have addressed the Society, at different times. We conclude, by expressing our hope, that our little mite may be of some service in the cause, in which you are engaged. Very respectfully, Your obdt. servants,

DAVID PECK Pres. J.A.S.S.
GEO. B. VASHON, Sec

Colored American (New York, N.Y.), 23 November 1839; *BAP*, 3:320–21.

30 THE UNION MISSIONARY SOCIETY

African American clergymen founded the Union Missionary Society to encourage the growth of Christian missions in Africa. They believed these missions would hasten the demise of slavery. Pittsburgh clergyman and black abolitionist Lewis Woodson was skeptical about

the new society and called on white philanthropist Lewis Tappan for
clarification.

Pittsburgh, P[ennsylvani]a
January 31st, 1842

My Dear Sir:
It is taken for granted that you are aware of the organization of the
Union Missionary Society at Hartford Conn. in August last; and that you
are acquainted with the general character of those who originated it, and
assisted in its organization.

So far as the nature and design of the Society is understood in this region,
it is generally approved of by all opposed to slavery; especially in regard
to its educating and sending out, as missionaries, persons of African ex-
traction. It is supposed that several causes combine to make these the most
proper persons for propagating the gospel in Africa, among which are their
national consanguinity, national identity, and a national sympathy. It is true
that these causes must be greatly modified, if not annihilated in those who
for many generations have inhabited the northern regions of the United
States; but they are certainly very applicable to those of the extreme south.

A strong desire to do something for the conversion and civilization of
Africa, is felt by several persons in this region; and they are now ready
and willing to co-operate with any organization of known integrity and efficiency . Residing at so great a distance from the seat of its operations, we
need scarcely inform you, that as yet, our knowledge of the general character of the Hartford Society is quite imperfect. We wish it however to be
understood, that we have never heard any thing said against it; but not quite
enough for it, to fully warrant its friends in demanding for it that support
which it requires for the great object which it proposes to accomplish.

All the colored people know you, and all their friends know you, and all
have confidence in you, in consequence of your past services; and some in
this city are anxious to know your views of the Union Missionary Society
organized at Hartford in August last. Among those who are anxious to know
your opinion are some of the most wealthy and influential Abolitionists in
this city.

I should be much obliged to you, to answer this letter at your earliest convenience, as there is to be a meeting of the West Pennsylvania AntiSlavery Society in this city on the 23rd of Feby. and some wealthy friends from the adjoining counties would like to see it.

My reluctance at troubling you with this letter is only overcome by my more ardent desire to promote the interests of my brethren in this country and in Africa. Your favourable opinion would bring to the assistance of the Society several additional friends, and it is therefore respectfully solicited. Your most sincere friend And humble servant,

LEWIS WOODSON

Weld-Grimké Papers, Clements Library, University of Michigan, Ann Arbor, Michigan; published by permission; *BAP*, 3:365–66.

31   BLACK ABOLITIONISM IN THE PULPIT

The American Home Missionary Society (AHMS) allocated small stipends to Henry Highland Garnet and Samuel Ringgold Ward, both prominent black clergymen and committed political abolitionists. When the AHMS reprimanded them for "preaching politics on the Sabbath," they responded with letters to church officials defending antislavery in the church.

Geneva, [New York]
Nov[ember] 10, 1843

Rev. J. A. Murray
Dear Sir:
Having heard that some objections arose in the Home Missionary Board, the other day, to my appointment, on the ground of doubts as to my political sentiments, and my preaching politics on the Sabbath &c., it seemed to me, but just that I should say in a word what the truth is on this point.

In preaching now, as heretofore, I frequently speak of national sins. Of course, I mention slavery among them. I call upon the people to do all in their power at the ballot box & elsewhere for the removal of this sin, or to expect the severe judgements of God for its continuance. I frequently say that since slavery is admitted to be a sinful institution that a man is no more at liberty (morally) to vote for it than he is to <u>pray</u> for it.

When the duty of doing <u>all</u> to the glory of God is under ~~consideration~~ consideration I sometimes demand that a man should glorify God, or at least endeavor to glorify God, in his civil relations as well and as much as elsewhere.

I preach that a man has no more right to commit sin with his vote, than with any other power or instrument. I plead for no party, no candidates, against no party, against no candidates, means nor measures on the Sabbath. But what I have described in the foregoing lines I do and <u>shall</u> preach, because I think it duty to rebuke <u>all</u> sins, and to plead for righteousness every where.

If the Board deem it best not to appoint me I submit to their decision, only asking that I may have a fair and a plain statement of the reason why I am not appointed. Your humble servant,

S A M L .   R .   W A R D

American Home Missionary Society Papers, Amistad Research Center, Tulane University, New Orleans, Louisiana; published by permission; *BAP*, 3:425–26.

Troy, N[ew] Y[ork]
June 28, 1844

Rev. C. Hall
Dear Bro. Hall:
At a meeting of our Presbytery a letter which you sent to Rev. Mr. Noble was read. You state in that communication that it had been reported that I had been much engaged in <u>political action</u> , and you therefore hesitate to renew my commission. I send this letter to [word crossed out] inform your committee that I withdraw my request.

It is true that I am an abolitionist, and when I speak of politicts I recommend all not to strengthen the Slave power. I have lifted up my feeble voice for my oppressed brethren—and what more or less could I do? My own kindred are this moment in Slavery—and I must speak for them—and do all that I can to break off their chains. This is all my crime. I hope the day will come when the American H. M. Society will not urge such an excuse. While I live I will raise my voice for Liberty. I am sorry that I have done so little. If I had a thousand lives I would spend them all for my bleeding people—for God tells me to remember them.

If it is thought that the $50. which I received the last year was improperly given I will refund the money. I have only to say that my conscience is void of offence in this matter. I have done nothing more than I would desire that others should do for me in like circumstances. Yours truly in Christian love,

HENRY H. GARNET

American Home Missionary Society Papers, Amistad Research Center, Tulane University, New Orleans, Louisiana; published by permission; *BAP*, 3:426.

32 FAIR IN AID OF THE IMPARTIAL CITIZEN

Subscriptions and advertisement revenue seldom met the publishing costs of the African American press; additional community support was needed. Black women in New York State, led by Julia Garnet, sponsored an antislavery fair in September 1849 on behalf of Samuel Ringgold Ward's Impartial Citizen.

That the press should be sustained when it boldly and fearlessly advocates our rights, and when it really and truly represents us, is evident to all. That a Reform Paper like the *Impartial Citizen* cannot sustain itself without the aid of its friends, has been demonstrated too often and too clearly to admit of a shadow of a doubt. And that it is the duty of Reformers to contribute of their means, time and talents for the sustenance of such a Press is equally unquestionable.

Feeling in some measure the force of these truths, the undersigned have determined, with the Divine assistance, to hold a FAIR to aid the self-sacrificing Editor and Publisher of the *Impartial Citizen*, in the City of Syracuse, on the 11th, 12th, and 13th days of September next (during the time of the State Agricultural Fair), in the Lecture Room of the Congregational Church.

The friends not only of SAMUEL R. WARD, but of the three millions of slaves, and the six hundred thousand nominally free colored citizens, with whom he is identified, and in whose behalf he has for years toiled, the friends of Liberty, and Human Progress, the friends of Christ and His crushed and insulted and outraged Poor, are earnestly entreated to give us their countenance and encouragement on the occasion.

During the evenings there will be speaking and singing of a superior order.

"Come over and help us." * * *

Impartial Citizen (Syracuse, N.Y.), 5 September 1849; *BAP*, 4:38–39.

PROBLEMS IN THE MOVEMENT

Through the 1830s, black abolitionists became increasingly frustrated with the antislavery movement's white leadership. They were dismayed by the antislavery schism of the late 1830s and questioned whether white abolitionists, engrossed in heated ideological debates, had forgotten their primary commitment to the slave. Above all, blacks sensed that their white allies had abandoned the struggle against racial prejudice in the North. They perceived a waning interest among white abolitionists in the fight against political disfranchisement, segregation, and discrimination. They admonished white reformers for ignoring the economic issues confronting free blacks and urged them to open their businesses to black apprentices and employees. Black leaders found disturbing evidence of racial prejudice within the antislavery movement, particularly in the patronizing attitude and social conduct of many white reformers. Prejudice, Sarah L. Forten concluded, "clings like a dark mantle to our professed friends." The apparent failings of white abolitionism eventually spurred blacks to a more independent and militant course of antislavery action.

33   HINTS ABOUT PREJUDICE

Samuel E. Cornish, editor of the Colored American, *challenged white abolitionists to measure their antislavery commitment by making racial prejudice "the test question."*

Now is the time for abolitionists to gird up the loins of their minds for a conflict with prejudice against color—to burnish the armour of truth, to supply themselves with the appropriate tracts and books which are the ammunition necessary for our warfare—for now their use is called for. The signs of the times indicate this. The recent outbreak of popular violence in Philadelphia—the recent affair in Newark, where a worthy Minister has been hunted from his charge, because he presumed to walk to meeting with a colored woman, and to seat her in a pew with his wife and family, one who was his own domestic, and a sister in the church (a most horrible sin truly!)—and the recent demonstration of sentiment in New Brunswick, because the Baptist Convention held at that place chose Brother Raymond of this City, to preach the introductory sermon. All these things place the question of prejudice against color, and the duty the abolitionists owe to their colored brethren, so prominently before the public, that it will be hard work, even should any be inclined to do it, to get around it or to dodge it. The time has come when the question has got to be met. When our friends must face it, if they are our friends; or do as some will, take to their heels and run. Prejudice against color, after all, is the test question—at least among us. The mere and direct question of slavery is not. For every man here says—"I am as much opposed to slavery as you are. But as for these *Niggers*, we don't want them here—let them go home to their own land." This is what we hear, and this is the feeling. Here comes the tug; and here our friends have to grapple with slavery, not at arms length, but with a back-hold. Here the slimy serpent is among them, coiled up in their own hearts and houses.

We see it, and have long seen it—that the real battleground between liberty and slavery is prejudice against color. The friends of humanity have as yet but possessed a few out-posts upon its frontiers. They have not yet undisputed possession of the field, even in their own hearts, as time will show; and we have been a little surprised that the phalanx of our friends have been so slow to see this.

We do not object of course to the tremendous cannonading which has been kept up on the citadel of slavery with the big ordinance and long-toms of our cause. Such as Emancipation in the West Indies—Bible *vs.* Slavery—Powers of Congress, and the like. But we suggest, whether the drill officers and the file leaders should not have inculcated a little more the importance and use of our abolition side arms and pocket weapons. That all may be as well prepared for the controversy, in close quarters as at a distance. Our abolition magazine is pretty well stocked. But yet there should be no slacking up in forging more. Brother Lewis' tract *on caste*, is a pocket pistol that no one should be without. "Goodell's Speech on Prejudice," and the *Appeal of the 40,000*, are both polished toledoes. *Rights of Colored Men* is a broadsword; and *The Negro Pew* an iron spear. Get your pistols and broad-swords brethren, and go to work.

Our figures are clumsy, and perhaps out of place. But our readers will understand what we mean. Now is the time to circulate books and tracts of the description we have spoken of. The public mind should be saturated with them.

Colored American (New York, N.Y.), 9 June 1838; *BAP*, 3:265–66.

34 PROFESSED FRIENDS

Samuel Ringgold Ward, in a letter to the National Anti-Slavery Standard, *accused many white abolitionists of failing to overcome their own racial prejudice.*

Peterboro, [New York]
June 27, 1840

Mr. Editor:

With all that has been done by our friends, we see ample reasons for efficient action on our own part. Abolitionists have met frequently, and held Town, County, State, and National Conventions. They have generally remembered us, scattered, peeled, disfranchised, and downtrodden, as we are. They have done much, very much, for the reformation of public opinion concerning us and our rights. Some of them have refused to sustain pro-slavery political parties, to give their suffrages to those who would not remember us in the halls of legislation. Yet the fact ought not to be concealed, that there are too many Abolitionists in *profession*, who have yet to learn what it is to crucify prejudice against color within their own bosoms. Too many who best love the colored man at a distance.

A fact or two in proof. From my own observation and painful experience, I am enabled to say, that a large proportion of the professed friends of the slave, the professed and recorded believers in the doctrine of immediate emancipation, give encouragement to prejudice against color, at the polls, in the social circle, and in the church.

At the polls, they sustain the pro-slavery laws which disfranchise us, and the pro-slavery parties that uphold and sanction those laws.

In the social circle, in company with white persons, they find it difficult to see a colored man, though they have spectacles on their noses.

In the church, they refuse to remonstrate against negro-pewism, and suffer colored persons to wander about the aisles unseated, till the sexton seats them *near the door*. A white person, of no greater respectability in appearance, enters next, and they offer him a good pew, with proper respect. Indeed, brother Gardner, of Newark, lately wrote me, that for seating and sitting with Rev. Mr. Williams (the pastor of the colored Methodist church of that city), in the free church of Newark, he was *reproved* by one of the *earliest Abolitionists* of New Jersey, [at] one of the sessions of that church.

Besides, Abolitionists have not so much regard for the rights of colored men as they think they have. When press, speech, and others of *their own rights* were jeopardized by the spirit of slavocracy, they raised their united voice, as men should, in self-defence. But now, when their own rights are somewhat secure, they appear to cease to feel identified with us. I know not how else to account for their strong and determined action in defence of their own rights, while now they are comparatively mute concerning *ours*.

I repeat, that these are facts which have come under my own observation; facts that are facts concerning a large proportion of the professed Abolitionists of this State and other States. Happy for us, however, there are many honorable exceptions, especially in Western New York. But viewing these facts as they are, and feeling their malign influence as we do, I must beg leave to dissent from the views expressed in an editorial article in the *Standard* of the 18th instant, concerning a Convention of colored people. I know that your intentions are correct; but had you worn a colored skin from October '17 to June '40, as I have, in this pseudo-republic, you would have seen through a very different medium. The continuation of wrongs, injustice, and ingratitude, inflicted upon us by the State government, the small share of sympathy evinced towards us by many of our professed friends, and the still smaller amount of efficient action put forth by them in our behalf, all render it indispensably necessary that the colored people of this State should convene and act for themselves. Yours, for pure and impartial Abolitionism.

SAMUEL R. WARD

National Anti-Slavery Standard (New York, N.Y.), 2 July 1840; *BAP*, 3:340–41.

3 5 THE NEED FOR A PRACTICAL
ABOLITIONISM

Stephen A. Myers, editor of the Northern Star and Freeman's Advocate, *questioned white abolitionist commitment to eradicating racial
prejudice in the North and called on white reformers to demonstrate
a "practical abolitionism" by training black apprentices in their shops
and businesses.*

For several years we have been astonished at the indifference mani-
fested by abolitionists, in regard to the adoption of some effectual measures
for advancing the welfare of free people of color. In observing the principles set forth by the abolition presses, the declarations of lecturers, and
the sentiments expressed to us in private in relation to these things, and
contrasting them with their daily practises we discover many gross inconsis-
tencies. They profess to possess the most generous and benevolent feelings
towards us, and deeply lament the unhappy situation in which we are placed
by unjust laws and a cruel and oppressive prejudice. They regret and acknowledge that we labor under a thousand disadvantages from which every
other class of community are exempt, and wonder that with all the accumulated hindrances to our progress to become intelligent and respectable
members of society, we possess moral fortitude sufficient to rise above the
surges of persecution.

Twenty-two thousand abolition votes were polled during the last year
in the states, in favor of persons opposed to southern slavery, and a large
number of those opposed to political action withheld theirs. Large numbers in this and other states, have also with us petitioned the legislatures,
for the repeal of those laws which were unjust, oppressive, anti-republican,
and inimical to the interests of the colored portion of the community. Now
with all this array of sentiment and feeling, and political action before us,
the natural inference would be, that the united wisdom, wealth, influence,
benevolence, and sympathy of so large a portion of our citizens, could and
would have devised some efficient means for bettering the condition of at
least a portion of the people of color.

Some twelve or fifteen years ago, when the spirit of immediate emancipation sundered the bonds by which it was bound, and arrayed itself with the immutable truth that all men are born free and equal, the veil which had covered the horrors of slavery and an unholy prejudice, was rent in twain; the corruption of almost the entire community was made palpable, and the hearts of men were found susceptible to the impressions of truth. The hopes of our people became exalted; their anticipations of future happiness and prosperity were high, and they believed that in a few years they should realize what for ages their fathers had fervently prayed for. But sad experience has taught us, that "it is a vain thing to trust in man." But yet amid all our expectations there are some things asserted of us, which we never expected nor ever desired. We never expected that abolitionists would place themselves upon a level even with the most intelligent and respectable of our people; neither did we desire their daughters in marriage. We did not expect to ride in their carriages, nor desire to mix in their parties of pleasure; but we did hope that they would do for us some things, which they have not only neglected, but what appears to us to have been foreign from their intentions. We supposed that while they advocated the rights of man and the cause of suffering humanity, that they would have been foremost in opening every avenue, and destroying every barrier in their power that was closed against us, or that retarded our progression; and that by doing so they would be enabled to present those with whom they plead for the restoration of the inalienable rights of man, a class of individuals rising from degradation, and striving to become good, intelligent, economical and industrious citizens. Probably there are no less than thirty thousand abolitionists in the states, and doubtless among them there are mechanics of every description; who, instead of endeavoring to break down prejudice and make a powerful thrust at slavery, by taking our youth and instructing them in the various branches, content themselves and suppose that *we* also are contented, by having them disseminate what they call *their* principles from one end of the country to the other. They profess to be opposed to slavery, but with the greater portion of them *we* believe that it is that slavery only which exists at the south.

Now we ask if the prejudice which exists at the north is not akin to the slavery of the south? *We* firmly believe it to be so, and if the prejudice of the northern abolitionists will not permit them to take as apprentices colored boys, or if their regard for the prejudices of others will not allow them so to do, *we also believe* that the influence of their example is more injurious to colored people at large, than the disinclination of the slave holder to release the victims of his avarice. And until abolitionists *eradicate prejudice from their own hearts*, they never *can* receive the unwavering confidence of the people of color. We do not ask for money, neither do we wish them to educate our children; these we will endeavor to provide for by the sweat of our brow, but we *do* ask that their workshops may be opened to our youth, and that those of us who are already in business may be patronized. These things (if there be any meaning in their language) we think we have a right to ask of those who are our professed friends, and if they will grant what we actually want (and what we know they can give) we shall the more readily believe them sincere in their professions.

The question is frequently asked us, why abolitionists do not give practical demonstrations of the sincerity of their regard for colored people, by making apprentices of our boys, &c., and the only answer which we have been able to give without exposing *what we* believe to be the real cause has been that we were unable to tell. We know a professed abolitionist of this city, upon whom a friend of ours called for the purpose of hiring a frame tenement which he owned in the lower part of the city, who refused to let him have it, for fear the neighbors would not like to have colored people living so near them; and at the same time this man was called by abolitionists a staunch friend of the cause, he could exclaim as loudly against southern oppression as the best of the party, and denounce others for developing in a different manner the very same principles which were dominant in his own bosom.

We hope that our friends will not be hasty and conclude that we are opposed to abolitionists because we express ourselves in a free and candid manner; we believe it to be a duty which we owe them and ourselves; and if others have neglected and feared to speak the truth, *we are determined* not to follow into their footsteps.

We are aware of and acknowledge that some very great sacrifices have been made for our brethren in slavery; that trial, persecution and calumny have been endured by many in their endeavors to diffuse the principles of justice and truth through society; but while *they* continue to express their disapprobation and indignation of prejudice on account of complexions, and consider it cruel and unjust in others, *we* shall labor to inform them that *we* are not insensible to the prejudice which exists in their minds.

Northern Star and Freeman's Advocate (Albany, N.Y.), 3 March 1842; *BAP*, 3:375–77.

Chapter 3

Black Independence

A NEW DIRECTION

Frustrated by the antislavery schism and white reformers' apparent indifference to the problem of prejudice and discrimination, black abolitionists grew convinced of the need for independent initiatives. They recognized that independence fostered racial pride and identity, as well as gave them greater control over antislavery strategies and objectives. A white-directed antislavery movement did little to nurture a sense of self-worth and self-confidence in the African American community. By the 1840s, most black abolitionists had accepted the practical and symbolic value of racially separate efforts in the fight against slavery and prejudice. African Americans had served a "faithful apprenticeship," William J. Watkins concluded, but the time had come to "hang out *our own shingle.*"

John W. Lewis, a lecture agent for the New Hampshire Anti-Slavery Society, used his letter of resignation to the society to express his weariness over white abolitionist infighting and his desire to continue antislavery work independently.

Concord, [New Hampshire]
Dec[ember] 28th, 1840

Gentlemen:
As I have concluded to resign to you my agency to your society, I

feel it my duty to give the reason why. I have for a long time past felt it my duty, in view of the useless controversy going on between the N.H. Anti-Slavery and Abolition Societies, to assume a strict neutral ground, not on the subject of slavery, but on a contentious spirit and action going on, in my view, to the great disadvantage of the anti-slavery cause. I am aware there are those in both societies, who are uncompromising and inflexible opponents of the foul system of slavery, and decided friends to the colored man. And, as a colored man, and representative of my people, I feel it a duty to make the advocacy of the cause the paramount question. Thus, in assuming a strict conservative ground, I do not discard the merits of the old platform on which the genuine *anti-slavery* rests. And I do not give up my agency with the intention of quitting the *anti-slavery* field, for I shall go on and lecture whenever and wherever the way is open to me, and hold myself amenable to God for the faithful discharge of my duty. But I shall not at any time attempt to discuss the merits or demerits of new or old organization. I do feel truly conscientious in taking this position, and think I can do more for the abused slave than to hold my agency with any society, unless one that agrees with me on the ground of neutrality; and, further, it is my humble opinion (and I value my own opinion as much as of others in guiding me to duty), that for the two societies to act as antagonists, and trying to build itself up on the ruins of the other, instead of spending all the moral strength to pull down slavery, has a direct tendency to bring our cause into disrepute before our enemies, and thus counteract all the good that is attempted to be done, and lead to alienation of feeling among those who ought to be an undivided host. I do not take this step through any sinister motive. I love the cause—it always has had, and still has the warmest affection of my heart. For while it tends to emancipate the slave, it also tends to enfranchise the nominally free colored man. Of course, I have some great interest in the cause, and have long learnt to trust those interests on the altar of freedom; then I cannot be recreant to anti-slavery; and I regret that any should. And while I fear there is an alarming degeneracy from genuine principles, I am wishing to stand in the breach, and use my influence to check the evil. Again my ideas of carrying on this work differ from some of the prominent men in your society. I think the preaching of the Gospel, as it is technically called, will open the way in those places where there is an aversion to hear anti-slavery. I have pursued this course, and for it have been censured as wasting time. I think if I am acting on my own hook, I can consult my own way and plan of operation; this is the main ground of my taking this stand. I hope your society will do much; and the new society do all they can. I bid both God speed to the rescue of suffering, bleeding humanity; and may both act for the slave, so that both may join in the general enthusiasm when the bondman shall go free. Yours truly, for human rights,

JOHN W. LEWIS

Liberator (Boston, Mass.), 15 January 1841; *BAP*, 3:352–53.

37 WILLIAM WHIPPER'S LETTERS

In a four-part series entitled "William Whipper's Letters," "Sidney" (probably Henry Highland Garnet) argued for separate black organizations and initiatives in the antislavery movement. He used William Whipper, a leading exponent of integration and moral reform, as a foil for his arguments.

Ought they not (the free people of color) to make one weak effort; nay, one strong, one mighty, moral effort to roll off the burden that crushes them?—*Wm. Hamilton*

The correctness of our views will further appear from a consideration of the essentially peculiar ability of the oppressed, and the necessary incapability of all others, even of the best of friends.

In an effort for freedom, there are several important and indispensable qualifications, which the oppressed alone can possess.

There must be, primarily, a keen sense of actual suffering, and a fixed consciousness that it is no longer sufferable. These are requisite, both to unite the entire feeling and purpose of those who suffer, and likewise to awaken the sympathy of those in power. It is absolutely important that there should be *such* a presentation of wrongs as may reveal to the power-holding body the enormity of their oppression; and at the same time, acquaint them that their outrages have so proved the vital seat of suffering, as to arouse the deepest feelings and most inflexible determination of their insulted victims. Now, from the nature of the case, this statement of grievance in all its fulness and power, can come from none other than those conscious of suffering. How is it possible, we ask, for men who know nothing of oppression, who have always enjoyed the blessedness of freedom, by an effort of imagination, by any strength of devotedness, by any depth of sympathy, so fully and adequately to express the sense of wrong and outrage, as the sorrowful presence and living desire of us who have drank the dregs of the embittered chalice?

The oppressed are ever their best representatives. Their short and even abrupt expression of intense feeling, is more effectual than the most refined and polished eloquence, prompted though it be, by deep humanity and strong human-heartedness. Sterne's description of slavery has always been considered very graphic; we can bring three millions of men who can give one still more natural and touching. Hence the expression of Mr. Buxton, in his recent letter upon Colonization, in which he calls us "the *natural* allies, and ABLEST CHAMPIONS of the slave!" And why? Because we are oppressed, and know what slavery is.

Again, it is one of the most malignant features of slavery, that it leads the oppressor to stigmatize his victim with inferiority of nature, after he himself has almost brutalized him. This is a universal fact. Hence the oppressed must vindicate their character. No abstract disquisitions from sympathizing friends, can effectually do this. The oppressed themselves must manifest energy of character and elevation of soul. Oppression never quails until it sees that the downtrodden and outraged "know their rights, and knowing, dare maintain." *This* is a radical assurance, a resistless evidence both of worth and manliness, and of earnest intention and deep determination.

We maintain that these evidences—these feelings, desires, and capacities, must stand out prominently, as coming from their proper source, to have their rightful influence. Thus exhibited, they can be employed with prodigious effect. But on the other hand, experience proves, that they lose by retailment or admixture. Let an expression of our wants and feelings be produced by others, and should there be anything of character, intellect, or dignity connected with it, it is not predicated of our ability. How pregnant with verification are facts in our history! where documents setting forth our views and demanding our rights, which were ostensibly the productions of colored men, have proved to have been written by whites. The base suspicion (to say nothing of the real knowledge of the fact) has caused the effort to fall powerless to the ground.

The elevation of a people is not measurably dependent upon external relations or peculiar circumstances, as it is upon the inward rational sentiments which enable the soul to change circumstances to its own temper and disposition. Without these, the aids of sympathizing friends, the whisperings of hope, the power of eternal truth, are of but little advantage. We take the case of an individual. His ancestors have been the objects of wrong and violence. In consequence, they become degraded. At the season of thought and reflection he feels a desire to escape from the degradation of his sires, and the oppressions of the many. The sympathy of friends is excited, and they make active exertions.

Now we affirm that their efforts and influence may be as potent as angels; yet vain that influence, vain their efforts. * * * It must exist in the man. The spirit that would elevate him above his circumstances, and gain him respect and manhood, must have all the strength of personal character.

And the same it is with a people. Our friends, abolitionists, may redouble their efforts, they may lavishly expend their means, they may strew their pamphlets over the country, thick as the leaves in some primeval forest, where the soil is undistinguishable from their thickly bedded masses—they may add to their numbers, and fill up their ranks. * * * Yet our condition will remain the same, our sufferings will be unmitigated, until we awaken to a consciousness of a momentous responsibility, which we shall manifest by giving it actuality. We occupy a position, and sustain relations which they cannot possibly assume. *They* are our allies—Ours is the battle.

In coming forth as colored Americans, and pleading for our rights, we neither preclude the necessity, nor forbid the action of our friends, no more than the Americans forbade the help of their French allies. We ask their sympathy, and entreat their prayers and efforts. The Americans received the aid and co-operation of their French allies; but they kept the idea of *American* resistance to oppression distinct and prominent. As wise men, they knew much depended upon that. They know not what evils—perhaps failure—might result from an admixture of extraneosities.

So the convention at Albany acted. They interdicted the presence and co-operation of no set of men, but they called for the exertion of a people peculiarly interested in its objects.

The necessity, nay, the DUTY of peculiar activity on the part of an aggrieved people, we conclude, is the dictate of reason and common sense, and the testimony of history.

And thus thought our fathers. In this way they acted for years. It was this conviction that led to the concentration of their energies in the annual conventions. The people generally acquiesce in their judgement, and follow in their wise and rational footsteps. Thus, throughout the country, we hear the sounds of their hearty, earnest labor. But lo! in the midst of our energetic and effectual exertions, we are called off from our efforts, when we have made considerable progress in undermining our great Bastille, a LEADER informs us, that not only we, but our fathers, yea, all mankind, have gone wrong, and that he has found out a better plan—a new *theory*.

He bids us disregard the voice of principle, to pay no heed to its historic affirmations, to repudiate the dictates of *reason* and common sense, to leave the path of our sires, and adopt a new theory, alike unsupported by reason, and unaffirmed by experience.

In speculating upon "heaven born truth," he comes to despising all specific actions or means, and can deal in nothing but generalities—universalities.

We differ from him. We do not think that by watering and preserving the plant that perfumes our room, that therefore we dislike all other plants in the world. We do not believe that in loving our own mother's sons, our brothers, that therefore we create a cord of caste, and exclude mankind from our rights. In fine, we have no sympathy with that cosmopoliting disposition which tramples upon all nationality, which encircles the universe, but at the same time theorizes away the most needed blessings, and blights the dearest hopes of a people.

And pray, for what are we to turn around and bay the whole human family? In the name of common sense, we ask for what have we to make this great radical change in our operations? Why are we to act different from all others in this important matter? Why, because we *happen* to be—COLORED—which we shall endeavor to look into by and by.

SIDNEY

Colored American (New York, N.Y.), 6 March 1841; *BAP*, 3:356–59.

3 8   AN ADDRESS TO THE COLORED PEOPLE OF THE UNITED STATES

At the 1848 black national convention in Cleveland, Ohio, a committee chaired by Frederick Douglass drafted "An Address to the Colored People of the United States." Douglass used the occasion to clarify the meaning of black independence.

* * * In the Northern states, we are not slaves to individuals, not personal slaves, yet in many respects we are the slaves of the community. We are, however, far enough removed from the actual condition of the slave to make us largely responsible for their continued enslavement, or their speedy deliverance from chains. For in the proportion which we shall rise in the scale of human improvement, in that proportion do we augment the probabilities of a speedy emancipation of our enslaved fellow-countrymen. It is more than a mere figure of speech to say, that we are as a people, chained together. We are one people—one in general complexion, one in a common degradation, one in popular estimation. As one rises, all must rise, and as one falls all must fall. Having now, our feet on the rock of freedom, we must drag our brethren from the slimy depths of slavery, ignorance, and ruin. Every one of us should be ashamed to consider himself free, while his brother is a slave. The wrongs of our brethren, should be our constant theme. There should be no time too precious, no calling too holy, no place too sacred, to make room for this cause. We should not only feel it to be the cause of humanity, but the cause of christianity, and fit work for men and angels. We ask you to devote yourselves to this cause, as one of the first, and most successful means of self improvement. In the careful study of it, you will learn your own rights, and comprehend your own responsibilities, and, scan through the vista of coming time, your high, and God-appointed destiny. Many of the brightest and best of our number, have become such by their devotion to this cause, and the society of white abolitionists. The latter have been willing to make themselves of no reputation for our sake, and in return, let us show ourselves worthy of their zeal and devotion. Attend Anti-slavery meetings, show that you are interested in the subject, that you hate slavery, and love those who are laboring for its overthrow. Act with white Abolition societies where-ever you can, and where you cannot, get up societies among yourselves, but without exclusiveness. It will be a long time before we gain all our rights; and although it may seem to conflict with our views of human brotherhood, we shall undoubtedly for many years be compelled to have institutions of a complexional character, in order to attain this very idea of human brotherhood. We would, however, advise our brethren to occupy memberships and stations among white persons, and in white institutions, just so fast as our rights are secured to us.

Never refuse to act with a white society or institution because it is white, or a black one, because it is black; but act with all men without distinction of color. By so acting, we shall find many opportunities for removing prejudices and establishing the rights of all men.—We say, avail yourselves of *white* institutions, not because they are white, but because they afford a more convenient means of improvement. * * *

Understand this, that independence is an essential condition of respectability. To be dependent, is to be degraded. Men may indeed pity us, but they cannot respect us. We do not mean that we can become entirely independent of all men; that would be absurd and impossible, in the social state. But we mean that we must become equally independent with other members of the community.

Report of the Proceedings of the Colored National Convention, Held in Cleveland, Ohio, . . . (Rochester, N.Y., 1848), 18–20.

THE AFRICAN
AMERICAN PRESS

From the first tentative call of *Freedom's Journal* in the 1820s to the refined, assertive voice of the *Weekly Anglo-African* thirty years later, the antebellum black press symbolized independence. By establishing and sustaining their own press, African Americans demonstrated their initiative and capacity for self-reliance and progress. The black press initially arose from the need for a public voice to counter racist diatribes and proslavery myths. But the editorial direction of Philip A. Bell, Samuel E. Cornish, Frederick Douglass, and others transformed its function and character. They developed the press's essential role in enhancing racial identity, nurturing African American culture, linking communities across the continent, and forging an independent place in the antislavery movement.

39 WHY WE SHOULD HAVE A PAPER

Samuel E. Cornish's 1837 editorial in the Colored American *outlined the reasons for establishing an independent black press.*

1. Because the colored people of these United States have to contend with all the multiplied ills of slavery, more cruel in its practice and unlimited in its duration than was ever before inflicted upon any people; and we are proscribed and pressed down by prejudice more wicked and fatal than even slavery itself. These evils not only pervade the length and breadth of the land, but they have their strong hold in the Church of Jesus Christ, where they abide and act themselves out, contrary to all its holy precepts. Colored men must do something, must make some effort to drive these "abominations of desolation" from the church and the world; they must establish and maintain the PRESS, and through it speak out in THUNDER TONES, until the nation repent and render to every man that which is just

and equal—and until the church possess herself of the mind which was in Christ Jesus, and cease to oppress her poor brother, because God hath dyed him a darker hue.

2. Because our afflicted population in the free states, are scattered in handfuls over nearly 5000 towns, and can only be reached by the Press—a public journal must therefore be sent down, at least weekly, to rouse them up. To call all their energies into action—and where they have been down trodden, paralyzed and worn out, to create new energies for them, that such dry bones may live.

Such an organ can be furnished at little cost, so as to come within the reach of every man, and carry to him lessons of instruction on religion and morals, lessons on industry and economy—until our entire people are of one heart and of one mind, in all the means of their salvation, both temporal and spiritual.

3. Because without such an organ we never can enlist the sympathy of the nation in our behalf, and in the behalf of the slave; and until this be done, we shall have accomplished nothing nor shall we have proved ourselves worthy to be freemen and to have our grievances redressed. Before the wise and good awake and consecrate themselves to our cause, we ourselves must have proclaimed our oppression and wrongs from the HOUSE-TOP. When did Greece and Poland win the sympathy of the world; after they had published their wrongs, asserted their rights and sued for freedom at the hands of their oppressors. Then, and only then, were they worthy to be freemen, nor should *we* expect the *boon*, until we feel its importance and pray for its possession. With us this is to be a great moral struggle, and let us brethren, be united in our efforts.

4. Because no class of men, however pious and benevolent, can take our place in the great work of redeeming our character and removing our disabilities. They may identify themselves with us, and enter into our sympathies. Still it is ours to will and do—both of which, we trust, are about to be done, and in the doing of which, this journal *as an appropriate engine*, may exert a powerful agency. We propose to make it a journal of facts and of instruction. It will go out freighted with information for all—it will tell tales of woe, both in the church and out of the church; such as are calculated to make the heart to bleed and the ear to burn. It will bring to light many hidden things, which must be revealed and repented of, or this nation must perish.

Colored American (New York, N.Y.), 4 March 1837; *BAP*, 3:216–17.

40 OBSTACLES FOR THE BLACK PRESS

Benjamin F. Roberts, a Boston printer, describes the thinly veiled hostility that he encountered from white abolitionists in his attempts to establish a black newspaper.

Boston, [Massachusetts]
June 19, 1838

Rev A. A. Phelps
Dear Sir:
At 25 Cornhill, I found a note addressed to myself, which on opening I was surprised to learn that you felt much dissatisfied with the recommendation you furnished—the impression I got showed it was undeserving. I return it as requested. But as it respects the facts alluded to, I am aware there has been and now is, a combined effort on the part of certain professed abolitionists to muzzle, exterminate and put down the efforts of certain colored individuals effecting the welfare of their colored brethren. The truth is respecting myself, my whole soul is engaged in the cause of humanity. I am for improvement among this class of people, mental and physical. The arts and sciences have never been introduced to any extent among us—therefore they are of the utmost importance. If anti-Slavery men will not subscribe to the advancement of these principles, but rail out and protest against them when took up by those who have a darker skin, why we will go to the heathen. The principle ground on which the anti-slavery cause is said to be founded (and boasting are not a few) are the elevation of the free colored people here. Now it is altogether useless to pretend to affect the welfare of the blacks in this country, unless the chains of prejudice are broken. It is of no use [to] say with the mouth we are friends of the slave and not try to encourage and assist the free colored people in raising themselves. Here is sir the first efforts of the colored man in this country of the kind, vis. the paper published, printed and edited by colored persons in Massachusetts—shall this be defeated? But it is contended the individual who started the enterprise has not taken it up from principle—he don't intend what he pretends. Base misrepresentations! false accusations!—I was not aware that so many hypocrites existed in the Anti slavery society. According to what I have seen of the conduct of some, a

black man would be as unsafe in their hands as in those of Southern slave-holders. I have found a few true to the righteous cause, and those were practical abolitionists as well as abolitionists by profession. I should like to become acquainted with some of the stories in circulation. Those in haste

B. F. ROBERTS

41 REPORT OF THE COMMITTEE ON A NATIONAL PRESS

James McCune Smith chaired the Committee on a National Press at the 1847 black national convention in Troy, New York. His commit-tee report underscores the fundamental role of the press in achieving black independence.

It being admitted that the colored people of the United States are pledged, before the world and in the face of Heaven, to struggle manfully for advancement in civil and social life, it is clear that our own efforts must mainly, if not entirely, produce such advancement. And if we are to advance by our own efforts (under the Divine blessing), we must use the means which will direct such efforts to a successful issue.

Of the means for advancement of a people placed as we are, none are more available than a Press. We struggle against opinions. Our warfare lies in the field of thought. Glorious struggle! God-like warfare! In training our soldiers for the field, in marshaling our hosts for the fight, in leading the onset, and through the conflict, we need a Printing Press, because a printing press is the vehicle of thought—is a ruler of opinions.

Among ourselves we need a Press that shall keep us steadily alive to our responsibilities, which shall constantly point out the principles which should guide our conduct and our labors, which shall cheer us from one end of the land to the other, by recording our acts, our sufferings, our temporary defeats and our steadily approaching triumph—or rather the triumph of the glorious truth "Human Equality," whose servants and soldiers we are.

If a Press be not the most powerful means for our elevation, it is the most immediately necessary. Education of the intellect, of the will, and of character, is doubtless a powerful, perhaps the most powerful, means for our advancement; yet a Press is needed to keep this very fact before the whole people, in order that all may constantly and unitedly labor in this, the right direction. It may be that some other means might seem even more effectual than education; even then a Press will be the more necessary, inasmuch as it will afford a field in which the relative importance of the various means may be discussed and settled in the hearing of the whole people, and to the profit of all.

The first step which will mark our certain advancement as a people, will be our Declaration of Independence from all aid except from God and our own souls. This step can only be taken when the minds of our people are thoroughly convinced of its necessity and importance. And such conviction can only be produced through a Press, which shall show that although we have labored long and earnestly, we have labored in too many directions and with too little concert of action; and that we must, as one man, bend our united efforts in the one right direction in order to advance.

We need a Press also as our Banner on the outer wall, that all who pass by may read why we struggle, how we struggle, and what we struggle for. If we convince the world that we are earnestly and resolutely striving for our own advancement, one half the battle will already be won, because well and rightly begun. Our friends will the more willingly help us; our foes will quail, because they will have lost their best allies—our own inertness, carelessness, strifes and dependence upon others. And there is no way except through a Press—a National Press—that we can tell the world of our position in the path of Human Progress.

Let there be, then, in these United States, a Printing Press, a copious supply of type, a full and complete establishment, wholly controlled by colored men; let the thinking writing-man, the compositors, pressman, printers' help, all, all be men of color; then let there come from said establishment a weekly periodical and a quarterly periodical, edited as well as printed by colored men; let this establishment be so well endowed as to be beyond the chances of temporary patronage; and then there will be a fixed fact, a rallying point, towards which the strong and the weak amongst us would look with confidence and hope; from which would flow a steady stream of comfort and exhortation to the weary strugglers, and of burning rebuke and overwhelming argument upon those who dare impede our way.

The time was when a great statesman exclaimed, "Give me the song-making of a people and I will rule that people." That time has passed away from our land, wherein the reason of the people must be assaulted and over-come; this can only be done through the Press. We have felt, and bitterly, the weight of odium and malignity wrought upon us by one or two promi-nent presses in this land; we have felt also the favorable feeling wrought in our behalf by the Anti-Slavery Press. But the amount of the hatred against us has been conventional antipathy; and of the favorable feeling has been human sympathy. Our friends sorrow with us, because they say we are unfortunate! We must batter down those antipathies, we must command something manlier than sympathies. We must command the respect and admiration due men, who, against fearful odds, are struggling steadfastly for their rights. This can only be done through a Press of our own. It is needless to support these views with a glance at what the Press has done for the downtrodden among men; let us rather look forward with the de-termination of accomplishing, through this engine, an achievement more glorious than any yet accomplished. We lead the forlorn hope of Human Equality; let us tell of its onslaught on the battlements of hate and caste; let us record its triumph in a Press of our own. * * *

Proceedings of the National Convention of Colored People, and Their Friends, Held in Troy, N.Y. . . . (Troy, N.Y., 1847); *BAP*, 4:7–10.

IN THE COMMON DEFENSE

Blacks in most large northern cities established vigilance committees to assist fugitive slaves who escaped via the underground railroad and to prevent the kidnapping of free blacks into slavery. The New York Committee of Vigilance, founded in 1835, proved one of the most active and best organized. It cared for fugitives, watched the waterfront for illegal slave ships, obstructed the work of slave catchers, exposed official connivance with kidnapping rings, and rallied the African American community to the antislavery cause. During its first three years, the committee was involved in over five hundred fugitive slave cases. Committees served as distribution centers for the underground railroad and directed fugitives to safe havens in the North or on to Canada. Blacks dominated this underground system, which reached into the upper South and labored with extraordinary bravery even in the shadow of the U.S. Capitol. The assistance and sacrifices of scores of black underground workers such as William Still, who directed the largest operation at Philadelphia, insured freedom for thousands of fugitive slaves.

42   KIDNAPPING IN THE CITY OF NEW YORK

David Ruggles, journalist and leader of the New York Committee of Vigilance, reveals the constant dangers African Americans faced and the initiative they took to guarantee their own safety.

It is too bad to be told, much less to be endured! On Saturday, 23d inst., about 12 o'clock, Mr. George Jones, a respectable free colored man, was arrested at 21 Broadway by certain police officers, upon the pretext of his having "committed assault and battery." Mr. Jones being conscious that no such charge could be sustained against him, refused to go with the officers; his employers, placing high confidence in his integrity, advised him

KIDNAPPING
AGAIN!!
A MAN WAS STOLEN LAST NIGHT BY THE
Fugitive Slave Bill COMMISSIONER!
HE WILL HAVE HIS
MOCK TRIAL
ON SATURDAY, MAY 27, AT 9 O'CLOCK,
In the Kidnapper's 'Court,' before the Hon. Slave Bill Commissioner,
AT THE COURT HOUSE, IN COURT SQUARE.
SHALL BOSTON STEAL ANOTHER MAN?
Thursday, May 25, 1854.

Poster announcing the seizure of a fugitive slave. Courtesy of the Trustees of the Boston Public Library.

to go and answer to the charge, promising that any assistance should be afforded to satisfy the end of justice. He proceeded with the officers, accompanied with a gentleman who would have stood his bail—he was locked up in Bridewell—his friend was told that "when he was wanted he could be sent for." Between the hours of 1 and 2 o'clock, Mr. Jones was carried before the Hon. Richard Riker, Recorder of the city of New York. In the absence of his friends, and in the presence of several notorious kidnappers, who preferred and by oath sustained that he was a runaway slave, Poor Jones (having no one to utter a word in his behalf, but a boy, in the absence of numerous friends who could have borne testimony to his freedom) was by the Recorder pronounced to be a slave!

In less than three hours after his arrest, he was bound in chains, dragged through the streets like a brute beast to the shambles! My depressed countrymen, we are all liable; your wives and children are at the mercy of merciless kidnappers. We have no protection in law—because the legislators withhold justice. We must no longer depend on the interposition of the Manumission or Anti-Slavery Societies, in the hope of peaceable and just protection; where such outrages are committed, peace and justice cannot dwell. While we are subject to be thus inhumanly practiced upon, no man is safe; we must look to our own safety and protection from kidnappers! remembering that "self-defence is the first law of nature."

Let a meeting be called—let every man who has sympathy in his heart to feel when bleeding humanity is thus stabbed afresh, attend the meeting; let a remedy be prescribed to protect us from slavery! Whenever necessity requires, let that remedy be applied. Come what will, anything is better than slavery! Yours, &c.

DAVID RUGGLES

Liberator (Boston, Mass.), 6 August 1836; BAP, 3:168–69.

43 THE RESCUE OF LUCY FAGGINS

The rescue of Virginia slave Lucy Faggins in New Bedford, Massachusetts, typified the response of most African American communities. In this case, a local black clergyman obtained a writ of habeas corpus for Faggins in July 1841 and took her to Boston where a state supreme court justice granted her freedom. William C. Nell, leader of Boston's black abolitionists, described the rescue in a letter to William Lloyd Garrison.

Mr. Editor:

The following facts in relation to the case of habeas corpus, heard before Judge Wilde on Saturday last, may not be uninteresting to the readers of the *Liberator*, especially as the pro-slavery press is industriously circulating stories which have no proximity to truth, and are therefore calculated to deceive many who may not have an opportunity to learn both sides of the question.

Henry Ludlam, of Richmond, Va., having urgent business that called him to the North, secured the services of the said Lucy, as a servant, making a contract with her owner, it is said, for the term of one year. On their arrival at New Bedford, some of the vigilant friends of liberty soon ascertained that Lucy was held as a slave, contrary to the statute provision of the Old Bay State; and further learned from her own lips, that she desired to be free. It would be well to state here that as soon as it was found that she had been conversing with colored persons, efforts were immediately made by the family to put an end to what they deemed a "foreign" interference, though it has been asserted that she was subject to no restraint while in New Bedford. The attempt, however, to deny her the opportunity to see and converse with friends, proved unsuccessful, for they, doubtless remembering that eternal vigilance was the price of liberty, were not to be deterred from their mission by any influences exerted to restrain a fellow being in bondage, and, that too, when the unhappy victim herself was panting for the invigorating atmosphere of liberty. Many strange stories are told of her being dragged from under Mr. Dunbar's bed, and of there being a great noise about the house, but they are *pro-slavery* facts. There was no noise. It was not generally known, even amongst abolitionists, the course that was to be taken to secure her right to freedom, and consequently but few were gathered near the house. Those without were quietly listening to the doings within. The Sheriff, however, served the writ of habeas corpus, and she was conveyed to Boston, where on Saturday morning Judge Wilde pronounced her free.

She retired from the court-house accompanied by a large concourse of friends, who proceeded with her to the Rev. Mr. Cannon's chapel in West Centre street, where she received their congratulations. Prayers were offered in gratitude to God, followed by remarks from several individuals. A collection was taken for her benefit, and the exercises concluded with a hymn of Praise for her escape from the *"delectable land of slavery."*

W . C . N .

Liberator (Boston, Mass.), 16 July 1841; *BAP*, 3:362–63.

44 THE UNDERGROUND RAILROAD

In southeastern Pennsylvania, African Americans and white Quakers maintained one of the best-organized sections of the underground railroad. The home of Quaker Elijah F. Pennypacker stood midway between two stops managed by blacks: Joseph C. Bustill's farm in Harrisburg and William Still's antislavery office in Philadelphia.

Harrisburg, [Pennsylvania]
March 24, [18]56

Friend Still:

I suppose ere this you have seen those five large and three small packages I sent by way of Reading, consisting of three men and women and children. They arrived here this morning at 8½ o'clock and left twenty minutes past three. You will please send me any information likely to prove interesting in relation to them.

Lately we have formed a Society here, called the Fugitive Aid Society. This is our first case, and I hope it will prove entirely successful.

When you write, please inform me what signs or symbols you make use of in your dispatches, and any other information in relation to operations of the Underground Rail Road.

Our reason for sending by the Reading Road, was to gain time; it is expected the owners will be in town this afternoon, and by this Road we gained five hours' time, which is a matter of much importance, and we may have occasion to use it sometimes in the future. In great haste, Yours with great respect,

JOS. C. BUSTILL

William Still, *The Underground Railroad* (Philadelphia, Pa., 1872), 24–25; *BAP*, 4:331–33.

Phila[delphia], [Pennsylvania]
Nov[ember] 2nd, [1857]

[Dr. Sir:]

With regard to those unprovided for, I think it will be safe to send them on any time toward the latter part of this week. Far better it will be for them in Canada, this winter, where they can procure plenty of work, than it would be in Pa., where labor s will be scarce and hands plenty, with the usual amount of dread & danger hanging over the head s of the Fugitive. From the place where the ten you referred to came, fourty four ~~have~~ have left within the last two weeks—16 of whom we have passed on, I trust safely.

After the middle of this week, I think you might venture to send them to us in "Small parcels"—that is, not over four or 5 in a company.

If convenient, you will confer a favor by dropping us a few lines informing us by what hour & train the arrivals will come. Yours truly,

W M   S T I L L

Elijah F. Pennypacker Papers, Friends Historical Library, Swarthmore College, Swarthmore, Pennsylvania; published by permission; *BAP*, 4:333.

ANTISLAVERY POLITICS

Most black abolitionists recognized the importance of political action to ending racism and slavery. But less agreement existed over which party—Whig, Liberty, Free Soil, or later, Republican —would best help to achieve African American goals. The Liberty party, founded in 1839, attracted many black leaders because of its unfailing commitment to emancipation and racial equality. But for other African Americans, it posed a dilemma—should they support a true antislavery party that was politically weak or work with moderate Whigs in the hope of securing a major party's support for limited black goals on the local level? Most black leaders rallied around the Liberty party (despite its ineffectiveness), the first American political organization to nominate and run African Americans for office. Individual black achievement carried immense symbolism, and the nomination and election of blacks to office directly challenged white beliefs of racial inferiority. When African Americans ran for office, as they did in Ohio, New York, and Massachusetts, they helped breach the wall of American racism.

45 PURE ANTISLAVERY POLITICS

Henry Johnson, a freeborn lecturer active in New England antislavery circles, wrote to Austin Willey, editor of the Liberty Standard, *to explain the commitment of many African Americans to the Liberty party.*

Augusta, [Maine]
Aug[ust] 31, 1843

Mr. Editor:
Having for some years been a strong supporter of first one and then the other of the two political parties of the day—believing that they,

according to their many professions, would remove this current system of American slavery from this our land, and finding to my satisfaction that slavery never would be removed by these parties—I came to the conclusion as a colored man, as a christian, as a friend to my country, and above all, as one who but a few years since left the Prison house of slavery to abandon them. I could not and would not go to the polls again in support of either the Whig or Locofoco party. I have been, and still remain, an uncompromising advocate of the Liberty party principles, believing it the duty of every true friend of liberty, and particularly every man of color, to do the same. I lectured at the Baptist church last evening, and in my lecture I stated some few reasons why I was turned out of employment in one of these parties, and stated that it was for no other reason than because I denounced both of these parties, and rushed through their midst and found my way to the Liberty party—and they give me the right hand of fellowship—not the left hand as the other two parties do. And in making these statements it seems that I trod upon the corns of your Whig editors, who stated, I was informed after the meeting, that these were not the reasons, that it was for some of my misconduct. I would inform that gentleman, through the columns of your Liberty paper, that my moral character stands as high in the town of New Bedford, as his does in the town of Augusta, and in proof of those facts, if that gentleman will call at my boarding house, I will produce documents signed by the leading men of both parties, setting forth my true character, both moral and religious. But to the question—my object in coming to this place was not to lecture on political matters, but to lay before this people, having been a slave myself, what is the condition of those whom I left behind me—and for this only. And it has been very often the case while lecturing on this part of the subject, that many persons have desired to know what they should do to better the condition of the slave, and when this question shall be asked me, God being my helper, I shall answer according to the dictates of my own conscience, without consulting each of the two political parties of the day. If I shall consult at all, I shall consult liberty, and not slavery. The first question to be proposed by me is not what shall be profitable to me, but what is right. Duty must be primary, prominent, most conspicuous among the objects of human thought and pursuit. We can never see the right clearly and fully, but by making it our first concern. And I hold that no judgement can be just and wise but that which is built on the conviction of the paramount worth and importance of duty. This is the fundamental truth upon which I believe the foundation of the Liberty party stands. And the mind which does not start from this in its inquiries into human affairs, is in my estimation doomed to fatal error. It has been long since decided in my own mind, what my duty is to God and my fellow men. And having been made sensible of those duties, I have now come to the conclusion to perform them. I will further state, as I did last night, if there is a colored man in the town of Augusta or Hallowell, who supports either of the two political parties instead of the Liberty party, let him come out like a man and show one reason why he should support either of those corrupt parties, and I will, notwithstanding a stranger in your town, pledge myself to show for every one of his reasons, five why he should not support them. Let such come forth in public print and show himself a man by good sound reasons, through this or any other public Journal of the day, and I will never give him up until I shall prove all of his reasons before this public to be worse than folly, so long as pen, paper and ink, can be found in the town of Augusta. Yours for the downtrodden slave,

HENRY JOHNSON

Liberty Standard (Hallowell, Maine), 14 September 1843; BAP, 3:413–14.

46 OUR PLATFORM OF PRINCIPLES

---

*Samuel Ringgold Ward, one of New York State's most effective expo-
nents of the Liberty party, helped lead the fight for African American
suffrage. His letter to Joseph C. Hathaway, secretary of an upcoming
Liberty party convention, warned against eroding the party's moral
foundation with political compromises.*

Ravenna, Ohio
Sept[ember] 15, 1851

My Dear Sir:
I find that I am obliged to deny myself the pleasure of attending your Convention. On my own account, I have abundant reason to regret

this. In the Convention, however, no such poor and obscure man as myself can be missed.

I take the liberty of addressing this line to suggest a word, on two or three points of some practical importance.

1. *In regard to our platform of principles.* My hope is that it shall be both radical and catholic. Insisting upon the inalienable rights of all men, and the equality of the whole brotherhood of the human race, denying the validity and the legality of any and all constitutions, enactments, compromises, compacts, and decisions which conflict with the doctrine of the inalienable rights of all men, it is to be hoped that we shall meanwhile insist upon nothing as a test of party fellowship, which does not necessarily conflict with this doctrine, and that we shall be ready and willing to cooperate with all who honestly embrace it, and who are willing to study its relations, and apply it to the entire range of civil duties.

But to yield up, compromise, or hold in abeyance, any of our great vital principles, for the sake of making it easy for others to unite with us, would be not only wounding to the hearts of those most devoted to our cause, but detrimental, also, to the very success which we should seek by such means. We learned a valuable lesson in 1848. Too many of our old coadjutors hastened to nominate and to vote for a Presidential candidate, who, within less than fourteen months of his nomination, and in less than ten months of his being voted for, was a member of one of the most corrupt pro-slavery parties that ever consented to, and aided in, the crushing and enslavement of man. That deed of folly, though done with the best of intentions, on the part of our brethren, ought to be a perpetual admonition to us, that we depend much less upon numbers than upon the integrity and steadfastness with which we shall maintain our principles. If we have a hearty and cordial belief in the principles which underlie our Heaven-originated cause, let us not be in haste to gather numbers, at the expense of the truth. The divine word assures us that "he that believeth shall not make haste," and also that "he that believeth shall not be made ashamed." Let us neither be ashamed of the paucity of our numbers, nor be in haste to increase them.

2. *As to Candidates.* The eyes of many, in my opinion, a great majority of the true and faithful, are turned towards our beloved Gerrit Smith as the standard-bearer of our ranks in the coming campaign. None can better represent our principles, in civil or social matters, than he. But for his unconquerable repugnance to being a candidate, it would seem unwise to convene and adjourn, without the placing of his great name before the people,

as the representative and embodiment of our principles, and a rebuke to the character of opposing candidates, and a protest against the truckling spirit of compromise which is working the ruin of our country.

It is a source of great joy, however, that we are not destitute of great names, bourne by good men. No party in the country, of whatever pretensions, will seek the elevation of better men than William Goodell, James H. Collins, George W. Johnson, Lindley M. Moore, or Samuel Aaron. Either of these gentlemen, as a nominee for Vice President, or, in case of Mr. Smith's irrevocable declinature for President, would form a ticket of which we might well be proud. What is most important, in my judgement, is the naming of men who are true-bred, unwavering, intelligent in the history and relations of the cause of freedom, and self-sacrificing in their devotion to the cause. What we should chiefly seek to avoid is the nominating of some halfway compromise candidate, to accommodate whom, we must lower our standard after the manner of October, 1847. May the God whom we serve save us from all such folly!

3. Allow me to say a word concerning *the aspects of our cause in several of the States*. In Maine, the Free Soil Party is but the old Liberty Party, with a very small addition from the two pro-slavery parties. It were not difficult, if tried, to cooperate and harmonize with our friends in Maine. In New Hampshire there is a growing anti-slavery sentiment among the Free Soilers, but the leaders of the party never were abolitionists. There is, consequently, more of the spirit of compromise, and less of radical tendency, in that State. The Free Soilers of Connecticut have so low a standard of action that but little may be hoped of them. Free Soil in that State, is but little else than modified, but not converted, spurious democracy. In Vermont and Massachusetts, the Free Soilers are not yet tired of uniting with Democrats for the sake of sharing in the results of victories which neither could achieve without the aid of the other. Rhode Island abolitionism always had the misfortune to be, as is abolitionism elsewhere in New England, too much attached to the tariff to be at liberty to embrace radical ideas of reform.

In the West, there are brighter signs of hope. Illinois is with us. Wisconsin is fighting for the same principles as ourselves. The mass of the Free Soilers of Ohio spurn the tendencies toward the Democratic party exhibited in the Southern, and the Whig-wise tendencies of some leading minds in the Northern part of that State. A paralytic stupor sits upon the bosoms of Michigan, Indiana, Iowa, New Jersey, and Pennsylvania.

4. *Laborers are needed.* They are needed in the last named States. In many

portions of the free States, the need of men to talk about our principles to the honest, laboring masses is but too apparent—too evident. Many of our best lecturers are abroad. Others will leave soon. The temptation to leave the country is greater, from the fact that compensation is so poor at home. Would that some more liberal plan could be adopted by the Convention, and recommended to the national committee, securing the employment of able young men (it were better that they be unmarried), to carry our principles to the people in all the free States.

Suffering from the disappointment of not being able to be with you, and praying for the Divine blessing on your deliberations, I am, dear sir, Your obedient servant,

SAMUEL R. WARD

Frederick Douglass' Paper (Rochester, N.Y.) 25 September 1851; *BAP*, 4:93–95.

47 AN EXTRAORDINARY EVENT

In the spring of 1855, John Mercer Langston, Ohio's premier black abolitionist, became the first black elected official in the United States. Although the light-skinned Langston was permitted to run because state laws defined him as white, he boldly described himself as African American and proudly announced that his victory represented evidence of the "steady march of the Anti-Slavery sentiment."

I have a news item for you. On the 2nd of this month, we held our elections. In our township, we had three distinct parties, and as many independent tickets. The Independent Democrats were wise for once, at least, in making and sticking to their own nominations. But more than this, and a thing which also exhibits their wisdom and virtue, they put upon their ticket the name of a colored man, who was elected clerk of Brownhelm Township, by a very handsome majority indeed. Since I am the only colored man who lives in this township, you can easily guess the name of the man who was so fortunate as to secure this election. To my knowledge, the like has not been

John Mercer Langston. Courtesy of Library of Congress.

known in Ohio before. It argues the steady march of the Anti-Slavery sentiment, and augurs the inevitable destruction and annihilation of American prejudice against colored men. What we so much need at this junction, and all along the future, is political influence; the bridle by which we can check and guide to our advantage the selfishness of American demagogues. How important, then, it is that we labor night and day to enfranchise ourselves. We are doing too little in this direction. And I make this charge against white Anti-Slavery persons, as well as colored ones. I hope that before a great while, we will all amend our ways in this particular.

JOHN MERCER LANGSTON

Frederick Douglass' Paper (Rochester, N.Y.), 20 April 1855; BAP, 4:281.

48 THE ISSUE PLAINLY STATED

William J. Watkins, the New York journalist, lecturer, and suffrage leader, advised African Americans to work within the Republican party to advance its antislavery principles. Although Watkins had been hired by the party to encourage blacks to vote the Republican ticket, his labors did not prevent him from censuring Republicans for equivocating on the issue of slavery.

Rochester, [New York]
Sept[ember] 5th, 1859

* * * Politically speaking, there are but two parties in this Republic. These are composed, on the one hand, of all those, at the North or at the South, at the East or at the West, who are *opposed* to slavery; and on the other of all those who are *in favor* of this accursed evil.

Those who view the present aspect of affairs with a philosophic eye, and whose range of vision enables them to descry, as in the strong, clear light of eternity, the resistless undercurrent which is upheaving the foundation of our already diseased and tottering body politic, will find no difficulty in discerning and assenting to the correctness of this plain and positive declaration. These are aware of the fact that the question of the life or the death of liberty in these United States is the all-absorbing, aye, the test question in American politics.

On the part of a majority of those composing the Democratic party, there is manifestly a disposition to ignore *the real* issue and substitute some other in its stead. A few bold and determined Southern politicians do not hesitate to avow their intention and determination to make slavery the "God over all and blessed forevermore" of this Republic, and to compel men and women everywhere in the land to fall down and worship this incarnation of crime and corruption—this embodiment of death and damnation. But a majority of the slaveocratic party, both at the North and at the South, hesitate, for certain reasons, to make this candid avowal.

The Republican party is likewise fearful, but for a different reason, of a presentation of the only true, living, real issue. With a few exceptions, its leaders are not disposed to take the broad, consistent, and righteous ground of opposition to the *existence* of slavery. They prefer to harp upon the popular and palatable doctrine of its nonextension to the Territories of the Republic, and appear exceedingly afraid of the imputation of Abolitionism. They talk of the slaveholder's rights *"under the Constitution"* about as flippantly as the slaveholders do themselves. But if they were to interpret the Constitution in accordance with the well established rules of legal hermeneutics, they would discover that the slaveholder, *as such*, has no more rights under the Constitution than he has under the shadow of the protecting wing of Heaven—has no more right, *as a slaveholder*, a human flesh-jobber, to live in the Republic, under a Constitution ordained to *"establish justice"* and *"secure liberty,"* than a wolf has in the cradle of a new-born babe.

Now, the Republican party is the only political party in the land in a position, numerically speaking, to strike a death-blow to American slavery—such a blow as will send it staggering to hell. It is important, then, that it assumes a defensible and right position in the present conflict. It does not deserve success, it ought not expect success, while in the occupancy of any other position. I believe it will take such a position. It *must* do so in order to preserve its distinctiveness, its vitality. If it is not right, let Abolitionists strive to make it right. More can be accomplished on the part of those who are right, by going into the party and renovating and revolutionizing it, than by standing outside harping upon a beautiful theory, but without the requisite machinery to crystalize it into practical life. If slavery is to be voted down in this Republic, it becomes a question of arithmetic. We must look at this question from the stand-point of common sense, and the single rule of three.

It is my opinion, founded upon actual observation, that the masses of the people of the free States are prepared to act in the right direction. I have just returned from a lecturing tour of four weeks through the Western part of this State and Vermont. What do I find to be the fact? That the most radical utterances which escaped my lips were the most cordially received and the most loudly applauded. Now, to those who reason from premise to conclusion, this is a fact truly significant—a fact which means something.

Let us, then, I repeat it, state the issue boldly. Let the people thoroughly understand it, and they will *lead their leaders*, and lead them on to victory. We all know that such are the dissimilarity and consequent antagonism existing between liberty and slavery, that there never can be a reconciliation between them. While slavery is allowed to exist anywhere in the land, it *will* develop itself; it *will* breathe its pestilential breath into the nation's lungs; it *will* cast its murky shadow across the path of liberty. Such is its nature. Just so with the spirit of liberty. It is jealous of its honor. The envenomed hatred of its antagonist cannot fail to be most cordially reciprocated. The two must be in perpetual conflict, in conformity with their respective instincts, in accordance with the changeless laws of their being.

If these premises be correct, the irresistible deduction is that the present bitter conflict must result in the extinction of the one or the other; and the fallacy of any theory based upon the assumption of the possibility of harmonizing their belligerent instincts, is as clearly demonstrated as the plainest mathematical problem. Either the two become one—one in nature, one in sympathy, one to all intents and purposes—or one or the other must cease to exist.

Then how absurd it is to attempt to ignore the issue! And how inconsistent the endeavor to oppose the further spread of slavery, while refusing to assume the position of hostility to its continuance in a certain locality! One might as well expect to thaw an iceberg by the cold, pale beams of a winter moon, as to expect to promote the peace and happiness of the nation by such a course of procedure.

The dividing line is already drawn. It may not be perceptible to the contracted and darkened vision of the mere politician; but no great truth ever evoked in the world of matter or of mind, stands out in more bold relief than this: *He who is not for slavery is against it, and must take his station accordingly.* Under which king, Benzonio—which king?

WM. JAMES WATKINS

Weekly Anglo-African (New York, N.Y.), 24 September 1859; *BAP*, 5:30–33.

BLACK ANTISLAVERY TACTICS

For black abolitionists, independence meant new strategies and initiatives. They struggled to achieve their goals by circulating petitions, lobbying sympathetic politicians, and, when permitted, taking their case before state legislatures. From the lecture platform to the streets, African Americans pursued all tactics that promised to advance racial equality and emancipation. The campaign against separate schools represented one such instance. Black abolitionists insisted that segregated schools were inherently unequal, perpetuated racial stereotypes, and crushed black aspirations. Beginning in 1840, Boston blacks began a fifteen-year campaign, including a complete boycott, against the city's separate educational facilities. Stephen A. Myers of Albany, New York, one of the most effective abolitionist lobbyists, met prominent politicians through his work as a journalist, temperance advocate, and manager of the local underground railroad. Through individual and group efforts, black abolitionists kept the issues of slavery and racism constantly before the public by publishing calls to action, demonstrating in the streets, or, like the well-to-do Robert Purvis, refusing to pay taxes to a town that practiced racial discrimination.

49 MORAL ELEVATION?

Peter Paul Simons, an outspoken New York City porter, reflected growing black impatience with the strategies inherited from the white-dominated abolitionist movement. While addressing the city's African Clarkson Association in 1839, Simons challenged the usefulness of moral reform as an antislavery tactic for blacks.

My Brother Clarksons:

I have on all occasions where I have had the honor to address an assemblage of our people, advocated in most strongest terms the benefit of our benevolent institutions and the object of our moral elevation. The reason why I advocated the first was that we have had practical proof of its benefit, while the latter has now carried its good to a climax.

In particular reference to our people, my language is inadequate to express the honor due to those who first introduced these institutions among us, all that I can say to those who still remain among us is, that heaven alone can justly pay them for their labors. It would be vain to endeavor the useless task to trace up the very many practical proofs derived from our benevolent associations, but there is one I cannot pass over, which is unity. Unity alone has elevated us to our present stand, and benevolent societies was the father of it; some thirty years back there was nothing to guide us but discord and enmity, but with the introduction of institutions, came virtue, benevolence, sympathy, brotherly affection, unity. It was this, exertions of our feeble selves (independent of other sources) that has brought us to our present stand.

But hark to the trumpet sound from the pulpit. Again it's thundered from the press, now it's the topic of our common arguments. What is this discording tone? MORAL ELEVATION. OUR MORAL ELEVATION.

It is sounded to be the prolific parent of all virtue, and he who would dare whisper in the faintest breath against it, is thought no less than the parent of all vice, crime, and degradation, that possibly could afflict humanity. But I my Brother Clarksons will venture to say that this long talk of our moral elevation, has made us a moral people, but no more. There is no nation of people under the canopy of heaven, who are given more to good morals and piety than we are. Show up to the world an African and you will show in truth morality. It is stamped in his countenance, it is in his word and action, he uses it mechanically for his principal tool to work by. But as it has progressed, it has carried along with it blind submission. Yes it's nothing but this moral elevation that causes us to have so little confidence in one another, it is this alone that puts white men at the head of even our private affairs, they are both judge and council for some of our people's transactions, and they can fill all offices where they can gain their ends. Yes Brothers, this moral elevation of our people is but a mere song, it is nothing but a conspicuous scarecrow designed expressly, I may safely say, to hinder our people from acting collectively for themselves. For long as it continues we will have a lack of confidence in one another, and if we suspect each other, how can we act together. No, we must lose sight of it entire, for it will deceive you if practiced any longer. I wonder much how our people could be regurgitated by this false philanthropy so long, for there is no such a thing as elevating a nation of people by good morals, it is contrary to common sense or any plan of elevation laid down in record. But it is practiced on our people as a means for to hinder them from acting in another way to obtain their rights. * * *

Why is it, that we never hear of a physical and a political elevation, because they both call for united strength. And these two must go together, for if you destroy the one you must unquestionably shock the other, and even when taken separately they require action, and we must act before we can be an independent people.

Physical and political efforts are the only methods left for us to adopt. * * *

Is it possible that this foolish thought of moral elevation suffers us to remain inactive? If so, then remain inactive, and you but raise another generation of slaves, and your children's children to the last posterity will spend their lives in as bitter oppression as ye do now today.

Remain inactive and your children will curse the day of their birth.

Remain inactive, and you will be the cause of rearing children for an eternal torment, for they in an ecstacy of despair will curse their maker for suffering such bitter oppression to be practiced upon them.

Remain inactive, and the almighty himself will spurn you, for lack of courage and not using properly your agency. No, we must show ACTION! ACTION! *ACTION!* and our will to be, or not to be; this we study, this we must physically practice, and we will be in truth an independent people.

Colored American (New York, N.Y.), 1 June 1839; *BAP*, 3:288–92.

5 0   A G A I N S T   S E P A R A T E   S C H O O L S

Persistent accusations of racism and brutal treatment of students by the headmaster and staff at Boston's Smith School led to demands by African American parents that it be closed. When the petition strategy failed to change city policy, they turned to boycotts, protest meetings, and legal action. They achieved victory in 1855 when the Massachusetts legislature desegregated the state's schools. Early in the campaign, Boston blacks met at the First Independent Baptist Church on 18 June 1844 and adopted the following resolutions.

Whereas, we, the Colored Citizens of the City of Boston have recently sent a petition to the School Committee respectfully praying for the abolition of the separate schools for colored children, & asking for the rights & privileges extended to other citizens in respect to the Common School System, viz: the right to send our children to the schools established in the respective Districts in which we reside, and

Whereas, the School Committee at their last meeting passed a vote, stating, in substance, that the prayer of our petition would not be granted, & that the separate schools for colored children be continued, and

Whereas we believe, & have the opinion of eminent counsel, that the institution & support of separate schools at the public charge for any one class of the inhabitants in exclusion of any other class is contrary to the laws of this Commonwealth, therefore,

Resolved, that we consider the late action of the School Committee in regard to our petition asking for the entire abolition of separate schools for colored children as erroneous & unsatisfactory.

Resolved, that while we would not turn aside from our main object, the abolition of the separate colored schools, we cannot allow this occasion to pass without an expression of our suprize & regret at the recent acquittal by the School Committee of Abner Forbes, Principal of the Smith School, & of our deep conviction that he is totally unworthy of his present responsible station; & that the colored parents of this City are recommended to withdraw their children from the exclusive schools established in contravention of that equality of priviliges which is the vital principal of the school system of Massachusetts.

Resolved, that a copy of the above preamble and resolutions be sent to the Chairman of the School Committee with a request that the petition heretofore presented may be reconsidered, & that we be allowed a hearing on said petition before them.

JOHN T. HILTON	President
HENRY L. W. THACKER	
JONAS W. CLARK	Vice Presidents
WILLIAM C. NELL	
ROBERT MORRIS JR.	Secretaries

5 1   L O B B Y I N G   T H E   L E G I S L A T U R E

Stephen A. Myers led the lobbying efforts on behalf of the New York State Suffrage Association to eliminate the $250 property qualification for black suffrage. In a letter to white abolitionist leader Gerrit Smith, Myers describes his activities and his attempt to defeat a bill to appropriate state funds for the New York State Colonization Society.

AntiSlavery office
168 third street
Albany, [New York]
March 22, 1856

Sir:

I have been striving hard this winter with the members of the Senate assembly and Legislator to recommend an amendment to the Constitution of this state so as to strik off the property qualifycation, and let us vote on the same footing of the white mail citizens. So as to hav it one more handed down to the people I hav got Senetor Cuyler some weeks a go to get up a resolution in the senat wich is now under discusin and will com up again on monday or tuesday. I shall hav one up in the assembly in a few days. I hav recieved pertitions from Colerd men from differant sections of the state wich I hav presented to Senate and assembly. I hav devided the partitions in the two houses. The partitions hav about 1600 names all together. I hav also devoted my time to defeat the Collenization bill to appropriate five thousand dollars to the colenization Society. I hav gotten about sixty members pledged to go against it on a final vote. It now under discussion. When it comes up again thy will iether vote it down or strike out the inacting clause wich will eventually kill the bill. Their is one thing that I am sorry to say: two thirds of my people want energy and more perseveranc. At the state convention of Colerd Citizens at troy it fell to me ~~to be~~ as one of the agents of the Suffrage association to attend the Capitol during the seting of the legislator. Thy were to furnish funds from the differant portions of the State to pay expenes during the winter. Thy hav not yet forwarded the first ~~Cen~~ Cent for that purpos. The only aid I hav received has been from

Fredrick Douglas. My people want a great deal done but thy are not willing to make any sacrifices. Yor speech at the Capitol on the ~~Canses~~ Kanses question last thursday night a week has left a lasting impresion on the people. It has been all the talk sinc you Sir made that famous speech. Their has been over fifty members of the Senate and assembly spoken to of your speech and dozens of our citizens hav talked to me of your speech and say that it was one of the greaest speeches made by any in the Capitol. The people say that you compleetily anhialated Judge Northrap. The Judge has spoken to me two or three time on that subject. The Judge says that he did not wish to speak but he was forced out unprepared. He said he thought that you was rather hard on him and is willing to admit that you are a sound and strong argurer. He said Mr Smith wanted to giv him a hard rap because he was a going to support Mr [Millard] Filmore. He said Mr Smith took that oppertunity to do it before a large audianc. He says never the less he likes Mr Smith. He says that you do not talk anything only what you practic and says that your check for three thousand dollars is the impuls of your noble Heart. And he says that your life is crowned with hundreds of Charitable acts. The members of assembly plague the Judge because he could not answer you. I forwarded you Sir one of the curculars that the Collenization agent is a curculating in the Senate and assembly. I hav had sinc Mr Smith was in our city [six] fugitives from Maryryland. They were more destitute of [c]lothing than any that hav reached here for many winters. The letter sir that you wrote to Topp and me[,] I hav never seen it. Topp and me differ a litle on the Garrison question. I am rather more favorable to Mr Douglass veiues and not to Mr Garrisons. Theirefore we differ. I remain your Humble Servat,

STEPHEN MYERS

Gerrit Smith Papers, George Arents Research Library, Syracuse University, Syracuse, New York; published by permission; *BAP*, 4:326–28.

5 2   L E T   U S   R O U S E   O U R S E L V E S

African Americans filled the reform press with protests, petitions, and calls to action. An anonymous black woman from Hartford, Connecticut, published this appeal to all women in the state.

Free women of Connecticut (for I speak not now to slaves, to the servile minions of pride, selfishness and prejudice), have you this fall signed the petitions in behalf of the dumb, and entreated *all* the women in your town to do the same? If you have not, I implore you to drop the work you have in your hand, or this paper, as soon as you shall have finished this article, and go to the work *now*, nor leave it till not one woman in your town shall have for excuse in the day of accounts, that she has not been *asked* to pray for the perishing.

Do you say you have so many family cares you cannot go? Thousands of your sisters may never hear the word *family* but to mock their desolation. But you must prepare your beloved children's *warm, winter clothing.* Look yonder. Do you not see that mother toiling with her *almost, or quite naked children, shivering in the keen blast?* Yet you cannot go, you must prepare the table for your family. The slave spends but little time in dressing her *"peck of corn per week."* Does your house need putting in order? Had you a house but *"fifteen feet by ten,"* furnished with a rough bench, a stool and a bunk, with a little straw and a blanket, and then, for cooking and table apparatus, a kettle, a spoon and a knife, it might not take you so long to set them in order. Why do you delay, and take up a book to read? Is it in derision of blighted intellect? Ah! throw it down in remembrance of the millions in whose bodies immortality has well nigh found a sepulchre. Do your precious babes demand your tender watchings, so that you cannot leave them? Hark! that shriek!! It proclaims the bursting of a heart, as the babe is torn from the frantic mother, and sold for *"five dollars the pound."* Still do you say *"I have not time?"* O! I pity you. You are yourself almost qualified to be a slave. Ay, *you are a slave*—a slave to hardness of heart. You have got a stone in your bosom, there is no flesh there, you are consumed by selfishness. Is this hard talk? How would *you* talk of *me*, were you allowed to speak, if I should wrap myself up in *"my own concerns"* and see your relatives and friends sold under the hammer, your clothing stripped from you, except perhaps, a mere rag, your mind smothered to almost utter extinction, and then the defaced remnant of your former self driven before the gory lash, till, exhausted, you cannot finish your task, and are bound down, shamelessly exposed, and a cat hauled up and down your back to gratify the revenge of some lustful brute of an overseer. I see all this, and know that our GREAT and WISE men (?) in the nation's BLACK LAW FACTORY have decided that *you have no right to ask for mercy* in their behalf. You know all this, and cry out, "O how I pity the poor creature. I can't bear to hear of such treatment. My feelings are so acute I cannot read such horrible cruelties; but I have so much to do, that I cannot carry this petition all around town; it will take so much time I shan't be able to finish this ruffle, or put the ribbon on this bonnet."

Women of Connecticut, I shall blush to acknowledge myself a woman, if women's souls have become so sear, so blighted, as to neglect this labor of humanity. But I cannot think it will be neglected. I cannot think there would be a falling off in this important work.

Let us rouse ourselves and pour an overwhelming flood of rebuke upon those beings who claim to be men, agents of those who style themselves the "FREEST NATION ON THE EARTH," and use their freedom to say, "For Four Hundred Dollars WASHINGTON may be a *Guinea coast for Texas.*" "For Four Hundred Dollars any wretch may trade in human flesh and bones, in slaves and the souls of men, in the Capital of 'THE REFUGE OF THE OPPRESSED.'" "For Four Hundred Dollars any human hyena may FATTEN ON THE BLOOD OF MEN, WOMEN AND CHILDREN, under the walls of our CAPITOL." Yes, worse still, they have made *robbery, adultery,* and *murder,* free game—ay, honorable sport—and he who holds the greatest number of trophies is deemed most noble. Up, my sister, speak while there is time. Millions are perishing, victims of your delay.

A COLORED WOMAN

Charter Oak (Hartford, Conn.), November 1839; *BAP,* 3:326–27.

53 AN UNJUST TAX

Robert Purvis, the wealthy black abolitionist, refused to accept the exclusion of his son from a segregated school supported by his property taxes. Although town officials attempted to circumvent his demands for integration by exempting him from payment, they could not long afford to keep one of the town's largest landowners off the tax rolls and eventually integrated the school.

Byberry, [Pennsylvania]
Nov[ember] 4th, 1853

Dear Sir:

You called yesterday for the tax upon my property in this Township, which I shall pay, excepting the "School Tax." I object to the payment of this tax, on the ground that my rights as a citizen and my feelings as a man and a parent have been grossly outraged in depriving me, in violation of law and justice, of the benefits of the school system, which this tax was designed to sustain. I am perfectly aware that all that makes up the character and worth of the citizens of this township, look upon the proscription and exclusion of my children from the Public School as illegal, and an unjustifiable usurpation of my right. I have borne this outrage ever since the innovation upon the usual practice of admitting *all* the children of the Township into the "Public Schools," and at considerable expense have been obliged to obtain the services of private teachers to instruct my children, while my school tax is greater, with a single exception, than that of any other citizen of the Township. It is true (and the outrage is made but the more glaringly and insulting), I was informed by a *pious Quaker* director, with a sanctifying grace, imparting doubtless an unctuous glow to his *saintly* prejudices, that a school in the village of Mechanicsville was appropriated for "*thine.*" The miserable shanty, with all its appurtenances, on the very line of the township, to which this *benighted* follower of George Fox alluded, is as you know the most flimsy and ridiculous sham which any tool of a skin-hating aristocracy could have resorted to, to cover or protect his servility. To submit by voluntary payment of the demand is too great an outrage upon nature, and with a spirit, thank God, unshackled by this, or any other wanton and cowardly act, I shall resist this tax, which before the unjust exclusion had always afforded me the highest gratification in paying. With no other than the best feeling towards yourself, I am forced to this unpleasant position, in vindication of my rights and personal dignity, against an encroachment upon them as contemptibly mean, as it is infamously despotic. Yours, very respectfully,

ROBERT PURVIS

Pennsylvania Freeman (Philadelphia), 10 November 1853; *BAP*, 4:187–88.

BY ALL JUST AND
NECESSARY MEANS

The steady escalation of racial violence—kidnappings, personal assaults, and rioting mobs—during the antebellum era prompted African Americans to reconsider their commitment to Garrisonian pacifism. As early as 1837, black abolitionists began to reject Garrisonian thought by refusing to "recommend non-resistance . . . when liberty is invaded and lives endangered." What use were "moral weapons," one black leader questioned, "in defense against a kidnapper or a midnight incendiary with a lighted torch in his hand"? Through the 1840s, African American leaders openly questioned the moral suasion principles of the antislavery movement. By 1850, only a few blacks remained ambivalent about the use of violence in self-defense, and before the end of the decade most had concluded that only violence could end the scourge of slavery.

54 WHAT ARE MORAL MEANS
GOOD FOR?

Augustus W. Hanson, an Episcopal clergyman born on the West African coast, questioned the practical and moral value of nonresistance in a letter to Garrison when he revealed that during a recent assault he had challenged his attacker and appealed to the legal authorities.

Saturday, 3rd November 1838

My dear Sir:
  With inexpressible feelings I now take up my pen to address you; and as a multiplicity of Subjects urge themselves upon my mind I hardly know with which to commence, but as the most recent occurrence is the most fresh undoubtedly upon your mind as well as my own, I will endeavor first to treat briefly upon that. Not having it in my power to avail myself of

the conversation of men of such exalted and enlightened views of morality and Christianity as yourself, and being necessitated to rely solely upon my own feeble resources, I consequently have not probably arrived at the conclusion touching some Subjects which probably under other circumstances I might have done. In this manner am I Situated respecting the doctrine of no Civil Government; with all becoming deference would I speak of your opinions on this Subject if at any time I may occasionally recur to them. On mentioning to you the other day the circumstance of the outrageous assault committed upon me, my object really was to procure advice—and to be governed thereby in case my own reason should accord thereto—and strange as it may seem to you that I should have acted in opposition to the advice given by you, I know you will allow me a few moments of your precious time to give my reason[s] for so doing. In the first place however, it is necessary that I should [assert] my belief that "the powers that be are ordained of God," as "a praise to them that do good, and a terror to Evildoers." Although therefore I would under no circumstances exercise physical force to the infliction of injury upon any fellow being. I do not believe that I should commit sin—that is transgress the law of God—by the exercise of the same physical powers merely to restrain that fellow being from inflicting an injury upon me. For instance a man comes with the avowed intention of striking me, and if possible by that blow to terminate my existence— no one will deny that he is thereby be doing wrong—and consequently if I return him the like injury—even though with the view to save my own life—I should be guilty of the like wrong. But Supposing that instead of retaliating blow for blow I merely put forth my arm to avert the intended injury—should I in this case be doing wrong? In my humble conception it appears not. Consequently the sin consists not merely in the application of physical force—but in the application thereof with a bad motive to gain a certain end at all hazard. If I be right in my view of this subject I think my course in this late affair of assault upon me with evident intent to injure will be perfectly justifiable—for my reason for appealing to the strong arm of the law for protection arose from the settled conviction that my life was in danger. And as I hold it my duty to protect and preserve that life as far as may be without infringing upon the laws of God—and also to prevent at any time the Commission of crime whenever it lies in my power so to do— I entered my protest that the law restrains that individual, and protect my life—not any more for the sake of my life than to prevent the commission of crime—and the periling of an immortal Soul to irretrievable and inevitable ruin. Self knowledge is undoubtedly the knowledge in which man has yet arrived at the least perfection but as far as I know myself this was my true and only motive in appealing to the law. I feel no personal enmity—nor have I at any time felt any against that individual. I am not aware that I have at any time infringed upon any prerogative of his—for with Cowper I hold that "a disputable point is no man's ground"—much therefore as I contemn and repudiate the [word illegible] sin-like conduct of this disgrace to man— I can freely forgive him. My aim is to arrive at the truth concerning the divine Sanction concerning human governments—and "j'espere que nous [ne] contredisons pas" [I hope we don't disagree].

The next point to which I would advert is the studiousness with which my name seems to have been shut out of the proceedings of the two last AntiSlavery Conventions (I allude to those in Worcester Co. & holden in the towns of Worcester & Northampton which I attended). In this private epistle I request to be informed by you of the reason for these proceedings. In Worcester the resolution I introduced in behalf of the "Mirror of Liberty" was not only not acted upon but Wendell Phillips deputed a Committee to take the unusual step of returning my resolution, on the false ground that the Mass. AntiSlavery Society never in their Conventions recommended any periodicals or other publications not published in New England. Need I say to you Sir that I am convinced this is not true fo[r] in the case of the Color'd American—and others which cant be mentioned they <u>have</u> acted upon publications <u>out</u> of New England. In Worcester my name was given in as a member of the Convention and my money—one dollar in amount— paid towards defraying the expenses of the Convention. Yet altho. my name was there read on the [note] it was shut out of the Liberator—tho. not I am convinced by <u>you</u>. [In the] minutes of the Northampton Convention published this week—everyone that made any remarks is mentioned excepting your humble Servant—not that I <u>wish</u> to be mentioned but I cannot help noticing and feeling the evident design in these proceedings. Altho. we are told that "there is Joy in the presence of the angels of God in heaven over one Sinner that repents"—<u>men</u> are not willing to cooperate with one however penitent for the errors of past ways. It is impossible for me to place the one twentieth part of my thoughts on paper—and I have no friend like yourself to whom I can disburden my mind of its many encumbrances. This of course does not concern the public & if at any time you can spare me or permit me one hour's interview wherever it may suit your convenience you will exceedingly oblige. My dear Sir, Your most obedient and humble Servant

AUGUSTUS WILLIAM HANSON

55 AN APPEAL FOR VIOLENCE

More than seventy delegates and scores of black and white observers at the 1843 black national convention in Buffalo, New York, heard Henry Highland Garnet eloquently and passionately advocate slave resistance and insurrection. The controversial speech was universally condemned by white abolitionists and was not published until 1848— and then at John Brown's expense.

ADDRESS TO THE SLAVES OF THE UNITED STATES OF AMERICA

Brethren and Fellow Citizens:

Your brethren of the north, east, and west have been accustomed to meet together in National Conventions, to sympathize with each other, and to weep over your unhappy condition. In these meetings we have addressed all classes of the free, but we have never until this time, sent a word of consolation and advice to you. We have been contented in sitting still and mourning over your sorrows, earnestly hoping that before this day, your sacred Liberties would have been restored. But, we have hoped in vain. Years have rolled on, and tens of thousands have been borne on streams of blood, and tears, to the shores of eternity. While you have been oppressed, we have also been partakers with you; nor can we be free while you are enslaved. We therefore write to you as being bound with you.

Many of you are bound to us, not only by the ties of common humanity, but we are connected by the more tender relations of parents, wives, husbands, children, brothers, and sisters, and friends. As such we most affectionately address you. * * *

SLAVERY! How much misery is comprehended in that single word. * * * TO SUCH DEGRADATION IT IS SINFUL IN THE EXTREME FOR YOU TO MAKE VOLUNTARY SUBMISSION. The divine commandments, you are in duty bound to reverence, and obey. * * * Your condition does not absolve you from your moral obligation. The diabolical injustice by which your Liberties are cloven down, NEITHER GOD, NOR ANGELS, OR JUST MEN COMMAND YOU TO SUFFER FOR A SINGLE MOMENT. THEREFORE IT IS YOUR SOLEMN AND IMPERATIVE DUTY TO USE EVERY MEANS, BOTH MORAL, INTELLECTUAL, AND PHYSICAL, THAT PROMISE SUCCESS. * * *

Brethren, it is as wrong for your lordly oppressors to keep you in slavery, as it was for the man thief to steal our ancestors from the coast of Africa. You should therefore now use the same manner of resistance, as would have been just in our ancestors, when the bloody footprints of the first remorseless soul thief was placed upon the shores of our fatherland. The humblest peasant is as free in the sight of God, as the proudest monarch that ever swayed a scepter. Liberty is a spirit sent out from God, and like its great Author, is no respecter of persons.

* * * Look around you, and behold the bosoms of your loving wives, heaving with untold agonies! Hear the cries of your poor children! Remember the stripes your fathers bore. Think of the torture and disgrace of your noble mothers. Think of your wretched sisters, loving virtue and purity, as they are driven into concubinage, and are exposed to the unbridled lusts of incarnate devils. Think of the undying glory that hangs around the ancient name of Africa—and forget not that you are native-born American citizens, and as such, you are justly entitled to all the rights that are granted to the freest. Think how many tears you have poured out upon the soil which you have cultivated with unrequited toil, and enriched with your blood; and then go to your lordly enslavers, and tell them plainly, that YOU ARE DETERMINED TO BE FREE. * * * Tell them in language which they cannot misunderstand, of the exceeding sinfulness of slavery, and of a future judgement, and of the righteous retributions of an indignant God. Inform them that all you desire, is FREEDOM, and that nothing else will suffice. Do this, and forever after cease to toil for the heartless tyrants, who give you no other reward but stripes and abuse. If they then commence the work of death, they, and not you, will be responsible for the consequences. You had far better all die—*die immediately*, than live slaves, and entail your

Henry Highland Garnet. Courtesy of Library of Congress.

wretchedness upon your posterity. If you would be free in this generation, here is your only hope. However much you and all of us may desire it, there is not much hope of Redemption without the shedding of blood. If you must bleed, let it all come at once—rather, *die freemen, than live to be slaves.* It is impossible, like the children of Israel, to make a grand Exodus from the land of bondage. * * *

Fellow men! patient sufferers! behold your dearest rights crushed to the earth! See your sons murdered, and your wives, mothers, and sisters, doomed to prostitution! In the name of the merciful God! and by all that life is worth, let it no longer be a debateable question, whether it is better to choose LIBERTY or DEATH!

In 1822, Denmark Vesey, of South Carolina, formed a plan for the liberation of his fellow men. In the whole history of human efforts to overthrow slavery, a more complicated and tremendous plan was never formed. He was betrayed by the treachery of his own people, and died a martyr to freedom. * * *

The patriotic Nathaniel Turner followed Denmark Vesey. He was goaded to desperation by wrong and injustice. By Despotism, his name has been recorded on the list of infamy, but future generations will number him upon the noble and brave.

Next arose the immortal Joseph Cinqué, the hero of the *Amistad.* He was a native African, and by the help of God he emancipated a whole ship-load of his fellow men on the high seas. And he now sings of Liberty on the sunny hills of Africa, and beneath his native palm trees, where he hears the lion roar, and feels himself as free as that king of the forest. Next arose Madison Washington, that bright star of freedom, and took his station in the constellation of freedom. He was a slave on board the brig *Creole,* of Richmond, bound to New Orleans, that great slave mart, with a hundred and four others. Nineteen struck for Liberty or death. * * *

We do not advise you to attempt a revolution with the sword, because it would be INEXPEDIENT. Your numbers are too small, and moreover the rising spirit of the age, and the spirit of the gospel, are opposed to war and bloodshed. But from this moment cease to labor for tyrants who will not remunerate you. Let every slave throughout the land do this, and the days of slavery are numbered. You cannot be more oppressed than you have been—you cannot suffer greater cruelties than you have already. RATHER DIE FREEMEN, THAN LIVE TO BE SLAVES. Remember that you are THREE MILLIONS.

It is in your power so to torment the God-cursed slaveholders, that they will be glad to let you go free. If the scale was turned and black men were the masters, and white men the slaves, every destructive agent and element would be employed to lay the oppressor low. Danger and death would hang over their heads day and night. Yes, the tyrants would meet with plagues more terrible than those of Pharaoh. But you are a patient people. You act as though you were made for the special use of these devils. You act as though your daughters were born to pamper the lusts of your masters and overseers. And worse than all, you tamely submit, while your lords tear your wives from your embraces, and defile them before your eyes. In the name of God we ask, are you men? Where is the blood of your fathers? Has it all run out of your veins? Awake, awake; millions of voices are calling you! Your dead fathers speak to you from their graves. Heaven, as with a voice of thunder, calls on you to arise from the dust.

Let your motto be RESISTANCE! RESISTANCE! RESISTANCE! No oppressed people have ever secured their Liberty without resistance. What kind of resistance you had better make, you must decide by the circumstances that surround you, and according to the suggestion of expediency. Brethren, adieu. Trust in the living God. Labor for the peace of the human race, and remember that you are three millions.

Henry Highland Garnet, ed., *Walker's Appeal, With a Brief Sketch of His Life* (New York, N.Y., 1848), 90–96; *BAP*, 3:403–11.

Chapter 4

Black Abolitionists
and the National Crisis

THE SLAVE POWER

Black abolitionists sought to convince the American public that slaveholding interests—the "slave power"—corrupted the South, caused racial prejudice in the North, and threatened American democracy. In the 1840s and 1850s, they witnessed slavery's growing influence on the federal government. The Fugitive Slave Law, the Kansas-Nebraska Act, the attempt to annex Cuba as a slave state, the movement to reopen the slave trade, and the Dred Scott decision all seemed to underscore the power of slaveholding interests at the national level. African Americans reacted with dismay, disbelief, and anger as the government policies upheld slavery and systematically eroded their civil rights. The federal government's conduct compelled African Americans to reassess antislavery tactics and goals and to question fundamental beliefs about the nation's institutions and democratic political principles.

56 SLAVERY—ITS EFFECTS UPON THE RIGHTS AND INTERESTS OF THE NORTH

Joseph C. Holly, a poet and antislavery lecturer, explored the political, economic, and moral costs of the federal government's "unhallowed

*connection" with slaveholding interests in an 1848 essay published in
Frederick Douglass's* North Star.

"If a people assist in fastening one end of a chain around the limbs
of another, inevitable fate will sooner or later fasten the other end around
their own necks."

We rejoice that it is an immutable law of Providence, in the regulation
of human affairs, to order that individuals or communities cannot disregard
and trample upon the rights of others without affecting their own rights
and interests; that he has established the indivisibility of the human race
an identity of their interest. We need no more infallible illustration of the
workings of this Providential law than is presented in reviewing the unhallowed connection and criminality of the North in relation to slavery, and
the effects of that institution on the rights and interests of the North.

In the formation of a constitution for the government of the confederacy, the North did not only mortgage every particle of its soil as a hunting
ground for the bloodhounds of slavery, biped and quadruped, to dog the
track of, and worry the panting fugitive from the worse than deathlike vale
of Southern oppression; they did not only pledge every strong arm at the
North to go to the South in case the slaves, goaded by oppression, should
imitate the "virtues of their forefathers," and vindicate their rights by sub-
scribing to the doctrine of Algernon Sydney—that "resistance to tyrants is
obedience to God"—and crush them in subjection to their galling yoke; but
in the spirit of compromise and barter, stipulated that the slaveholder should
have additional power in proportion as he became the great plunderer of
human rights, the more insolent to the great declaration of fundamental
principle, the substratum of all democratic institutions.

They agreed, in Art. 1st, Section 2d, of the Constitution, that representatives, and direct taxes, shall be apportioned among the several States which
may be included within this Union, according to their respective numbers,
which shall be determined by adding to the whole number of free persons,
including those bound to service for a term of years, and excluding Indians
not taxed, three-fifths of all other persons.

This provision allows slaveholders to count every five of their victims as
three freemen in the apportionment of representatives to the popular branch
of Congress—a representation which the lamented late John Q. Adams declared was an outward show, a representation of persons held in bondage;

in fact, a representation of the masters—the oppressor representing the oppressed—an exemplification of the art of committing the lamb to the tender custody of the wolf. By this arrangement, a slaveholder claiming two hundred of his fellow beings as property, "in a government professedly free," has the same weight in the national council as one hundred and twenty of his Northern brethren.

The advantage that the North supposed they would derive as a consideration for this bargain, was that the South should contribute in like proportion to the support of the government; "but here they got their foot in it," for armed with this overwhelming and consolidating political power, the South soon departed from this system, and *decreed* the indirect tax system, by which they threw the burden of supporting government almost entirely upon the shoulders of the North. * * *

Having shorn Sampson of his locks, Delilah set about to get the green wisps wherewith to bind him; the first that presented itself to her comprehensive vision was Louisiana. It was in vain that [Thomas] Jefferson, "who was not overscrupulous," declared that the Constitution was framed for the government of territory defined to be United States territory by the treaty of 1783; that the framers of that instrument never contemplated in its provisions the admission of England, Holland, or any foreign State into the Union. For a time our Sampson struggled. The North stood up boldly for the Constitution; but the coy maiden insisted on having this jewel to decorate her casket, and what could he do—poor impotent soul—but yield; and thus was the constitutional barrier broken down, and the South strengthened and secured for a time in her political ascendancy. But owing to the influence of slavery upon the industrial classes, the tide of emigration rolled North-westward, where it would not come in competition with that institution. Territorial governments were springing up as if by magic of a wand, and knocking for admission into the confederacy of States; the Northern Sampson's locks were growing out, and Delilah was fearful of losing her power over him. The Constitution having been broken down, it was an easy matter to march through the breach. Florida and Texas were other wisps to bind the North with—were other jewels to decorate the political casket of the South. Against each of these the North made a *faint* resistance; passed any number of "rhetorical" resolves, well guarded with compromising "buts and ifs," and might have exclaimed, "Thy genius has triumphed, oh Delilah!" And Sampson bows him to the dust; for these resolves were as impotent as the famous "white man's resolution" in relation to President Polk's indemnity will prove to be.

But in the national Constitution are incorporated some guarantees for freedom—the right of speech, the freedom of the press, the right of a citizen of one State to the privileges and immunities of citizenship in another State; these have been carried out extensively at the North; for although the hand of violence has been raised against those that should dare be so bold as to contend for a practical application of the principles of "76," the sons of the South may stand over the very graves of those who struggled and fell in defence of these principles, on the very spot enriched by their patriot blood, and insult their hallowed memory by declaring that "slavery is the corner-stone of democracy," that "all communities must settle down into classes of employers and laborers, and that the former will sooner or later own the latter," and no hand of violence will be raised against them. This is right. We want no weapons but those of truth and right to combat these deluded sophistries, even when backed by the learning, talents and sagacity of the Calhouns, McDuffies and Rhetts, or any other of the "model" republicans of the Palmetto State. Cannons, brickbats, clubs and proscription, are the weapons of tyranny and wrong.

But should any descendant of those who fought for liberty when it meant something else than a "rhetorical flourish," who felt as the French Republicans of '48 (honor to them!) felt, that liberty is the boon of heaven, the birthright of man. Go to South Carolina or most any of the slaveholding States, and advocate a practical application of these principles to the toiling masses; we are informed by modern democrats that "they will be seized upon, tried and hung, in spite of the interference of all governments, not excepting the general government of the United States."

In 1812, this government contended with the most powerful maritime nation on the globe for "free trade and sailor's rights," the immunity of national flags, and yet in several of the Southern States, in violation of the Constitution, citizens, seamen from the North, are imprisoned, and if their captains, after being unjustly deprived of their services, will not pay the ransom of slavery, they are sold as chattels. The fact that they stand upon an American vessel, with an American commander, with the world-renowned stripes and stars floating above their heads, is no indemnity against such outrage.

Old Massachusetts, among whose granite hills are lurking whatever principle of freedom that remains to the degenerate sons of the pilgrim fathers, felt aggrieved at this treatment. With a Faneuil Hall and a Boston harbor in her, how could she fail to see that the right to imprison one of her citizens involved the right to imprison another, and with these old-fashioned, obsolete views, she sent commissioners to South Carolina and Louisiana to take cognizance of such cases, with a view of bringing them before the supreme tribunal for adjudication. But these ambassadors, on this peaceful and lawful mission, were driven from the soil of a sister State (!) by threats of violence, and one who felt his puritanic blood, and was not easily affrighted, was promised a coat of tar and feathers to assist him in making his flight, by a committee of Southern gentlemen! And thus was the sovereignty of a State insulted, in the person of her representative, and her constitutional rights trampled under foot. Had some barbarous state in the Indian Archipelago, or in the Gulf of Mexico, refused to acknowledge the aristocratic titles of some American agent, the thunders of the Northern would cooperate with the Southern line in pronouncing vengeance upon the barbarians, and the cry of indemnity for the past and security for the future would resound through the executive and legislative halls, and be re-echoed in every grog-shop throughout the land. The Constitution is everything in its compromises in favor of the peculiar institution, but nothing in its guarantees for freedom.

When a Northern member, on the presentation of the Constitution of the State of Florida for the ratification of Congress, very politely suggested that one of its provisions conflicted with the national Constitution, a Southern representative rose with that air of command and arrogance peculiar to Southerners, and said: "We of the South sometimes find it necessary to enact laws for our personal safety, and when we find it so necessary, we care not how many clauses there are in *your constitution* allowing or disallowing it, we will enact them." The Constitution is but another proof of the futility of any attempt at compromise between liberty and slavery, right and wrong; they are incompatible, incongruous, and wrong must ever strengthen at the expense of right. * * *

North Star (Rochester, N.Y.), 12 May 1848; *BAP*, 4:18–23.

57 IN THE WAKE OF DRED SCOTT

Robert Purvis, a Philadelphia businessman and community leader, spoke on the proslavery character of the government and the U.S. Constitution at the American Anti-Slavery Society's 1857 annual meeting in New York City. His speech imparts the anger and indignation felt by African Americans following the Dred Scott decision.

In allowing my name to be published as one of the speakers for this morning, which I have consented to do, at the earnest request of the Committee, it is due to myself to say that I have acted with great reluctance. Not that I am not deeply interested in this cause, nor that I have not clear convictions and strong feelings on the subject. On the contrary, my interest is too intense for expression, and my convictions and feelings are so vivid and overpowering that I cannot trust myself in attempting to give them utterance. Sir, I envy those who, with cooler blood or more mental self-command, can rise before an audience like this, and deliberately choose their words and speak their thoughts in calm, measured phrase. This is a task, sir, to which I am not adequate. I must either say too much or too little. If I let my heart play freely and speak out what I think and feel, I am extravagant, as people call it. If I put a curb on my feelings and try to imitate the cool and unimpassioned manner of others, I cannot speak at all. Sir, how can any man with blood in his veins, and a heart pulsating in his bosom, and especially how can any coloured man, think of the oppression of this country and of the wrongs of his race, and then express himself with calmness and without passion. (Applause.)

Mr. Chairman, look at the facts—here, in a country with a sublimity of impudence that knows no parallel, setting itself up before the world as a *free country*, a *land of liberty!*, "the *land of the free*, and the *home of the brave*," the "*freest country in all the world!*" Gracious God! and yet here are millions of men and women groaning under a bondage the like of which the world has never seen—bought and sold, whipped, manacled, killed all the day long. Yet this is a *free country!* The people have the assurance to talk of their *free institutions.* How can I speak of such a country and use language of moderation? How can I, who, every day, feel the grinding hoof of this despotism, and who am myself identified with its victims? Sir, let others, who can, speak coolly on this subject; I cannot, and I will not. (Applause.)

Mr. Chairman, that I may make sure of expressing the precise sentiment which I wish to present to this meeting, I will offer a resolution. It is one which I had the honour of presenting to a meeting lately held in the City of Philadelphia, but to which I did not speak as I could have desired, for the reasons which I have already stated. The resolution is as follows:

> Resolved, That to attempt, as some do, to prove that there is no support given to slavery in the Constitution and essential structure of the American Government is to argue against reason and common sense, to ignore history and shut our eyes against palpable facts; and that while it may suit white men, who do not feel the iron heel, to please themselves with such theories, it ill becomes the man of colour, whose daily experience refutes the absurdity, to indulge in any such idle phantasies.

Mr. Chairman, this resolution expresses just what I think and feel about this newfangled doctrine of the anti-slavery character of the American Constitution. Sir, with all due respect to the Hon. Gerrit Smith, who is a noble and a good man, and one whom, from my soul, I honour with all due respect—I say to the nobleminded, largehearted Gerrit Smith, I must say, that the doctrine of the anti-slavery character of the American Constitution seems to me one of the most absurd and preposterous that ever was broached. It is so contrary to history and common sense, so opposite to what we and every man, and especially every coloured man, feel and know to be the fact, that I have not patience to argue about it. I know it is said that the word "slave" or "slavery" is not to be found in the document. Neither are these words to be found in the Fugitive Slave law. But will any man pretend, on this account, that that infamous statute is an anti-slavery statute, or that it is not one of the most atrocious and damnable laws that ever disgraced the annals of despotism. (Applause.) I know, sir, that there are some fine phrases in the Preamble about "establishing justice" and "securing to ourselves and our posterity the blessings of liberty." But what does that prove? Does it prove that the Constitution of the United States is an anti-slavery document? Then Mr. [James] Buchanan's late Message was an anti-slavery document, and Mr. Buchanan himself a great Abolitionist. Then were all the Messages of your contemptible President Pierce anti-slavery documents, and your contemptible President Pierce was not contemptible, but a much misunderstood and misrepresented Abolitionist. If these fine phrases make the Constitution anti-slavery, then all the Fourth of July orations delivered by pro-slavery doughfaces at the North, and Democratic slave-breeders at the South, all these are anti-slavery documents. Sir, this talk about the Constitution being anti-slavery seems to me so utterly at variance with common sense and what we know to be facts that, as I have already intimated, I have no patience with it. I have no particular objection, Mr. Chairman, to white men, who have little to feel on this subject, to amuse themselves with such theories; but I must say that when I see them imitated by coloured men, I am disgusted! Sir, have we no self respect? Are we to clank the chains that have been made for us, and praise the men who did the deed? Are we to be kicked and scouted, trampled upon and judicially declared to *"have no rights which white men are bound to respect,"* and then turn round and glorify and magnify the laws under which all this is done? Are we such base, soulless, spiritless sycophants as all this? Sir, let others do as they may, I never will stultify or disgrace myself by eulogizing a government that tramples me and all that are dear to me in the dust. (Applause.)

Sir, I treat as an absurdity, an idle phantasy, the idea of the Constitution of this American Union being anti-slavery; on the contrary, I assert that the Constitution is fitting and befitting those who made it—slaveholders and their abettors—and I am free to declare, without any fears of successful contradiction, that the Government of the United States, in its formation and essential structure as well as in its practice, is one of the basest, meanest, most atrocious despotisms that ever saw the face of the sun. (Applause.) And I rejoice, sir, that there is a prospect of this atrocious government being overthrown, and a better one built up in its place. I rejoice in the revolution which is now going on. I honour, from the bottom of my soul, I honour this glorious Society for the part, the leading part, it has taken in this noble work. My heart overflows with gratitude to the self-sacrificing men and women of this Society who have been pioneers in this cause—men and women who, from the beginning till this time, in storm and whatever of sunshine they have had, through evil report and good report, have stood by the side of the slave and unfalteringly maintained the rights of free men of colour. Sir, I cannot sufficiently express, the English language has not words strong enough to express, my admiration of the Abolitionists of this country, and my gratitude to them for what they have done for the confessedly oppressed coloured people in it. And in saying this, I believe I utter the sentiments of all the true coloured men in the country. I know, sir, there are coloured men, some of them occupying prominent places before the public, who lose no opportunity of traducing and misrepresenting the character and course of the Garrisonian Abolitionists; but, sir, these are men without principle, men who are actuated by the basest selfishness, and in whose hearts there is not a spark of genuine love for the cause of freedom. They value anti-slavery not for what it is in itself, or for what it is doing for the slave, but for what it does or fails to do for themselves personally. Sir, I should be ashamed and mortified to believe that these men represented truly the views and feelings of the people of colour in this country. They do not. * * *

National Anti-Slavery Standard (New York, N.Y.), 23 May 1857; BAP, 4:362–65.

THE FUGITIVE SLAVE LAW

Passage of the Fugitive Slave Law in 1850 marked a dramatic and difficult moment for African Americans. The law deprived fugitive slaves of any safe haven in the northern states and threatened all African Americans—fugitives and freeborn—with arbitrary arrest and enslavement. The new law prompted a fresh examination of antislavery tactics. Black leaders, including devotees of Garrisonian principles of nonresistance and moral suasion, openly endorsed the right of self-defense and the use of force to protect fugitive slaves. The law radicalized black abolitionism, mobilized northern black communities, and unleashed angry protests. In cities throughout the North, African Americans gathered in unprecedented numbers to express their outrage and affirm their commitment to organized resistance.

58 AFRICAN AMERICANS RESPOND TO THE FUGITIVE SLAVE LAW

The defiant resolutions adopted by a meeting of Philadelphia blacks in October 1850 signified the reaction of northern blacks to the Fugitive Slave Law.

Whereas, the Declaration of American Independence declares it to be a self-evident truth, "that all men are created equal, and are endowed by their Creator with certain inalienable rights, among which are life, liberty, and the pursuit of happiness"; and whereas, the Constitution of the United States, Art. 1, sect. 9, declares that "the privilege of the writ of habeas corpus shall not be suspended"; and in Art. 5 of the Amendments, that "no person shall be deprived of life, liberty, or property, without due process of law"; and whereas, the late Fugitive Slave Bill, recently enacted by the Congress of the United States, is in clear, palpable violation of these several provisions; therefore,

Armed resistance to the Fugitive Slave Law of 1850 at Christiana, Pennsylvania, September 1851. From William Still, Underground Railroad *(Philadelphia, 1872).*

1. Resolved, That while we have heretofore yielded obedience to the laws of our country, however hard some of them have borne upon us, we deem this law so wicked, so atrocious, so utterly at variance with the principles of the Constitution; so subversive of the objects of all law, the protection of the lives, liberty, and property of the governed; so repugnant to the highest attributes of God, justice and mercy; and so horribly cruel in its clearly expressed mode of operation, that we deem it our sacred duty, a duty that we owe to ourselves, our wives, our children, and to our common nature, as well as to the panting fugitive from oppression, to resist this law at any cost and at all hazards; and we hereby pledge our lives, our fortunes, and our sacred honor so to do.

2. Resolved, That we deem the laws of God at all times paramount to any human laws; and that, in obedience to the command, to "hide the outcast, and betray not him that wandereth," we shall never refuse aid and shelter and succor to any brother or sister who has escaped from the prison-house

of Southern bondage, but shall do all we can to prevent their being dragged back to a slavery inconceivably worse than death.

3. Resolved, That whenever a Government "frameth mischief by law," or "decrees unrighteous decrees," or concentrates all its power to strengthen the arm of the oppressor to crush the weak, that Government puts itself in an attitude hostile to every principle of justice—hostile to the liberal spirit of the law, hostile to that God who "executeth righteousness and judgment for all that are oppressed."

4. Resolved, That in our resistance to this most cruel law, we appeal to our own boasted Declaration of Independence, to the inherent righteousness of our cause, to the moral sense of enlightened nations all over the world, and to the character of that God, who by a series of the most astounding miracles on record, declared his sympathy for the oppressed and his hatred of the oppressor.

5. Resolved, That feeling the need in this trying hour of the Wisdom that erreth not, and the arm that is invincible to defend and guide us, we therefore call upon all the colored pastors of our churches in the Free States (so called) to set apart the first Monday night in each month for public prayer and supplication, that the hearts of this people may be so turned to the weak and the oppressed, that the operation of this cruel law may be powerless, and that the time may soon come when "liberty shall be proclaimed throughout ALL the land unto ALL the inhabitants thereof."

6. Resolved, That we will hold up to the scorn of the civilized world that hypocrisy which welcomes to our shores the refugees from Austrian tyranny, and at the same time would send the refugees from American Slavery back to a doom, compared with which, Austrian tyranny is mercy.

7. Resolved, That we endorse, to the full, the sentiment of the Revolutionary patriot of Virginia, and should the awful alternative be presented to us, will act fully up to it—"Give me Liberty or give me Death."

8. Resolved, That a Committee be appointed to draft an appeal to the citizens of the Commonwealth of Pennsylvania, setting forth the Anti-Republican, Anti-Christian, Anti-human nature of the Fugitive Slave Bill, and asking of them their sympathy and succor.

9. Resolved, That having already witnessed to some extent the cruel operations of this law; having felt such anguish as no language can describe in seeing the wife flying from her home and the embraces of her husband, and the husband compelled to fly from his wife and helpless children, to gain that security in the land of a Monarchy which they could not enjoy

in this Republic; we ask, calmly and solemnly ask, the American people, "What have we done to suffer such treatment at your hands?" And may we not, in the sight of that God with whom there is no respect of persons, appeal to your sense of justice and mercy to have this most cruel law repealed as soon as Congress shall reassemble, and in the meantime may we not ask you to create, by all lawful means, such a public sentiment as shall render its operation upon us powerless?

10. Resolved, That, not in the spirit of bravado, neither of affected unconsciousness to the cruelties of public sentiment and law, in regard to our unfortunate and abused race, but seeing clearly, and knowing fully, the unjust prejudice existing against us, and using only those moral means of truth, sufficient as we deem them by a certain process, to the "pulling down the stronghold" of the injustice and wrong that now afflict us; yet in view of the unheard of atrociousness of the provisions of this infernal FUGITIVE SLAVE BILL, we solemnly declare before the Most High God, and the world, to resist to the death any attempt to enforce it upon our persons. * * *

Pennsylvania Freeman (Philadelphia), 31 October 1850; *BAP*, 4:68–70.

59   W H O   A R E   T H E   M U R D E R E R S ?

William J. Watkins, assistant editor of Frederick Douglass' Paper, *defended antislavery violence in an 1854 editorial entitled "Who are the Murderers?" His comments came in response to the unsuccessful attempt by abolitionists to rescue Anthony Burns, a Virginia fugitive slave arrested in Boston under provisions of the Fugitive Slave Law and returned to slavery.*

RIOTS AT BOSTON—The opponents of the Fugitive Slave Law, murdered a Deputy U.S. Marshal, on Friday night, in order to prevent the delivery of a slave to his master. See telegraph head. *Rochester American*

Slavery is murder in the highest degree. Every slaveholder is a murderer, a wholesale murderer. Those who apologise for them are worse than murderers. If one of these midnight and noonday assassins were to rush into the house of a white man, and strive to bind him hand and foot, and tear God's image from his brow, and be shot in the attempt, no one would characterize the act as murder. Not at all. It would be considered an act of righteous retribution. The man who sent a bullet through the tyrant's heart would be almost extravagantly lauded. This would be done, we remark, if the man to be enslaved, or murdered, which is the same thing, were a white man. Now take the following case. A colored man is living quietly in Boston, one mile from Bunker Hill Monument. He is a free man, for God created him. He stamped His image upon him. Slavery has well nigh murdered him. He has contrived to break loose from its iron grasp. He is pursued by his murderers. The hall of justice has become a den of thieves. A man leaves the honorable occupation of driving horses, and consents, for a "consideration," to be appointed Deputy Marshal, consents to be invested with power to rob him of his God-given rights. The miserable hireling is shot in the attempt. Is that man a murderer who sent the well-directed bullet through his stony heart? He would not be so considered if the parties were white. If he be a murderer, then was Gen. Washington; then were all who wielded swords and bayonets under him, in defence of liberty, the most cold-blooded murderers. We believe in peaceably rescuing fugitive slaves if it can be peacably effected; but if it cannot, we believe in rescuing them forcibly. We should certainly kill the man who would dare lay his hand on us, or on our brother, or sister, to enslave us. We would feel no compunction of conscience for so doing. We cannot censure others for doing what we would be likely to do, under the same circumstances, ourselves.

W

Frederick Douglass' Paper (Rochester, N.Y.), 2 June 1854; *BAP*, 4:227–29.

60 A GOOD REVOLVER

Frederick Douglass expressed the growing militancy of black abolitionists in an editorial entitled "The True Remedy for the Fugitive Slave Bill."

A good revolver, a steady hand, and a determination to shoot down any man attempting to kidnap. Let every colored man make up his mind to this, and live by it, and if needs be, die by it. This will put an end to kidnapping and to slaveholding, too. We blush to our very soul when we are told that a negro is so mean and cowardly that he prefers to live under the slave driver's whip—to the loss of life for liberty. Oh! that we had a little more of the manly indifference to death, which characterized the Heroes of the American Revolution.

Frederick Douglass' Paper (Rochester, N.Y.), 9 June 1854.

BLACK EMIGRATION

Most black abolitionists rejected emigration on principle. For them, leaving the United States meant abandoning the antislavery struggle, which they were not prepared to do. Yet for many fugitive slaves, emigration was a practical necessity. The constant threat of reenslavement made life in the northern states uncertain and precarious. The pressure to emigrate intensified immediately following passage of the Fugitive Slave Law in 1850. Canada offered the most accessible sanctuary for fugitive slaves, and several thousand crossed over the Canadian border in the years before the Civil War. Emigration also appealed to some free blacks who joined the exodus to settlement sites in Canada, the Caribbean, and West Africa. The willingness of thousands of blacks to abandon their American home reflected a profound loss of hope for racial progress.

6 1   THE CANADIAN HAVEN

Lewis Richardson, an escaped slave of Kentucky Senator Henry Clay, paid tribute to the Canadian sanctuary in his 1846 speech before an antislavery gathering in Amherstburg, Canada West.

Dear Brethren,

I am truly happy to meet with you on British soil (cheers), where I am not known by the color of my skin, but where the Government knows me as a man. But I am free from American slavery, after wearing the galling chains on my limbs 53 years 9 of which it has been my unhappy lot to be the slave of Henry Clay. It has been said by some, that Clay's slaves had rather live with him than be free, but I had rather this day, have a millstone tied to my neck, and be sunk to the bottom of Detroit river, than to go back to Ashland and be his slave for life. As late as Dec. 1845, H. Clay had me stripped and tied up, and one hundred and fifty lashes given me on my naked back: the crime for which I was so abused was, I failed to return home on a visit to see my wife, on Monday morning, before 5 o'clock. My wife was living on another place, 3 miles from Ashland. During the 9 years living with Mr. Clay, he has not given me a hat nor cap to wear, nor a stitch of bed clothes, except one small coarse blanket. Yet he has said publicly his slaves were "fat and slick!" But I say if they are, it is not because they are so well used by him. They have nothing but coarse bread and meat to eat, and not enough of that. They are allowanced every week. For each field hand is allowed one peck of coarse corn meal and meat in proportion, and no vegetables of any kind. Such is the treatment that Henry Clay's slaves receive from him. I can truly say that I have only one thing to lament over, and that is my bereft wife who is yet in bondage. If I only had her with me I should be happy. Yet think not that I am unhappy. Think not that I regret the choice that I have made. I counted the cost before I started. Before I took leave of my wife, she wept over me, and dressed the wounds on my back caused by the lash. I then gave her the parting hand, and started for Canada. I expected to be pursued as a felon, as I had been before, and to be hunted as a fox from mountain to cave. I well knew if I continued much longer with Clay, that I should be killed by such floggings and abuse by his cruel overseer in my old age. I wanted to be free before I died—and if I should be caught on the way to Canada and taken back, it could but be death, and I might as well die with the colic as the fever. With these considerations I started for Canada.

Such usage as this caused me to flee from under the American eagle, and take shelter under the British crown. (Cheers.) Thanks be to Heaven that I have got here at last: on yonder side of Detroit river, I was recognized as property; but on this side I am on free soil. Hail, Brittania! Shame, America! (Cheers.) A Republican despotism, holding three millions of our fellow men in slavery. Oh what a contrast between slavery and liberty! Here I stand erect, without a chain upon my limbs. (Cheers.) I now feel as independent as ever Henry Clay felt when he was running for the White House. In fact I feel better. He has been defeated four or five times, and I but once. But he was running for slavery, and I for liberty. I think I have beat him out of sight. Thanks be to God that I am elected to Canada, and if I don't live but one night, I am determined to die on free soil. Let my days be few or many, let me die sooner or later, my grave shall be made in free soil.

Signal of Liberty (Ann Arbor, Mich.), 30 March 1846; *BAP*, 2:101–2.

6 2   STANDING ON FREE GROUND

---

*Thomas H. Jones, a fugitive slave, expressed his relief upon reaching
the safety of British soil. His letter, sent from New Brunswick, was
addressed to Daniel Foster, a Methodist clergyman who had aided his
flight to freedom.*

St. John, N[ew] B[runswick]
May 5, 1851

Dear Brother:

From my knowledge of your generous nature and kind Christian
hospitality, I know it will be a source of pleasure to you to be informed of
my safe arrival here on British ground. Quite free from terror, I now feel
that my bones are a property bequeathed to me for my own use, and not for
the servitude or gratification of the white man, in that gloomy and sultry
region, where the hue of the skin has left my race in thraldom and misery
for ages.

O, my dear friend! how good it is to live on the poorest fare, where the
mind may apply its immortal powers to the contemplation of heaven and
heavenly things, unawed by the monsters who would tie us to a tree and
scourge us in our nakedness for attempting to worship the Creator in spirit
and truth!

The atrocity of the hideous system under which I groaned for more than
forty years was never so strikingly demonstrated to my mind as it has been
by breathing under the auspices and protection of a Government that allows
all its children to go abroad in the true liberty of nature, every person free
to frequent the altar or the sanctuary to which Conscience would lead him;
no cause for degradation but vice, and no lever of promotion but virtue and
intelligence.

I begin to see clearly, and to hope with reason, that the Refugee Law has
or will awaken the world to a sense of our deep wrongs; and I feel warranted
in saying, that the nations of the earth will soon give an expression of opinion upon our cause which will shame the Southern white man out of his
cruelty, and cause him to unchain his sable victims. The Ethiopian will ere

long be redeemed from his bondage, for Jehovah will be his Emancipator, as he is his King, Creator and Judge.

As to this Province, I have found a home of refuge, full of true, warm, generous Christians, whose hearts, abounding with the love of God, are full of sympathy for the slave, whom they will help to free in due time, as far as human means can extend. The citizens of St. John have received me in the spirit of brotherhood, and only that my mission calls me beyond the seas, I might remain here, and be an instrument of good for many years to come.

In a few days, I proceed to Halifax, and thence to England, as soon as circumstances will permit. Hoping that you will remember me to every kind friend taking an interest in my destinies, I am, Your brother in Christ,

THOMAS H. JONES

P.S. Wherever I preach or lecture, I am followed by enthusiastic houses.

T. H. J.

Liberator (Boston, Mass.), 30 May 1851; *BAP*, 2:133–34.

63 COME TO CANADA

Mary Jane Robinson, a New York City laundress living in Buxton, Canada West, contrasted her newfound freedom to the racial oppression in the northern states. Her letter was addressed to a friend, Sarah Ann Harris, of Weeksville, New York.

Buxton, Canada West
March 23, 1854
Mrs. Sarah Ann Harris
Weeksville
Care of W[illia]m Dolly
Zion's Church
New York

My Dear Mrs. Harris:

I take up my pen to write you a few lines, after so long a delay. I suppose you all thought that we were all dead, but it is not so, I can assure you, although we have been quite sick since we arrived in Canada. I have been quite ill with the pleurisy, and, in the Fall, we all had the dumb ague and fever; but now we are enjoying good health, except my son John; it left him feeble and a pain in the side; but he never was strong in health. This is a healthy place—but little sickness except the ague and fever. We arrived in Chatham on the 13th May, after a pleasant journey. It's really beautiful to travel in the Spring, and to behold the different faces of nature's beauty. In the steamboat we went to Troy; then took the cars to Buffalo, and there we put up until Monday from Friday, and I found Buffalo a very pretty place indeed; then we took the steamboat for Detroit—a beautiful sail across the Lake—Erie—and out of sight of land, it seems to me as on the sea; and then we took the steamboat again for Chatham—then we were done and at our journey's end. Now, Chatham is a fine place indeed, a town pleasantly situated on the banks of the Thames; and there we kept house six weeks—we had a small house—much cheaper than to board; and then my husband went to Buxton, to the coloured settlement, a distance of six miles, and purchased a farm of fifty acres, with nine acres cut down and one all cleared. The man who had taken it has to give it up, or build; it's a pleasant place. So, my husband liked it, and bought it and paid the money on the spot. He had to pay for the improvements and the balance of the ground—but if you buy a farm with no improvements on it, then it is two dollars and a half an acre. And he hired his house put up, and on the first of July, we moved on our farm. O, my dear friend, how I do want to see you again; I do wish you would try to come to Buxton, Canada West. *Come to a land of liberty and freedom, where the coloured man is not despised nor a deaf ear turned to them. This is the place to live in peace and to enjoy the comforts of life.* In September, we got a fine cow, with a heifer calf ten months old. So I have been quite a country-woman. I both churned my own butter and milked my own cow. We have got three nice sows, and, by and by, I shall have some geese, and chickens, and ducks, and all those things. Here is nine thousand acres of land now taken up by coloured people in Buxton, where we live; and Mr. King, the government agent, who sells the land, has purchased eight thousand more to sell at the same rate; and the people are coming in from all parts, and the place is filling up fast. I hear that OLD FILLMORE *is a screwing you all up tighter still,* but don't stay there, come to *Queen Victoria's land, where they are not making laws to oppress and to starve you.* I raised a fine sight of tobacco. We had turnips as big as the crown of your husband's hat, and cabbage as large as a water-pail. O, don't laugh, for it's a fact—for the ground is so rich it raises everything up in no time. We were late, so we had only Fall things. There is a saw-mill and grist-mill building in Buxton, and a school now here, with seventy or eighty scholars. *O, we are just beginning to live well enough without the white man's foot on our necks. Away with your King Fillmore, I am for* QUEEN VICTORIA. GOD SAVE THE QUEEN. We have all kinds of game, deer, raccoon, ground-hogs, black-squirrels, hens, pheasants, quails, wild turkey, wild duck, woodcock and red-headed woodpeckers, and sapsuckers, wild red raspberries and plumbs, crabapples and wild gooseberries, and all kinds of nuts. *Not as cold as I thought.* We have Methodist, Baptist and Presbyterian meetings, too. We are to have a log-rolling soon, and then we will have ten acres cleared. They (the people) all will help you to raise and log, and you help them again. Whatever you raise in the ground, you can sell it in Chatham, six miles from here. There is a number come from Toronto to this place, as land can be got cheaper— 20s. an acre and ten years to pay it in, and land that will bring anything you plant just as I did in Weeksville (only it wanted more manuring); only put in the seed and *pray to the Giver of rain*, and they will come up. O, dear, how I want to see you again. Do come to Buxton, Canada West.

MARY JANE ROBINSON

Provincial Freeman (Chatham, Canada West), 13 January 1855; *BAP*, 2:279–81.

64 CALL FOR EMIGRATION

Granville B. Blanks, a Michigan free black, offered a public justification for emigration in his bleak assessment of American race relations.

Syracuse, [New York]
Aug[ust] 12, 1852

Sir:

I desire through your columns to make a few statements to the citizens of Syracuse, and to the public in general. I am a colored man, now forty years of age. I was born in Virginia, a free man, my father having purchased his freedom and that of my mother before my birth. About sixteen years ago I removed to Michigan, in which state I have since resided, with the exception of an absence for the most part of the last two years.

The question of the condition and prospects of the colored race is one which has long been agitating the public mind. The position of this government in relation to this portion of its population has afforded a theme for discussion the most intense and exciting both in this and other lands. The passage of the Fugitive Slave Law in 1850 aroused my mind and excited in me a purpose to examine for myself what would be the probable future history of my people. This examination has led me to certain conclusions which by your permission I desire here to express.

In the first place it is my deliberate conviction that, with our present Constitution and prejudices, it is impracticable, not to say impossible, for the whites and blacks to live together, and upon terms of social and civil equality, under the same government. In a mixed community, the white man has a superiority, and the black man is forced into a subordinate condition. Disabilities thus lie upon him which, with very rare exceptions, have crushed down the whole colored population of this country. Many of these disabilities are of such a nature, that no change of legal enactments, no force of education, no favor of public sentiment seems adequate to remove them, for they originate in the actual distinctions of the two races, which have been constituted by another than human power. Under this view of the subject I see no possible alternative for the mass of the colored population now, but a state of continual degradation or a removal to some land where they may hope to attain a condition of permanent freedom and of progressing civilization. Yet the negro is a *man*, although downtrodden. He must have, like the white man, a country he can call his own, where he may enjoy the opportunity of developing all his faculties under those just and equal laws which God has given to all mankind. And in passing, allow me to state that after long consideration I have adopted the opinion that the western coast of Africa, and especially the Republic of Liberia, offers the most controlling inducements to our emigration. Other regions, I know, have been mentioned, as Canada, the West India Islands and Central America, but a glance at the present condition of Africa and the prospect of her future civilization and christianization, together with the instrumentalities to be employed in an enterprise so noble and Godlike, will serve to show the paramount motives to our people which lie in that direction. I am not, however, pleading for the American Colonization Society, or for any other organization, as I am connected with none of any description. I hope all these associations will do good, and promote the paramount welfare of humanity. Nor have I been bought up by any individual or set of individuals to put forth these sentiments. Not all the money in the country could purchase these convictions, deliberately formed in my own mind, and not only from my own sad personal experience, but also from a close and attentive observation of the condition of my colored brethren in this nation. From that spirit of cupidity and that mercenary influence which is so prevalent and polluting, and which, while it corrupts the laws and customs of the American people, at the same time casts its dark suspicions on the purest motives and the most disinterested actions, I desire to be delivered. If any judge that the black man cannot think and feel for himself without the bribe of the designing, and without being bought, as his labor, and even his body and his soul are bought for the comparatively paltry considerations of filthy lucre, I hope the time will come when we shall demonstrate the libel of such an opinion.

It is true, I differ widely from many of my oppressed people who are longing for deliverance, but my judgement is formed in candor, and not, I hope in the bitterness of prejudice. It is painful for me to hold sentiments which others and especially those of my own race may feel bound to oppose—but if I stand alone, I cannot do otherwise than proclaim my honest convictions. Every day's experience has confirmed me in those convictions. I have been traveling now for a period of 18 months in various portions of the country, and the facts I have gathered up and not any delusive imagination are the basis on which I establish my opinions. In the State of Kentucky last summer I saw free colored men competent to do business and anxious to obtain a livelihood, but laboring under those distressing inequalities which must inevitably attend them among the white people. I found them, in many respects, surpassed by another class of colored men who were naturally no more adequate or enterprising, but who being slaves derived even from their masters a protection to labor, which is denied to the free people of color in that State. This advantage I do not ascribe to the system of slavery as such, but to the more humane disposition of certain masters in spite of the system itself. These are reasons which lead me to believe that the two races cannot, even if both were free, continue together in a condition of social and civil equality. To illustrate this more in detail, I will give, out of an abundance of similar proofs, one or two instances.

While in Louisville, Kentucky, I became acquainted with a colored man, an industrious and excellent mechanic. In conversation with him, I learned that he had once been worth a considerable property, but the tide of public prejudice was such as to render it impossible for him to compete with those of the same class of white laborers, or to secure the same degree of confidence or the same amount of patronage. The result was, he had become reduced in purse and dejected in spirit, and would gladly have left the place for some asylum where labor and economy shall be as sacred in the person of the black man as in that of the white man. I will specify a single other instance. A man in Louisville had bought himself from his master, a hardware merchant in that city, and was desirous to do business for himself. But such was the known prevalent disposition of the white men to tyrannize over the black, he stipulated with his master to extend to him that protection in his everyday business, now that he was free, which he would have enjoyed in the service of his master had he remained a slave. He provided himself with a horse and cart and became a drayman. Soon after, having been employed to cart goods to a certain place by another white man, his employer under the impression that he was a free negro doing business for himself, insisted that he should take such an amount of loading each time as it was plainly beyond the strength of his horse to draw. Upon this requisition the drayman remonstrated, at which his employer commenced the most outrageous abuse of him, threatening personal violence. The drayman soon left the cart standing there with the unreasonable load and called his old master to his aid. And when it appeared by a legal stipulation the drayman had still the protection of his master, then and then only were things set to rights and the poor drayman suffered to take such loads as it was possible for his horse to draw. This may be regarded of no account, but it is to my mind a circumstance similar to numberless others which prove beyond a question the existence of those difficulties which stand ever in the way of the black man in this country.

After leaving Kentucky, I resolved to visit those parts of the country where the sentiments of the white people were said to be more favorable to the interests of the colored people. I went into the Western States for the purpose of observing their condition in that section and noting the degree of progress to which they had attained. I invariably found them laboring under the same burdens. I then returned through the Eastern and older States where Slavery as a legal system had been longest abolished and where I was entitled to expect a more improved condition and a greater equality of privilege among the colored people, but in this I have been mainly disappointed. I have found but one or two colored men, and those in the city of New York, who have even the appearance of that prosperity and position which belong to the white citizen. I find then the colored population of this country, as a whole, in a most abject and degraded condition. They are mostly in ignorance and corrupted by many vices. Even the most enterprising and active of them, hold subordinate and menial positions. Some few there are like FREDERICK DOUGLASS, or PROFESSOR [WILLIAM G.] ALLEN, or DR. PENNINGTON, who may have partially risen above the obstacles which beset us, but even these men are compelled to mortifications which the white man knows nothing of, while the great mass of our people are totally shut out from the immunities and regards of the highest circles of society.

In view of this, to what conclusions could I, or any rational person, or any lover of his race, come upon this subject other than those I have already formed! I feel a deep interest in the future welfare of my colored brethren. I wish to see them in a condition where they can emulate any other portion of humanity in all the great interests of human life. I am persuaded they cannot do so, as long as they remain among the whites. It is my solemn judgment that they must have a country and laws and privileges of their own, in order to take that rank among the people of the earth to which they are entitled to aspire. Holding these sentiments, can I stand by in silence with folded arms, and look upon the certain degradation and ruin of the colored people, without an effort to relieve them. Too keenly do I feel in myself and too clearly do I see in my brethren the evils of our condition, and as long as strength endures I cannot rest, but must with my whole heart labor for the redemption of the colored race, feeling sacredly bound to proclaim these opinions everywhere by my obligations to myself, my people and my God. Truly, your obedient servant,

G. B. BLANKS

Syracuse Daily Standard (N.Y.), 12 August 1852; *BAP*, 4:131–35.

BLACK NATIONALITY

Martin R. Delany reopened the debate on black emigration with the publication of *The Condition, Elevation, Emigration and Destiny of the Colored People* in 1852. Delany, a physician and newspaper editor, advocated the establishment of a separate black nationality. He argued that a strong, independent black nation in the Western Hemisphere would help undermine slavery and gain respect for blacks everywhere. Later, Delany promoted West Africa as a possible area for settlement. James Theodore Holly, an Episcopalian clergyman, also called for a black nationality but focused specifically on Haiti, the first independent black republic, as the best site. The ideas of Delany, Holly, and other black nationalists encouraged the growth of black separatism and focused attention on nation building in Africa and the Caribbean.

65 CALL FOR A BLACK NATIONALITY

In the closing pages of The Condition, Elevation, Emigration and Destiny of the Colored People, *Martin R. Delany argued that emigration was central to the question of African American destiny.*

* * * The time has now fully arrived when the colored race is called upon by all the ties of common humanity, and all the claims of consummate justice, to go forward and take their position, and do battle in the struggle now being made for the redemption of the world. Our cause is a just one; the greatest at present that elicits the attention of the world. For if there is a remedy; that remedy is now at hand. God himself as assuredly as he rules the destinies of nations, and entereth measures into the "hearts of men," has presented these measures to us. Our race is to be redeemed; it is a great and glorious work, and we are the instrumentalities by which it is to be done. But we must go from among our oppressors; it never can be done by staying among them. God has, as certain as he has ever designed any thing, designed this great portion of the New World, for us, the colored races; and

Martin R. Delany in his Civil War uniform. From W. J. Simmons, Men of Mark *(Cleveland, 1887).*

as certain as we stubborn our hearts, and stiffen our necks against it, his protecting arm and fostering care will be withdrawn from us.

Shall we be told that we can live nowhere, but under the will of our North American oppressors; that this (the United States) is the country most favorable to our improvement and progress? Are we incapable of self-government, and making such improvements for ourselves as we delight to enjoy after American white men have made them for themselves? No, it is not true. Neither is it true that the United States is the best country for our improvement. That country is the best, in which our manhood can be best developed; and that is Central and South America, and the West Indies—all belonging to this glorious Continent.

Martin R. Delany, *The Condition, Elevation, Emigration and Destiny of the Colored People of the United States* (Philadelphia, Pa., 1852), 183–84.

66 THOUGHTS ON HAYTI

James T. Holly made his most comprehensive argument for Haitian immigration in a six-part series, "Thoughts on Hayti," written in 1859 for the monthly Anglo-African Magazine.

The Important position that this Nationality holds in relation to the Future Destiny of the Negro Race.

The recent bloodless revolution through which Hayti has passed and which has resulted in the dethronement of Faustin I and the elevation of Geffard to the chair of the Chief Magistracy; together with the revival of the subject of Haytian emigration among colored Americans, have contributed to bring the claims of this negro-nationality prominently before the public mind.

I, therefore, propose to profit by the attention which is now being bestowed upon the affairs of that country, to furnish some food for the public mind, by exposing some of my own thoughts derived from a somewhat careful and extended study of the history of the Haytian people. These thoughts, I will give in a short series of articles on various topics; such as may be of the most important consideration; and shall begin in this one to speak of *the important relation that this sovereign people hold to the future destiny of the negro race.*

In the first place, then, let me say, that *the successful establishment of this negro nationality; the means by which its establishment was sought and accomplished; and the masterly vigilance by which the same has been maintained for upwards of a half-century,* present us with the strongest evidence and the most irrefragable proof of the equality of the negro race, that can be found anywhere, whether in ancient or modern times. Among all the nationalities of the world, Hayti stands without any question the solitary prodigy of history. Never before in all the annals of humanity has a race of men, chattelized and almost dehumanized, sprung by their own efforts, and inherent energies from their brutalized condition, into the manly status of independent, self-respecting freemen, at one gigantic bound; and thus took their place at once, side by side with nations whose sovereignty had been the mature growth of ages of human progress. The ancient glory of Ethiopia, Egypt, and Greece, grows pale in comparison with the splendor of this Haytian achievement. Because civilization having grown to gradual maturity under the most favorable circumstances on the banks of the Ganges, rolled its slow length along until it penetrated into Ethiopia, and from thence following the course of the Nile passed into Egypt; coursed onward into Greece; and finally has rolled its restless tide over Modern Europe and the Western world. But the people of Hayti, without the elevating influence of civilization among them; without a favorable position for development; without assistance from any quarter; and in spite of the most powerful combination of opposing circumstances, in which they found themselves, at times contending against the armies of France, England and Spain; these people, I say, in the face of all these obstacles, aroused themselves to the consciousness of their own inherent dignity, and shook off from their limbs the shackles and badges of their degradation, and successfully claimed a place among the most enlightened and heroic sovereignties of the world. Such, in short, is the important position that Hayti holds when compared with the nations of all ages, past and present, that have figured in the world's history.

But this importance does not diminish in the least if we take a more circumscribed view of her relations. Let us confine ourselves to this continent alone and compare her with the nationalities of the New World. She is second on the list of independent sovereignties in the Western Hemisphere that have successfully thrown off European domination during the last 80 years. And if the United States can claim to have preceded her in this respect, Hayti can claim the honor of having contributed to the success of American Independence, by the effusion of the blood of her sable sons, who led by the gallant Rigaud, a man of color, fought side by side with the American heroes in the Battle of Savannah. And, if since her independence, her government cannot claim the same stability of administration as that of the United States and Brazil, yet she can claim to have been far superior in this respect to all the Hispano-American nationalities that surround her.

Hence, then, with this living, breathing nationality rearing its sovereign head aloft over the Caribbean sea; and presiding as the Queen of the Antilles, we need not resort to any long drawn arguments to defend negro-Ethnography against the Notts and Gliddons of our day. Let them prove, if they can, to the full satisfaction of their narrow souls and gangrened hearts, that the black faced, wooly haired, thick lipped and flat nosed Egyptians of Ancient times did not belong to the same branch of the human family that those negroes do, who have been the victims of the African Slave-trade for the past four centuries. Let them prove by the subtlest refinement of reasoning that those ancient darkies were pure white men; and without stopping to expose the fallacies of their argument we may grant their conclusions; and adduce the people of Hayti, as the most unexceptionable specimen of the degraded negro race, and prove their equality, nay, may I not say, their superiority to any other nation of men that have ever sprung into existence.

From these thoughts, it will be seen that whatsoever is to be the future destiny of the descendants of Africa, Hayti certainly holds the most important relation to that destiny. And if we were to be reduced to the dread alternative, of having her historic fame blotted out of existence, or that celebrity which may have been acquired elsewhere by all the rest of our race combined; we should say preserve the name, the fame, and the sovereign existence of Hayti, though everything else shall perish. Yes, let Britain and France undermine, if they will, the enfranchisement which they gave to their West Indian slaves; by their present Apprenticeship system; let the lone-star of Liberia, placed in the firmament of nationalities, by a questionable system of American philanthropy, go out in darkness; let the opening resources of Central Africa, be again shut up in their wonted seclusion; let the names and deeds of our Nat Turners, Denmark Veseys, Penningtons, Delanys, Douglasses and Smiths be forgotten forever; but never let the self-emancipating deeds of the Haytian people be effaced; never let her heroically achieved nationality be brought low; no, never let the names of her Touissaint, her Dessalines, her Rigaud, her Christophe, and her Petion be forgotten, or blotted out from the historic pages of the world's history.

The vantage ground given us in the former cases can be dispensed with rather than in the latter, because the White race can claim credit for having aided us to attain thereto; and thus they have ground to say that without them we could not have made this advancement; they might still continue to argue that when left to ourselves, we retrograde into barbarism. But in the case of Hayti the question of negro capacity stands out a naked fact, as vindication of itself, not only without any aid whatever from the white man, but in spite of his combined opposition to keep down in brutal degradation these self-emancipated freemen. From this view of the matter it may be seen that if Haytian independence shall cease to exist, the sky of negro-destiny shall be hung in impenetrable blackness; the hope of Princes coming out of Egypt and Ethiopia soon stretching forth her hands unto God, will die out; and everlasting degradation become the settled doom of this downtrodden, long-afflicted, and then God-forsaken race.

Therefore to despise the claims of Hayti, is to despise the cause of God, by which he promises to bring deliverance to the captives and to those who are bound; to be indifferent to these claims is to neglect the holiest duties that Providence imposes upon us; and to refuse to make any and every sacrifice to advance the interest and prosperity of that nation is to be a traitor both to God and humanity. Hence, then, let that tongue cleave to the roof of its mouth that could dare speak against her; and let that arm wither that would not be upraised to defend her cause, against a sacrilegious desecration by the filibustering tyrants of mankind, and the sworn enemies of God. And to this solemn prayer let every manly heart that beats within a sable bosom respond, Amen.

Anglo-African Magazine (New York, N.Y.), June 1859; *BAP,* 5:6–9.

BLACKS AND JOHN BROWN

John Brown's raid on the federal arsenal at Harpers Ferry, Virginia, in October 1859 had special meaning for black abolitionists. Over the years, Brown had developed strong ties with many African Americans, who extended him financial aid and moral support for his free-state activities in Kansas and for his plans to foment a slave revolt in the South. Five blacks fought with Brown at Harpers Ferry—two were killed in the raid and two others followed him to the gallows. In the months after the raid, African American communities across the northern states commemorated John Brown and his comrades as antislavery martyrs. Public gatherings paid homage to the fallen heroes and proclaimed slavery's imminent demise. Fired by the audacity of the Harpers Ferry raid, African American leaders spoke openly of armed resistance, slave insurrection, and the impending conflict between North and South.

67 GLORIOUS WORK

James N. Gloucester, a Presbyterian minister in New York City, and his wife Elizabeth offered their support to John Brown in correspondence during the year before the Harpers Ferry raid.

Philadelphia, [Pennsylvania]
Feb[ruary] 19, 1858

Most Esteemed Friend:
Being called away from home by death—to Philadelphia—I have not as yet sent any answer to your first communication. I do so now. I was pleased to hear from you at last after so long silence. I thought perhaps you might have passed to your more immediate field of Premeditated Labour—having not seen or heard anything from you, for so long a time—but I rejoice that you are still, in life and health—with the same vigorous hopes as formerly. Your very commendable ~~Letter~~ measure to deliver the slave, has

yet my heartiest consent and cooperation. I have never as yet faltered, in my previous asserted interest to you in the matter. All I need is the clear, inteligent watch-word of that Gallant Hero—distinguished in former triumphs—and then in David Crocket style. I can go ahead, but you speak in your Letter of the people. I fear there is little to be done in the masses. The masses suffer for the want of inteligence—and it is difficult to reach them in a matter like you propose. So far as is necessary to secure their cooperation, the Colored People are impulsive—but they need Sagacity— Sagacity to distinguish their proper course.

They are like a Bark at sea without a commander or rudder ready to catch port—or no port just as it may be—and it is so difficult to strike a line to meet them. No one knows better than Mr. Douglass the truth of this. But however, I do not despair, I only note it—as it may form a part of the history of your undertakings—and that it may not otherwise dampe ardor.

I wish you sir Gods speed in your Glorious work—may nothing arise to prevent accomplishing. Your intended visit to this city will be cheering. Please to make my house your home. I am not at home now but will be in a few days. Your sincere Friend,

JAMES N. GLOUCESTER

John Brown Collection, Manuscripts Department, Kansas State Historical Society, Topeka, Kansas; published by permission; *BAP*, 4:377–78.

Brooklyn, [New York]
March 9, 1858

Captain Brown:
Esteemed Sir, I regret that I cannot at this time be with you and friends convened in Philadelphia but you have my heartiest wish, with all the true friends here, for your success.

I hope sir, you will find in that city, a large response—both in money and men—Pepared at your command to do battle to that ugly foe.

I am more and more convinced that now the day and now the hour, and that the proper mode is at last suggested, practically.

Long enough have we had this great evil in our land discussed in all its possible aspects. Long have we applied to it, as we have thought[,] all those the moral means that enlightened men are capable. But yet this evil, as a system[,] remains the same. They have not phased it, as yet, in one material point .

What then shall we do, is the only sensible question—to every true lover of God and man. Shall we go on—and still prosecute under these means— and thus as we have done for years signally fail, or shall we in the Language of that noble Patriot of his country (Patrick Henry), now use those means that God and nature has placed within our power. I hope Sir to this sentiment sir in Philadelphia there is but one response—for in that city reside some noble men and women whose hearts are always warmed and cheered at every rising hope for the slave . But Sir your measure anticipates not only for the abject slave, but to those colored men, north and south, who are but virtually slaves . There is in no truth no black man , north, or south of mason and Dixion Line—a freeman whatever be his wealth, position, or worth to the world . This is but the result of that hellish system , against which every honest man and woman in the Land should be combined. I hope Sir you will be able, assisted by those Eminent Gentlemen who accompany you—to make these things plain—and take their hold upon the Philadelphia mind, and join with you, in holy Energy and Combat against the all damnable foe . Let them see the Little Book you presented to me, and so disipate their doubts and fears.

Please to put me down for (25) more to begin with. Yours for struggling universal rights,

J . N . G L O U C E S T E R

P.S. Please to read to the friends assembled if thought best.

John Brown Collection, Manuscripts Department, Kansas State Historical Society, Topeka, Kansas; published by permission; *BAP*, 4:378–79.

Brooklyn, [New York]
Aug[ust] 18, 1859

Esteemed Friend:
I gladly avail myself of the opportunity afforded by our friend, Mr. F. Douglass, who has just called upon us previous to his visit to you, to

inclose to you for the cause in which you are such a zealous laborer a small amount, which please accept with my most ardent wishes for its and your benefit.

The visit of our mutual friend Douglass has somewhat revived my rather drooping spirits in the cause; but seeing such ambition and enterprise in him, I am again encouraged. With best wishes for your welfare and prosperity, and the good of your cause, I subscribe myself, Your sincere friend,

MRS. E. A. GLOUCESTER

P.S. Please write to me. With best respects to your son.

Anglo-African Magazine (New York, N.Y.), December 1859; *BAP*, 4:379.

68 IF DIE I MUST

John A. Copeland, Jr., captured at Harpers Ferry and tried for treason, wrote to his family on the eve of his execution.

Charlesto[w]n, V[irgini]a
Nov[ember] 26, [18]59

Dear father & mother:

I now take my pen to address you for the first time since I have been in the situation that I am now in. My silence has not been occasioned by my want of love for you but because I wished to wait & find what my doom would be. I am well at this time & as happy as it is possible to be under the circumstances. I received your kind and affectionate letter, which brought much consolation to me, & the advice that you have therein given me. I thank God I can say I have accepted, & I have found that consolation which can only be found by accepting & obeying such advice.

Dear father & mother, happy am I that I can now truthfully say that I have sought the Holy Bible & have found that everlasting Life in its holy advice, which man can from no other source obtain. Yes, I have now in the

John A. Copeland, Jr. Courtesy of Library of Congress.

eleventh hour sought for & obtained that forgiveness from my God, whose kindness I have outraged nearly all my life.

Dear Parents, my fate so far as man can seal it, is sealed, but let not this fact occasion you any misery; for remember the <u>cause</u> in which I was engaged; <u>remember it was a holy cause</u>, one in which men in every way better than I am, have suffered & died. Remember that if I must die, I die in trying to liberate a few of my poor & oppressed people from a condition of servitude against which God in his word has hurled his most bitter denunciations, a cause in which men, who though removed from its direct injurious effects by the color of their faces have already lost their lives, & more yet must meet the fate which man has decided I must meet. If die I must, I shall try to meet my fate as a man who can suffer in the glorious cause in which I have been engaged, without a groan, & meet my Maker in heaven as a christian man who through the saving grace of God has made his peace with Him.

Dear Parents, dear bros & sisters; miserable indeed would I be if I were confined in this jail awaiting the execution of the law for committing a foul crime; but this not being the case, I must say (though I know you all will feel deeply the fate I am to meet), that I feel more deeply on acc't of the necessity of myself or any other man having to suffer by the existence of slavery, than from the mere fact of having to die. It is true I should like to see you all once more on the earth, but God wills otherwise. Therefore I am content, for most certainly do I believe that God wills everything for the best good, not only of those who have to suffer directly, but of all, & this being the case I beg of you not to grieve about me. Now dear Parents I beg your forgiveness for every wrong I have done you, for I know that I have not at all times treated you as I ought to have done. Remember me while I shall live & forget me not when I am no longer in this world. Give my love to all friends. There are some little matters that I would give most anything to have settled & made right. There have been misrepresentations of things which I have said; & if I can I shall correct them.

Oh brothers, I pray you may never have to suffer as I shall have to do: stay at home contentedly, make your home happy not only to yourselves but to all with whom you may be connected.

Dear Brothers & sisters, love one another, make each other happy, love, serve & obey your God, & meet me in heaven. Now, dear father & mother, I will close this last—or at present I think last letter—I shall have the pleasure of writing to you.

Good-bye Mother & Father, Goodbye brothers & sisters, & by the assistance of God, meet me in heaven. I remain your most affectionate son,

JOHN A. COPELAND

Oswald Garrison Villard Collection, Rare Book and Manuscript Library, Columbia University, New York, New York; published by permission; BAP, 5:43–47.

69 JOHN BROWN, THE MARTYR

At a public gathering in Detroit on 2 December 1859, African Americans paid tribute to Brown and celebrated his martyrdom as a call for action.

Whereas, We, the oppressed portion of this community, many of whom have worn the galling chain and felt the smarting lash of slavery, and know by sad experience its brutalizing effects upon both the body and the mind, and its damaging influence upon the soul of its victim; and

Whereas, We, by the help of Almighty God and the secret abolition movements that are now beginning to develop themselves in the southern part of this country, have been enabled to escape from the prison house of slavery, and partially to obtain our liberty; and having become personally acquainted with the life and character of our much beloved and highly esteemed friend, Old Capt. John Brown, and his band of valiant men, who, at Harpers Ferry, on the 16th day of October, 1859, demonstrated to the world his sympathy and fidelity to the cause of the suffering slaves of this country, by bearding the hydra-headed monster, Tyranny, in his den, and by his bold, effective, timely blow is now causing the whole South to tremble with a moral earthquake, as he boldly and freely delivered up his life today as a ransom for our enslaved race and thereby, "solitarily and alone," he has put a liberty ball in motion which shall continue to roll and gather strength until the last vestige of human slavery within this nation shall have been crushed beneath its ponderous weight. Therefore,

Resolved, That we hold the name of Old Capt. John Brown in the most sacred remembrance, as the first disinterested martyr for our liberty, who, upon the true Christian principle of his Divine Lord and Master, has freely delivered up his life for the liberty of our race in this country. Therefore will we ever vindicate his character throughout all coming time, as our temporal redeemer, whose name shall never die.

Resolved, That, as the long lost rights and liberties of an oppressed people are only gained in proportion as they act in their own cause, therefore are we now loudly called upon to arouse to our own interest, and to concentrate our efforts in keeping the Old Brown liberty ball in motion and thereby continue to kindle the fires of liberty upon the altar of every determined heart among us, and continue to fan the same until the proper time, when a revolutionary blast from liberty's trump shall summon them simultaneously to unite for victorious and triumphant battle.

Resolved, That we tender our deepest and most heartfelt sympathy to the family of Capt. John Brown in their sad bereavement, and pledge to them that they shall ever be held by us as our special friends, in whose welfare we hope ever to manifest a special interest.

Weekly Anglo-African (New York, N.Y.), 17 December 1859; *BAP*, 5:51–53.

70 BREAKING INTO A STATE

Thomas Hamilton, founding editor of the Weekly Anglo-African, *justified John Brown's raid as an attempt to recover "stolen property."*

Burglary is common, but State breaking is a new species of crime; and in the case to which we shall make reference some have been bold enough to term it a virtue. Men generally build, bolt and bar their houses so strongly that access is had with great difficulty; and it is only in extreme cases, or by the most expert operators, that it is at all accomplished. But the business of State-breaking, it seems, is less difficult, though we fear far more hazardous.

John Brown, with twenty-one other men, a few days ago threw himself against the State of Virginia, and in less time than it has taken to record the fact, the partition gave way, and he had and held possession of the Ancient Dominion and the terror-stricken chivalry, chattels and all, and might have continued possession but for the interference of Uncle Sam's troops.

But the idea of State-breaking for the purpose of winning what might be won, is, considering the hazard, novel indeed. The burglar breaks into your house that he may despoil you of your goods; but if we were asked why John Brown broke into Virginia we would answer that it was to bring stolen goods out of the State—goods and chattels that had been stolen and pent up there for past centuries. Surprising as it may seem, it is, nevertheless, true.

Here in the North we spend annually thousands of dollars in catching thieves and robbers and preventing theft and robbery, but John Brown and his few surviving followers, on the other hand, are to forfeit their lives for simply endeavoring to obtain and restore stolen chattels to their proper owners—to restore the slave to himself.

What right has Virginia to protect theft and punish with death him who, from honest conviction, attempts to do just what every law of right, humanity and true religion prompted him to do? What is done with every other species of interest? But it may be claimed that the law stands in the way of all such attempts. What right has Virginia to legalize theft in the bodies and souls of men?

It was a mercy to the property holders that the stolen goods—the chattels—did not tumble out of the State through the breach made by Brown; and as one step makes way for another, it may occur to the chattel some day to make a breach for itself. With an eye to this possibility, and to the future John Browns who may take it into their heads to again break into the State of Presidents, or some other of her sister States, it is now proposed that the whole South wheel out of the Union, and build a strong barrier against future inroads, and set up for itself. Out of what materials this barrier is to be erected, does not appear.

Whatever may have been the mistakes of the South on the subject of Slavery, and the sentiments of the North upon it, we scarcely think it will be guilty and blind enough to add the fatal error of disunion to the already fearful list, or accept from their Northern toadies advice leading to that end.

For a State like Virginia, whose partition gives way at the slightest touch of the arm of an aged man, whose inhabitants become frantic before the face of twenty-two men, whose military find it impossible to collect their scattered senses sufficiently to make even a semblance of resistance, whose authorities lose all dignity, and the sleep of whose inhabitants has been murdered—to talk of wheeling out of the Union, is one of the thinnest and meanest scarecrows ever set up before the eyes of sensible men.

Weekly Anglo-African (New York, N.Y.), 19 November 1859; *BAP*, 5:41–42.

71 CALL TO ARMS

George Lawrence, Jr., who succeeded Hamilton as editor of the Weekly Anglo-African, *expressed the appeal to violence rekindled by the Harpers Ferry raid.*

"One man in the right is a majority." Frederick Douglass crystalized the heroism that animates practical Abolitionists in those ringing words. They were forcibly brought to our minds by hearing a prominent orator say, that, being in the minority, it was no use trying, for colored men to attempt stemming the current. We wonder if he thought *that*, when, but a few years since, as a slave, he fled the land of bondage. Five hundred black men, divided into guerilla bands, and working their way through the mountain Ranges of Virginia, Kentucky, Tennessee, Arkansas, and the swamps of the Atlantic Coast, can do more to destroy slavery than five-thousand Regulars. It only wants men determined to do or die. White men had this spirit at Harpers Ferry, on that memorable October morn. We want Nat Turner—not speeches; Denmark Vesey—not resolutions; John Brown— not meetings.

Weekly Anglo-African (New York, N.Y.), 13 April 1861; *BAP*, 5:111–12.

Chapter 5

Civil War

DEBATING THE WAR

After the fall of Fort Sumter in April 1861, thousands of northern blacks rushed to enlist in the Union cause, only to be turned away by the Lincoln administration. The stinging rejection of African American patriotism incited an intense controversy within the black community. For several months, blacks debated their proper role in the conflict, searching for a policy that would end slavery and gain equality and citizenship for all African Americans. A full and influential discussion took place in the pages of New York's *Weekly Anglo-African* in the fall of 1861. The following letters illustrate the controversial issue among African Americans: Should northern blacks fight for a government that guaranteed slavery?

72 FORMATION OF COLORED REGIMENTS

"R. H. V."—most likely Robert H. Vandyne, a frequent New York City contributor to the Weekly Anglo-African—*argued that African Americans should avoid military service until emancipation became a northern war aim.*

Mr. Editor:

The duty of the black man at this critical epoch is a question of much importance, deeply interesting the friends of liberty, both white and black. The most imposing feature of this duty, I am told, is in relation to military organizations. This question, I am told, is forced upon us by our eminent, educated, farsighted leaders, who, anxious for our elevation and zealous for our reputation, in connection with our white brothers would have us write our names side by side with them upon the immortal book of fame, won by well-contested and desperate encounters upon the battlefield. Claiming that any omission on our part to exhibit that patriotism so noticeable in the whites, will, when history shall record the doings of this memorable country, leave our names without one deed of patriotism or expressed desire for the success of the cause of liberty. * * * Have not two centuries of cruel and unrequited servitude in this country, alone entitled the children of this generation to the rights of men and citizens? Have we not done our share towards creating a national existence for those who now enjoy it to our degradation, ever devising evil for our suffering, heart-crushed race?

Who that will carefully note the many historical reminiscences, made mention of by those who are ready to do justice to us, can doubt our bravery? Who that has heard of the many privations, hair-breadth escapes, and the unflinching determination of our enslaved brethren seeking the free shores of Canada, can doubt our love of liberty? True patriotism does not consist in words alone, neither do patriotic demonstrations always contribute to the end alone, independent of material aid. I do not suppose any people have been taxed heavier or more than the poor colored people for the cause of liberty, with such small results to themselves. Now, if we have contributed our share to support and establish a government, that we are not entitled to a share in the benefits thereof, what becomes our duty when that government is menaced by those they have cherished at the expense of our blood, toil and degradation?

Let your own heart answer this question, and no regiments of black troops will leave their bodies to rot upon the battlefield beneath a Southern sun— to conquer a peace based upon the perpetuity of human bondage—stimulating and encouraging the inveterate prejudice that now bars our progress in the scale of elevation and education.

I claim that the raising of black regiments for the war would be highly impolitic and uncalled for under the present state of affairs, knowing, as we do, the policy of the government in relation to colored men. It would show our incompetency to comprehend the nature of the differences existing between the two sections now at variance, by lending our aid to either party. By taking such measures, we invite injustice at the hands of those we prefer to serve; we would contribute to the African colonization scheme, projected a half century ago, by ridding the country of that element so dangerous to the charming institution of negro slavery.

* * * [W]hat do we enjoy, that should inspire us with those feelings towards a government that would sooner consign five millions of human beings to never-ending slavery than wrong one slave master of his human property? Does not the contemplation of so flagrant a wrong cause your blood to boil with Christian indignation, or bring tears to the eyes of your brokenhearted old men, whose heads, now silvered by time or bleached by sorrow, can no longer shoulder the weightier responsibilities of a young man's calling?

Not only that. Any public demonstration (for this could not well be done in a corner) would only embarrass the present administration, by stirring up old party prejudices which would cause the loss of both sympathy and treasure, which the government cannot well afford to lose at present. By weakening the arm of the government, we strengthen that of the slave power, who would soon march through these States without fear of forcible resistance. * * *

I maintain that the principle of neutrality is the only safe one to govern us at this time. When men's lives are in their hands, and so little inducement as there is for us to cast ourselves into the breach, our work for the present lies in quite a different channel from assuming war responsibilities uninvited, with no promised future in store for us—a dilemma inviting enmity and destruction to the few, both North and South, among our people, enjoying partial freedom.

The slave's only hope—his only help—is his suffering brother at the North. When we are removed, the beacon light which directs and assists the panting fugitive is darkened and obscured—his once bright hope, that gave comfort to him as he pressed on to liberty's goal, is shadowed o'er forever. Our own precipitous, unwise zeal must never be the cause to stay the car of freedom, but ever let it roll onward and upward until earth and heaven united shall become one garden of paradisal freedom, knowing no color, no clime, but all one people, one language, one Father, Almighty God.

Once under army discipline, subject to the control of government officers or military leaders, could we dictate when and where the blow should be struck? Could we enter upon Quixotic crusades of our own projecting, independent of the constituted authorities, or these military chiefs? Will the satisfaction of again hearing a casual mention of our heroic deeds upon the field of battle, by our own children, doomed for all that we know to the same inveterate, heart-crushing prejudice that we have come up under, and die leaving as a legacy unto our issue—all from those for whom you would so unwittingly face the cannon's mouth to secure to them a heritage denied you and yours.

Is this country ready and anxious to initiate a new era for downtrodden humanity, that you now so eagerly propose to make the sacrifice of thousands of our ablest men to encourage and facilitate the great work of regeneration? No! no!! Your answer must be: No!!! No black regiments, unless by circumstances over which we have no option, no control; no initiatory war measures to be adopted or encouraged by us. Our policy must be neutral, ever praying for the success of that party determined to initiate first the policy of justice and equal rights.

Who can say that in another twelve months' time the policy of the South will not change in our favor, if the assistance of England or France will by it be gained, rather than submit to Northern dictation or subjugation? Did that idea ever suggest itself to your mind? Strange things happen all the while. Look back for the last twenty-four months, and ask yourself if you could have foretold what today you are so well informed has actually transpired when coming events cast their shadows before?

In these days, principle is supplanted by policy, and interest shapes policy, I find by daily observation, both in high and low places. Although to many the above idea may seem idle and delusory, inconsistent with the present spirit and suicidal policy of the South, yet I for one would feel justified in entertaining it equally with the idea that the North would proclaim a general emancipation so long as she supposed it a possibility to reclaim the disaffected States of the Southern Confederacy.

And, if an impossibility, what would all proclamations to that effect avail?

I believe with the act of emancipation adopted and proclaimed by the South, both England and France (and in fact, I might safely say, all Europe) would not only recognize their independence, but would render them indirectly material aid and sympathy.

To get the start of the Northern slave-worshippers, as they are sometimes termed, who can say that, as a last resort, these rebel leaders have not had that long in contemplation, knowing that should they succumb to this government through force of circumstances, or the uncertain chances of war, their lives would be valueless only as a warning to future generations.

Then, why may we not hope that such is their ultimatum in case of a series of defeats—the liberation of four millions of our poor, heart-crushed, enslaved race. One or two large battles will decide the future policy of both the contending parties—the sooner it comes, the sooner we will know our fate. It is in that scale it hangs.

Then let us do our duty to each other—use care in all our public measures—be not too precipitous, but in prayer wait and watch the salvation of God.

R. H. V.

Weekly Anglo-African (New York, N.Y.), 28 September 1861; *BAP*, 5:117–21.

7 3   THE NECESSITY OF ACTION

Alfred M. Green, a popular Philadelphia lecturer, believed that if blacks failed to serve in the military they would irreparably harm the antislavery cause.

Mr. Editor:

In your issue of September 28th appears an able and elaborate article on the "Formation of Colored Regiments." I have no desire for contention at a time like this with those who differ honorably from me in opinion; but I think it just, once in a while, to speak out and let the world know where we stand on the great issues of the day, for it is only by this means that we can succeed in arousing our people from a mistaken policy of inactivity, at a time when the world is rushing like a wild tornado in the direction of universal emancipation. The inactivity that is advocated is the principle that has ever had us left behind, and will leave us again, unless we arouse from lethargy and arm ourselves as men and patriots against the common enemy of God and man. For six months, I have labored to arouse our people to the necessity of action, and I have the satisfaction to say not without success. I have seen companies organized and under the most proficient modern drill in that time. I have seen men drilled among our sturdy-going colored men of the rural districts of Pennsylvania and New Jersey, in the regular African Zouave drill, that would make the hearts of secession traitors or prejudiced Northern Yankees quake and tremble for fear.

Now, I maintain, that for all practical purposes, whatever be the turn of the war, preparation on our part, by the most efficient knowledge of the military art and discipline, is one of the most positive demands of the times. No nation ever has or ever will be emancipated from slavery, and the result of such a prejudice as we are undergoing in this country, but by the sword, wielded too by their own strong arms. It is a foolish idea for us to still be nursing our past grievances to our own detriment, when we should as one man grasp the sword—grasp this most favorable opportunity of becoming inured to that service that must burst the fetters of the enslaved and enfranchise the nominally free of the North. We admit all that has been or can be said about the meanness of this government towards us—we are fully aware that there is no more soul in the present administration on the great moral issues involved in the slavery question, and the present war, than has characterized previous administrations; but, what of that; it all teaches the necessity of our making ourselves felt as a people, at this extremity of our national government, worthy of consideration and of being recognized as a part of its own strength. Had every State in the Union taken active steps in the direction of forming regiments of color, we should now, instead of numbering eight regiments or about eight thousand five hundred men, have numbered seventy-five thousand—besides awakening an interest at home and abroad, that no vascillating policy of the halfhearted semi-secessionists of the North could have suppressed.

It would have relieved the administration of so much room for cavil on the slavery question and colored men's right to bear arms, &c. It is a strange fact that now, when we should be the most united and decided as to our future destiny, when we should all have our shoulders to the wheel in order to enforce the doctrine we have ever taught of self-reliance and ourselves striking blows for freedom, that we are most divided, most inactive, and in many respects most despondent of any other period of our history. Some are wasting thought and labor, physical and intellectual, in counseling emigration (which I have nothing against when done with proper motives); others are more foolishly wasting time and means in an unsuccessful war against it; while a third class, and the most unfortunate of the three, counsel sitting still to see the salvation of God. Oh, that we could see that God will help no one that refuses to help himself; that God will not even help

Recruitment poster for black troops. Courtesy of Chicago Historical Society.

a sinner that will not first help himself. Stretch forth thy hand, said the Saviour to the man with a withered hand. He did so and was healed. Take up thy bed and walk, said he, and the man arose; go and wash, said he to the blind man, and he did it. How many are the evidences of this kind. God is saying to us today as plainly as events can be pointed out, stretch forth thy hand; but we sit idly, with our hands folded, while the whole world, even nations thousands of miles distant across the ocean, are maddened by the fierceness of this American strife, which after all is nothing less than God's means of opening the way for us to free ourselves by the assistance of our own enslavers, if we will do it.

Can we be still or idle under such circumstances? If ever colored men plead for rights or fight for liberty, now of all others is the time. The prejudiced white men, North or South, never will respect us until they are forced to do it by deeds of our own. Let us draw upon European sentiment as well as unbiased minds in our own country by presenting an undaunted front on the side of freedom and equal rights; but we are blindly mistaken if we think to draw influence from any quarter by sitting still at a time like this. The world must know we are here, and that we have aims, objects and interests in the present great struggle.

Without this we will be left a hundred years behind this gigantic age of human progress and development. I never care to reply to such views as those which set up the plea of previous injustice or even of present injustice done to us, as a reason why we should stand still at such a time as this. I have lived long enough to know that men situated like ourselves must accept the least of a combination of difficulties; if, therefore, there is a chance for us to get armed and equipped for active military service, that is one point gained which never could be gained in a time of peace and prosperity in this country; and that could have been done months ago, and can now be done in a few weeks, if we adopt the measure of united effort for its accomplishment.

Does anyone doubt the expediency of our being armed and under military discipline, even if we have always been sufferers at the hands of those claiming superiority? But enough of this. As to public demonstrations of this kind weakening the arm of the Federal Government, I must say that I was prepared to hear that remark among Democratic Union-savers, but I am startled to hear it from among our own ranks of unflinching abolitionists.

Indeed, sir, the longer the government shirks the responsibility of such a measure, the longer time she gives the rebel government to tamper with the free colored people of the South, and prompt and prepare their slaves for shifting the horrors of Saint Domingo from the South to the North; and, in such an event, could we rid ourselves from the responsibility of entering the field more than any other Northern men whom the government chose to call into active service?

Could we more effectually exercise proper discretion without arms, without drill, without union, than by availing ourselves of all these at the present time, looking boldly forward to that auspicious moment.

The South (as I have said in an article written for the Philadelphia *Press*, and copied into several popular journals) can mean nothing less than emancipation, by the act of her having thousands of free colored men, as well as slaves, even now under the best military discipline. England and France of course would favor such a project should the South thus snatch the key to a termination of this rebellion from the hands of the Federal Government. But how much better off would we be, sitting here like Egyptian mummies till all this was done, and then drafted and driven off, undisciplined, to meet well-disciplined troops, who will then truly be fighting for freedom; and while we could have no other motive than to help conquer a peace for the *"Union still"* in its perfidious unregenerate state? Tell me not that it will be optional with us, in the event of emancipation by the South, whether we fight or not. On the contrary, there is no possible way to escape it but to either commit suicide or run away to Africa, for even the climate of Canada, in such an event, would not be cool enough to check the ardor of fighting abolitionists against the hell-born prejudice of the North, and the cowardly black man would sit here quietly with his arms folded, instead of taking advantage of the times, till even the emancipated slaves of the South, rigorous in their majesty, force him to rise and flee to Canada to save his unsavory bacon. Let us then, sir, hear no more of these measures of actual necessity inaugurating a "dilemma, inviting enmity, and destruction to the few, both North and South, among our people enjoying partial freedom." That is a work that cannot be accomplished by loyal patriotic efforts to prepare a hundred thousand men to do service for God, for freedom, for themselves. Sitting still, shirking the responsibility God has thrown upon our shoulders, alone can engender such a dilemma.

Your correspondent also asks whether: "Once under army discipline, subject to the control of the government officers or military orders, we could dictate when and where the blow should be struck. Could we enter upon Quixotic crusades of our own projecting, independent of the constituted authorities or these military chiefs?" Sir, it appears to me that, under whatever changes of governmental policy, our favor would be courted more under such circumstances, and our dictation received with more favor and regard, both by the authorities, chiefs, and the people at large, than by our weak, effeminate pleadings for favor on the merits of our noble ancestry, rather than nerving our own arms and hearts for a combat that we have long halfheartedly invited by our much groanings and pleadings at a throne of grace.

The issue is here; let us prepare to meet it with manly spirit; let us say to the demagogues of the North, who would prevent us now from proving our manhood and foresight in the midst of all these complicated difficulties, that we will be armed, we will be schooled in military service, and if our fathers were cheated and disfranchised after nobly defending the country, we, their sons have the manhood to defend the right and the sagacity to detect the wrong; time enough to secure to ourselves the primary interest we have in the great and moving cause of the great American Rebellion. I am, as ever, yours, for truth and justice,

ALFRED M. GREEN

Weekly Anglo-African (New York, N.Y.), 19 October 1861; *BAP*, 5:121–24.

THE EMANCIPATION
PROCLAMATION

When President Abraham Lincoln issued the Emancipation Proclamation on 1 January 1863, black abolitionists finally could claim
the Civil War as their own struggle—a battle for liberation. Despite
its bland language and severe limitations, the text offered hope that
slavery would end. As the jubilant celebrations across the North
waned, African Americans paused to consider the document's full
meaning. Many viewed it as a call to action and an obligation to help
transform some four million slaves into American citizens. Others
saw with equal clarity that it was a product of military necessity
that left thousands of slaves in bondage. They judged the proclamation by the standards of justice and moral right and found it
wanting. The following documents measure the various sentiments
among African Americans over Lincoln's act.

74   LESS THAN COMPLETE FREEDOM

*James H. Hudson, an agent for the San Francisco Pacific Appeal,
expressed the black abolitionist critique of the Emancipation Proclamation. Although he had earnestly supported the war, Hudson deeply
regretted that Lincoln's action failed "to include every bondsman."*

Suisun City, [California]
Feb[ruary] 25, 1863

Mr. Editor:
I object. I think our view of the Freedom Proclamation, its sig-
nificance and its consequences, is incorrect, not to say wrong, and I will
state, in brief, my opinions on the subject, without venturing to intrude
a lengthy argument upon your space. I am one of those who think the
President has been too dilatory in seizing, for the use of the public, such

potent means of oppressive warfare as a declaration of emancipation would have been 12 months ago, and even now, so far from perceiving the full requirements of the occasion—as, for instance, the necessity for complete and decisive measures for reducing the strength of the rebellion—our honest but incompetent President adopts a halfway measure, which purports to give freedom to the bulk of the slave population beyond the reach of our arms, while it ignores or defies justice, by clinching the rivets of the chain which binds those whom alone we have present power to redeem. The proclamation should have been made to include every bondsman on the soil of America; every chain should have been broken, and the oppressed bidden to go free. Then, indeed, believing we were obeying the divine law, we might have invoked God's blessing upon our arms, and we could then have boldly claimed the services of every loyal man, white or black, in suppressing this hell-born and heaven-defying rebellion. The proclamation has been brought forth by timid and heaven-doubting midwives, and proved an incompetent and abominable abortion. "Put not your trust in princes," says the inspired writer, and he might have added with truth, acknowledged by the wrongs of a long-suffering people, "nor in the rule of republics—their strength is nought, and burnt-offerings are offensive in my sight." Oh that the scales might drop from their eyes, and that they could pray, and work, and rule and fight with the fervor, the steadfastness, the wisdom and the righteousness that have characterized God's chosen people in olden times.

J . H . H .

Pacific Appeal (San Francisco, Calif.), 7 March 1863; *BAP*, 5:184–85.

7 5   T H E   D A Y   O F   J U B I L E E ?

Frederick Douglass, speaking at the Spring Street African Methodist Episcopal Zion Church in Rochester, New York, on 28 December 1862, warned that the end of slavery did not mean the end of racism and the ordeal of African Americans.

My Friends:

This is scarcely a day for prose. It is a day for poetry and song, a new song. These cloudless skies, this balmy air, this brilliant sunshine (making December as pleasant as May) are in harmony with the glorious morning of liberty about to dawn upon us. Out of a full heart and with sacred emotion, I congratulate you my friends, and fellow citizens, on the high and hopeful condition, of the cause of human freedom and the cause of our common country, for these two causes are now one and inseparable and must stand or fall together. We stand today in the presence of a glorious prospect. This sacred Sunday in all the likelihoods of the case, is the last which will witness the existence of legal slavery in all the Rebel slaveholding states of America. Henceforth and forever, slavery in those States is to be recognized, by all the departments [of] the American Government, under its appropriate character, as an unmitigated robber and pirate, branded as the sum of all villainy, an outlaw having no rights which man white or colored is bound to respect. It is difficult for us who have toiled so long and hard, to believe that this event, so stupendous, so far reaching and glorious is even now at the door. It surpasses our most enthusiastic hopes that we live at such a time and are likely to witness the downfall, at least the legal downfall of slavery in America. It is a moment for joy, thanksgiving, and Praise.

Among the first questions that tried the strength of my childhood mind— was first why are colored people slaves, and the next was will their slavery last forever? From that day onward, the cry that has reached the most silent chambers of my soul, by day and by night has been How long! How long oh! Eternal Power of the Universe, how long shall these things be?

This inquiry is to be answered on the First of January 1863.

That this war is to abolish slavery I have no manner of doubt. The process may be long and tedious but that that result must at last be reached is among the undoubted certainties of the future! Slavery once abolished in the Rebel States, will give the death wound to slavery in the border States. When Arkansas is a free State, Missouri cannot be a slave State.

Nevertheless. This is no time for the friends of freedom to fold their hands and consider their work at an end. The price of Liberty is eternal vigilance. Even after slavery has been legally abolished, and the rebellion substantially suppressed, even when there shall come representatives to Congress from the States now in rebellion, and they shall have repudiated the miserable and disastrous error of disunion, or secession, and the country shall have reached a condition of comparative peace, there will still remain an urgent necessity for the benevolent activity of the men and the women who have from the first opposed slavery from high moral conviction.

Slavery has existed in this country too long and has stamped its character too deeply and indelibly, to be blotted out in a day or a year, or even in a generation. The slave will yet remain in some sense a slave, long after the chains are taken from his limbs, and the master will yet retain much of the pride, the arrogance, imperiousness and conscious superiority, and love of power, acquired by his former relation of master. Time, necessity, education, will be required to bring all classes into harmonious and natural relations.

But the South will not be the only part of the country demanding vigilance and exertion on the part of the true friends of the colored people. Our chief difficulty will [be] hereafter, as it has been heretofore with proslavery doughfaces, at the North. A dog will continue to scratch its neck even after the collar is removed. The sailor a night or two after reaching land feels his bed swimming from side to side, as if tossed by the sea. Daniel Webster received a large vote in Massachusetts after he was dead. It will not be strange if many Northern men whose politics, habits of thought, and accustomed submission to the slave power, leads them to continue to go through the forms of their ancient servility long after their old master slavery is in the grave.

Law and the sword can and will, in the end abolish slavery. But law and the sword cannot abolish the malignant slaveholding sentiment which has kept the slave system alive in this country during two centuries. Pride of race, prejudice against color, will raise their hateful clamor for oppression of the negro as heretofore. The slave having ceased to be the abject slave of a single master, his enemies will endeavor to make him the slave of society at large.

For a time at least, we may expect that this malign purpose and principle of wrong will get itself more or less expressed in party presses and platforms. Pro-Slavery political writers and speakers will not fail to inflame the ancient prejudice against the negro, by exaggerating his faults and concealing or disparaging his virtues. A crime committed by one of the hated race, [words missing] while any excellence found in one black man will grudgingly be set to his individual credit. Hence we say that the friends of freedom, the men and women of the land who regard slavery as a crime and the slave as a man will still be needed even after slavery is abolished.

Douglass' Monthly (Rochester, N.Y.), January 1863.

76 THE PRESENT—AND ITS DUTIES

Robert Hamilton, the brilliant editor of the Weekly Anglo-African, *charged northern blacks with the responsibility of carrying freedom to the South.*

After the feast, comes the reckoning. The good things served up to and by our people in the way of hearty and spontaneous rejoicing over the PROCLAMATION OF FREEDOM should be immediately followed by such practical results as will show that the rejoicing was not a mere outburst of feeling. Let us therefore endeavor to see our relations and duties in regard to this great event.

It is well known that in the great battle of Waterloo, Wellington held in reserve until late in the afternoon the bravest and most effective of his British troops, and when the final moment came to turn the doubtful fortunes of the day, he exclaimed to them, *"Up Guards, and at them!"* We long ago took ground, that, in our present war, the black man is the "reserved guard," and the hour has come when our Commander-in-chief has exclaimed to them, "up blacks, and at them!"

What, therefore, the hour demands of us is action, immediate, pressing action! And the kind of action required is well described in one of the outbursts of Mr. Garnet's eloquent speech at the Cooper Institute—"We must fight! fight! fight!" It is a fight for freedom and we are bound to go in. Let us organize one regiment in every large northern city, and send our offer of services directly to the President or the Secretary of War. We have been pronounced citizens by the highest legal authority, why should we not share in the perils of citizenship? What better field to claim our rights than the field of battle? Where will prejudice be so speedily overcome? Where will brotherhood be so quickly and firmly cemented? It is now, or never: now, if ever. A century may elapse before another opportunity shall be afforded for reclaiming and holding our withheld rights. If freedmen are accepted as soldiers to man the forts in the Mississippi and the Southern coast, why shall not free men be also accepted? If freedmen are accepted to man the fleets of the United States, why shall not free men also be received?

Let us at this moment get rid of one great difficulty in our way; let us understand thoroughly that we have got to do our own work. It is no time to stop, with Professor Wilson, and cast about in search of the duties of Abolitionists in the matter of our advancement; we must depend on no one under God for our elevation. It is our own work, and always has been. All we wanted was OPPORTUNITY and that, blessed be GOD, has come! Freedom is ours. And its fruit, equality, hangs temptingly on the tree, beckoning our own brave arms to rise and clutch it. If we rise in tens of thousands, and say to the President, "here we are, take us!" we will secure to our children and children's children all that our fathers have labored and suffered and bled for! But if we tamely suffer this hour to pass, then will we sink, in the public estimation, lower down than the vilest slanders of our foes could carry us. We know that there are partial military organizations in most of our large cities, let those having them in charge bestir themselves, assured that this time they will work for something.

There are other labors also which we must undertake. The process of transforming three millions of slaves into citizens requires the aid of intelligent colored men and women. We are, and can be, nearer to them than any other class of persons; we can enter into their feelings and attract their sympathies better than any others can. We can more patiently help and teach, and more jealously defend them, than any others can. We are manifestly destined for this work of mercy. It is for this trial God has given us the partial freedom, and such education, and the irrepressible desire for equality which consumes our souls. This labor of love and humanity His Providence has assigned to us; and we will be false to our destiny if we fail to do it. Our brethren are strangers, and naked, and hungered and athirst, and woe be unto us if we fail to minister to their wants. We are bound to be foremost in this good work; not pushing others aside, nor suffering others to push us aside, but straining every nerve to do our whole duty. We know that some of us are now engaged in this good work; what we claim is that *all* should be engaged in like manner.

And as no work can be carried on efficiently without organization, so all these separate efforts should be combined under one great national organization, which shall have power and authority to do the work thoroughly. Our leading men and women should, by correspondence, or convention, immediately get up this organization. We feel jealous of this good work, jealous that our people shall do it, and thereby assert before the world the high character which is really ours. We have started so many good organizations, and suffered the other class to enjoy the fruits of them, that this effort should be guarded at all points. No nobler work could engage the labors of men or angels. Among the objects which should engage the attention of this organization should be,

1. The furnishing of clothing to the freedmen.
2. The furnishing and supporting teachers among them.
3. The furnishing and supporting physicians among them.
4. The furnishing and supporting of instructors in household labors, economics and industries.

An organization for these and kindred purposes, got up and managed by colored persons, would command the sympathies, support and pecuniary aid of the benevolent throughout this land and all christendom. Especially would it have a claim on the great Avery fund which has hitherto laid dormant so far as its American legatees are concerned.

Weekly Anglo-African (New York, N.Y.), 17 January 1863; *BAP*, 5:175–77.

BLACKS AND LINCOLN

Lincoln was the "Great Emancipator" to the former slaves, but northern blacks judged him more harshly. Black abolitionists saw that the president had done nothing to secure all African Americans their full rights as citizens. Black disillusionment began early in the war and grew as Lincoln rebuked Union military commanders who interfered with slavery, then advocated colonization and enforcement of the hated Fugitive Slave Law. The 1864 election magnified divisions among blacks over Lincoln. More pragmatic leaders supported Lincoln, while antislavery purists promoted the candidacy of the antislavery Union general, John C. Frémont. Lincoln's assassination, however, profoundly changed the terms of the debate. African Americans quickly fathomed the catastrophe his death represented.

77 A DEFENDER OF SLAVERY?

Philip A. Bell, editor of the Pacific Appeal, *conveyed blacks' initial disappointment with the president's "Pro-slavery Proclamation." He charged that the failure to adopt emancipation as a war aim encouraged slaveholders, perpetuated slavery, and supported the Confederacy.*

We have refrained, hitherto, from commenting on President Lincoln's Pro-slavery Proclamation in reference to the proclamation issued by Gen. Hunter, declaring the slaves free in the department of the South, over which he had military command, in hopes that the President only denied that Gen. Hunter had "been authorized by the Government to make any proclamation declaring slaves free," in order that action in the premises might come from the highest source, *i.e.* the President himself, moreover, he intimates in his proclamation that he is yet undecided. He says "whether it is competent for him, as Commander-in-Chief of the army and navy, to declare slaves in any State free, and whether at any time it shall become necessary and indispensable for the maintenance of Government to exercise such supposed power, are questions which he reserves to himself, and which he cannot feel justified in leaving to the decision of commanders in the field."

The President exhibits as much tergiversation as ever did our New York Magician, as Martin Van Buren was called, in former days. He is as noncommittal as that "Northern man with Southern principles."

Recent dispatches, however, have given us to understand that the Cabinet has revoked Gen. Hunter's proclamation, and hence slavery is still recognized in the department of the South. We thought from President Lincoln's confiscation messages, his emancipation recommendations and other liberal actions, that it was his intention to strike at the root of the tree of strife. We supposed he was possessed of judgment sufficient to know that it was useless to lop off the extraneous branches, and leave the trunk of the Upas of discord and disunion—slavery—still standing to branch forth again and diffuse its malignant and pestiferous poison over the land; and we still hope he will abide by the principles he has hitherto avowed, on the strength of which he was elected.

The success of the Republican party in the Presidential election of 1860 was predicated on the resolutions passed by the Convention which nominated Mr. Lincoln, commonly called the Chicago Platform, and on the principles therein enunciated, and the President has frequently declared that he would abide and be governed in his administration by these principles.

How does the present action of President Lincoln agree with the Chicago Platform? The 7th and 8th resolutions of that Convention, passed unanimously, read as follows:

7. That the new dogma, that the Constitution, of its own force, carries slavery into any or all of the Territories of the United States, is a dangerous political heresy, at variance with the explicit provisions of that instrument itself, with contemporaneous expositions, and with legislative and judicial precedent, is revolutionary in its tendency, and subversive of the peace and harmony of the country.

8. That the normal condition of all the territory of the United States is that of freedom: That as our Republican fathers, when they abolished slavery in all our national territory, ordained that "No person should be deprived of life, liberty or property, without due process of law," it becomes our duty, by legislation, whenever such legislation is neces-

sary, to maintain this provision of the Constitution against all attempts to violate it; and we deny the authority of Congress, of Territorial Legislature, or of any individuals, to give legal existence to slavery in any Territory of the United States.

An adherence to these resolutions gives the President power over the institution of slavery in the Territories, as they declare freedom to be the "normal condition of all the territory of the United States." The action of the President in appointing Military Governors over the rebellious States, and subjecting them to martial law, reduces such States to the condition of Territories, the "normal condition" of which is "freedom."

We fear the Administration is pursuing a course detrimental to the best interests of the country, and encouraging the Rebels in their efforts to overthrow the Union, and perpetuate slavery.

Generals who are on the ground where slavery exists, and see what effects emancipation would produce, are the best judges when to strike the blow, and, by eradicating the evil, end the war.

We also fear, by the course he is pursuing, the President will alienate his ablest generals from him, and he will be unable to find capable men to take command of departments most infected with the evil. He must either grant them unrestricted power, or appoint such ingrates as Edward Stanly.

Pacific Appeal (San Francisco, Calif.), 14 June 1862; *BAP*, 5:143–46.

78 THE BEST CHOICE AVAILABLE

The black abolitionist and clergyman J. W. C. Pennington stressed Lincoln's integrity and judged his worth against the actions of his political enemies.

New York, [New York]
June 9th, 1864

Mr. Editor:

The prospect of having HIS EXCELLENCY ABRAHAM LINCOLN for our next President should awaken in the inmost soul of every American of African descent emotions of the most profound and patriotic enthusiasm. There was a kind and wise Providence in bringing Mr. Lincoln into the Presidential chair, and I believe that the same all-wise Providence has directed him in everything he has done as our President. I say OUR President, because he is the only American President who has ever given any attention to colored men as citizens. I believe that his renomination by the Convention is not only sound policy, but that it is equivalent to reelection, and especially if colored men will do their duty at the ballot box next November.

It lies with colored men now to decide this great issue. The wisest, the safest, and the soundest policy for colored Americans is to exert all our influence to keep our present Chief Magistrate where he is for four years from next March.

There are many reasons why we, as colored men, should prefer Mr. Lincoln for our next President. Among the many I may say: 1. He is an honest President. 2. He is faithful to the whole nation. 3. He commands the respect of the world. 4. He is more cordially hated by the Copperheads of the North and the rebels of the South than any other living man. 5. His reelection will be the best security that the present well-begun work of negro freedom and African redemption will be fully completed. May God grant us four long years more of the judicious administration of that excellent man, ABRAHAM LINCOLN, and when I speak thus I believe I speak the sentiments of nine-tenths of my colored fellow-citizens. What say you, Mr. Editor?

J. W. C. PENNINGTON

Weekly Anglo-African (New York, N.Y.), 25 June 1864; *BAP*, 5:276–77.

79 JOHN C. FRÉMONT, A BETTER CHOICE

"Africano," an anonymous soldier in the Fifth Massachusetts Cavalry who had suffered the inequities of administration policy toward African American soldiers, looked to General John C. Frémont—"one of liberty's most radical sons"—as blacks' best hope.

Point Lookout, M[arylan]d
July 18, 1864

Mr. Editor:

Coinciding with my brother soldier of the 54th Mass., I would say a few words as to the necessity of colored men, soldiers particularly, voting, if such is allowed, for the creator of the Emancipation proclamation. Many of our intelligent colored men believe in Mr. Lincoln; but *we*, who have studied him thoroughly, know him better, and as *we* desire to conglomerate in the land of our nativity, and not be severed from the ties we hold most dear, we hail the nomination of one of liberty's most radical sons—John C. Fremont. Mr. Lincoln's policy in regard to the elevation and inseparability of the negro race has always been one of a fickle-minded man—one who, holding anti-slavery principles in one hand and colonization in the other, always gave concessions to slavery when the *Union* could be preserved without touching the peculiar institution. Such a man is not again worthy the votes of the voting portion of the colored race, when the intrepid Fremont, explorer of the Mariposa Valley, the well-known freedom-cherishing, negro-equalizing patriot, is the competitor. The press, like Mr. Lincoln, has always been, and will ever be, in favor of negro colonization; for, like him, they fear competition, and it is not extraordinary if the press should now uphold Mr. Lincoln, though dissatisfied with his vacillating administration, to keep John C. Fremont from occupying the presidential chair. The loyal and truehearted people of the North will, no doubt, weigh the two men now before the public, and choose the one not found wanting. We are within ourselves satisfied that the Cleveland Convention will carry its object— that of electing Freedom's son—while the Baltimore Convention, with its nominee for reelection, will return to the plowshare.

While we thank Mr. Lincoln for what the exigencies of the times forced him to do, we also censure him for the non-accomplishment of the real good this accursed rebellion gave him the power to do, and which if he had done, instead of bartering human sinews and human rights with slaveholding Kentucky, the world would have looked upon him as the magnanimous regenerator of American institutions, and the benevolent protector of human freedom.

AFRICANO

Weekly Anglo-African (New York, N.Y.), 6 August 1864; *BAP*, 5:277–78.

80 ASSASSINATION OF PRESIDENT LINCOLN

Dr. S. W. Rogers's editorial in the New Orleans Black Republican *revealed how rapidly African Americans sanctified "the name of 'Abraham, the Martyr.'"*

The 13th of April will be a day forever memorable in history by an act of atrocity that has no parallel in the annals of men. On the evening of that day, the President of the United States of America, while sitting quietly in his box at the theater—almost his only relaxation—in the capital of the country, in the company of his wife, in the very midst of his friends, at the zenith of his power, was shot to death by an assassin, who, after the deed of blood, leaped from the box to the stage, and exclaimed: "Now the South is avenged—be it so to all tyrants," and succeeded in escaping. At the same hour, the Hon. William H. Seward, Secretary of State, while lying hopelessly ill in his bed, in his own house, in the same city, is assaulted by a desperate accomplice of the murderer of Mr. Lincoln, and cut nearly to death, in the midst of his family and attendants, several of whom were seriously if not fatally wounded.

In the face of crimes so appalling, men are stunned. "Who next?" is the whispered inquiry.

These dreadful deeds are a fitting finale of this brutal and bloody rebellion. They are the natural results of it. By the rebellion, these men were instigated to the perpetration of crimes that are but the *great* crime compressed into individual acts. They are the fell spirit of slavery breaking from the knife of the assassin—slavery, that for two hundred years has educated whole generations in cruelty and the spirit of murder; that, in the end, drove half a nation to a rebellion to destroy liberty, now whets the knife of the assassin to murder, in cold blood, the most illustrious exemplar of freedom.

Rebels may condemn these horrible acts; they may seek to run down the responsibility to some individual insanity, but they can never clear the skirts of the rebellion of the responsibility for the madness of the murderers. The assassins are the natural outcrop of that vast stratum of cruelty and of crime which slavery has been so long depositing below the surface of society. The greatest earthly friend of the colored race has fallen by the same spirit that has so long oppressed and destroyed us. In giving us our liberty, he has lost his own life. Following the rule of the great and glorious in the world, he has paid the penalty of Apostleship. He has sealed with his blood his Divine commission to be the liberator of a people. Hereafter, through all time, wherever the Black Race may be known in the world; whenever and wherever it shall lay the foundations of its power; build its cities and rear its temples, it will sacredly preserve if not deify the name of "*Abraham, the Martyr.*"

Black Republican (New Orleans, La.), 22 April 1865; *BAP*, 5:315–16.

THE BLACK MILITARY
EXPERIENCE

African Americans interpreted the Civil War as a momentous struggle between the forces of slavery and freedom. Once the North adopted emancipation as a war aim and allowed blacks to fight, the vast majority of eligible, northern black males volunteered for military service. The Fifty-fourth Massachusetts Regiment became the standard-bearer of the black abolitionist commitment. Created in February 1863, the Fifty-fourth represented blacks' best hope to free the slave, secure equal rights, and affirm their worth to a skeptical nation. The regiment's extraordinary valor at the 18 July 1863 battle of Fort Wagner, South Carolina, dissolved doubts about black soldiers and facilitated the enlistment of nearly 180,000 more—some 10 percent of all Union troops. But heroism did not guarantee equal treatment. For African Americans, the issue of unequal pay symbolized the government's general mistreatment of black soldiers. Although they assured the Lincoln administration that they fought "for God, liberty and country, not money," black troops ignored threats of retribution to expose the demoralizing injustice of the pay crisis.

This letter by Meunomennie L. Maimi, a soldier of mixed white, black, and Native American blood, is deeply personal and intensely analytical, reflecting faith among blacks that the war would decide their fate.

Buckingham Legion, Co. I, 20th Reg[imen]t., C.V.
Camp near Stafford C[ourt] H[ouse], [Virginia]
March, 1863

My Dear Wife:

When I wrote you the last letter I was quite sick, and did not know as I should ever be able to write to you again; but I am better now and write to relieve your mind, in case you might worry too much about me. When I wrote my last letter, I did not expect to be able to write another; but some good news which I received and the kind usage of a few friends, who came to my hut and did what was needed for me, have saved you your husband, and I am enabled to write again. There is one thing which your selfish love for your husband has made you forget, and that is, that he is naturally a soldier, and in time of war, and particularly in times like the present, a good soldier has something else to do besides enjoying himself at home with his family. I shall come, if permitted to go home, but as soon as my health will admit, will return to duty.

Do you know or think what the end of this war is to decide? It is to decide whether we are to have freedom to all or slavery to all. If the Southern Confederacy succeeds, then you may bid farewell to all liberty thereafter and either be driven to a foreign land or held in slavery here. If our government succeeds, then your and our race will be free. The government has torn down the only barrier that existed against us as a people. When slavery passes away, the prejudices that belonged to it must follow. The government calls for the colored man's help and, if he is not a fool, he will give it.

The present is different from the Revolutionary war, for that was to decide between a king and a part of his subjects, who had fled from religious persecution in his land to a new land. He claimed even there to still hold them and sought by cruel and unjust taxation to subdue these people. They then rebelled; and after a long and bloody war won their independence and established a free government of their own. It was intended to be free to all, even to the few slaves who were in the land, brought there by the English government. The Constitution of the United States was such that it allowed each State to make its own laws, as long as they did not infringe upon the laws of the general government. Some of the Northern States in a few years set their slaves free. The other States would have followed their example, but they were in a warmer climate and, unfortunately for us, foreigners came from France and Spain, who were slaveholders, and soon found out that some parts of this country would grow cotton, rice, sugar and indigo. They then had to decide who should cultivate those plants that would produce so much wealth. They considered the climate and came to the decision that the white man could not stand it and the attendant fevers, and so they must have some other race of people beside the paleface, for he was only fit to rule in that line of business. They cast their eyes on the red men, the natives of the country and natural kings of the land. Why did they not take them? they were used to the climate—the reason was, the Indians, of whom I am in part a descendant, as well as yourself, were warriors or soldiers whose savage natures, when they found out the white man's intentions, would not submit to be chained down to them and their system of labor. They looked upon them as robbers, who came to deprive them of their natural rights and liberties; and became bitter enemies, fighting them by night and by day, surprising them at all times and everywhere, at labor or at prayer, in sunshine or storm. The white man was not safe at all; they scorned his paper treaties of peace and broke them as fast as they were made. But their bravery could not prevail; their weapons were inferior to those of the palefaces, and the want of union among them gave the victory to the white man.

The white man thought again how to get his money without his own dear self having to broil beneath a hot sun or see his wife or delicate child stoop to the labor of picking the cotton from the field or gathering rice from its damp bed. The Indian had failed him; the few captives they took died when they came to force labor upon them, thus proving the red man unable to do the labor in those climes. His fiend-like eyes fell upon the black man. Thought he, "I have it. We will get some of the States that cannot grow these plants, and do not need as many hands to help them as we do, to raise blacks for us, and we will purchase these of them, and they will keep their mouths shut about this liberty that was only meant for us and our children." They denied that God made the black man a man at all, and brought their most learned judges and doctors of the gospel and laws to attempt to prove by them that the sons of Africa were not even human. They tried to convince the world that the black man sprang from the brute creation; that the kings and princes and noble sons of the sunny land sprang from the loins of monkeys and apes, who made war with each other and slaves of each other in their mother country, and it was but right to buy and steal the children of apes or monkeys and to enslave them.

How do you fancy, wife, the idea of being part ape or monkey? I have often heard our grandmother tell what a noble man your great-grandfather was, how much he knew and was respected by his neighbors and the white man that owned him, and how her own father, who followed the condition of his father, who died a slave, suffered before he bought his freedom; how she and her little sisters and brothers were robbed of her hard-earned property by one who cared not for the rights of the black child. Tell grandmother that Maimi will strike for her wrongs as well as for those of others. * * *

They shall see these gentle monkeys, that they thought they had so fast in chains and fetters, coming on a long visit to them, with rifle, saber, and all the terrible trappings of war. Not one at a time, cringing like whipped hounds as we were, but by thousands, and if that doesn't suffice, by millions. Like Pharaoh's lice, we shall be found in all his palaces, will be his terror and his torment; he shall yet wish he had never heard of us. We will never forsake him, until he repents in sackcloth and ashes his crime of taking from us our manhood and reducing us to the brute creation. We will accept nothing but, without any mental or other reservation, our rights and liberties. He shall give up his monkeyizing, his demoniac, infernal plan of ruining our country and destroying our race. The black man shall yet hold up his head and be a man; not a poor, despised brute. But his own good hands must help strike the blows and gain the victory through blood, before the American slavery-taught white man can believe that the poor, oppressed slave and the downtrodden black man is his true friend and brother-man. With all his books and the vast amount of learning and the light of civilization shining on his path, he is still in the dark. In spite of his suffering at the hands of the slave power, the loss of his sons, who have fallen in the defense of his insulted flag, his loss of treasures and the threatened loss of his country, he is yet blind. He still bows down to these murdering slaveholders and is willing to kiss their feet, if they will but return to the Union as it was and kindly rule over him.

This is what the blind copperheads ask of them, but the slaveholder despises them and their offers, because they do it in the name of Democracy, which they hate, as there are yet some few sparks of freedom in that, and they hate everything which is free or points towards justice for any but themselves and their institutions. They ask, with arms in their hands, the right to buy and sell, to rob and murder all that are poor enough to labor for their daily bread, without respect to color or blood. They are selfish and care for no one but themselves.

These are my enemies, my flag's enemies, the flag I was born under, have suffered so much under—the enemies to God and our government. It is they who have struck down the flag which so long has defended their institutions before they left our Union. It has by them been cast to the earth and trampled under foot, because it professed to be the flag of liberty and freedom, although it was only liberty for the white man, but it included the poor white man as well the rich and noble sons of the South, the monkey-raisers and drivers. They tore that flag from its staff and in its place put their rebel rag, and swore by it that freedom should die. But they shall find that it cannot die, that its black sons as well as its loyal white sons are faithful, and will shed the last drop of blood in defense of the starry banner that is to be the emblem of freedom to all, whether black or white.

Now, wife, although I love you and would grant anything in reason to one who has been so kind and so faithful and true to her husband, yet there is something which the true man should hold dear and for which he should be willing to die, besides the wife of his bosom or the children of his loins: first, his God; then his country or his government, when it is a just one; and if he cannot do that he is no man, but a useless piece of machinery. If I did not know why you spoke those words, I would be very angry indeed. I know that it was your wifely anger at the mean treatment which your dearly beloved husband has suffered at the hands of some of his fellow soldiers that made you speak so quick and without forethought, bidding me desert my flag and leave my country to fall into the hands of its worst enemies. You did not speak such words as those on the day when I stood before you with the uniform of a volunteer, the uniform of a free man on. You told me at the door, with a smile on your face, but a tear in your eye, that if I thought it was my duty to go to what was then a white man's war, to "go, and may God bless you!" I was prouder of you that day than the day the minister bid me salute my wife.

You have never doubted my true and faithful love for you; it is still the same, or else I would come running home like a little cur that some large dog had badly frightened, and leave you to become a slave to those wretches who hate us. For if these Southern demons conquer, then you, with your Indian and Negro blood mixed in your veins, must bow down to them and become their slave or perhaps some white man's mistress, not an honored wife, loved and respected by her husband, but a mere plaything, to be cast aside as soon as he discovers a fresh victim to administer to his beastly lusts, and bear more monkeys for him to sell to others, to be used in the same way. This he has been doing for years, and the only cure that can or will relieve this disease is the present war, which he in his foolish and wicked plan began.

I do not blame you altogether for what you said about returning home, as it was cowardly in me to complain to you of the fools' bad usage. I forgive you, as it was prompted by your too-selfish love for your husband. But I want you to remember hereafter that you are a soldier's wife, a warrior's bride—one who has not a single drop of cowardly blood in his veins, and who will not desert his flag, or country, or his brother in bonds, not even for his dearly beloved wife, the friend of his bosom. Ponder this well; take the right sense of it and be proud that you have such a man for a husband. What is money but trash? and is trash to be compared to a country's and my own liberty? If the government gets so poor, before the war ends, that it cannot pay but $10 per month and no bounties, I will take that and fight on. That will buy bread for you and my poor old grandmother. If I return at all, let me come back to your arms a free man, of a free country and a free flag, and my brothers free, or else let me rest in death on the battlefield, with my face to the slaveholders, a continual reproach and curse unto him, as long as the world shall stand or a slaveholder breathe. This from your soldier-husband,

M . L . M A I M I

Weekly Anglo-African (New York, N.Y.), 18 April 1863; BAP, 5:187–91.

8 2   B R A V E R Y   A N D   I T S   R E W A R D S

Two letters from members of the Fifty-fourth Massachusetts Regiment—one by Lewis Douglass, son of Frederick Douglass, and one by black journalist George E. Stephens—describe the Fort Wagner, South Carolina, assault and explain how the crisis over equal pay embodied the African American struggle for justice and equality.

Morris Island, S[outh] C[arolina]
July 20th, 1863

My Dear Father and Mother:
Wednesday July 8th, our regiment left St. Helena Island for Folly Island, arriving there the next day, and were then ordered to land on James

Island, which we did. On the upper end of James Island is a large rebel battery with 18 guns. After landing we threw out pickets to within two miles of the rebel fortification. We were permitted to do this in peace until last Thursday, 16th inst., when at four o'clock in the morning the rebels made an attack on our pickets, who were about 200 strong. We were attacked by a force of about 900. Our men fought like tigers; one sergeant killed five men by shooting and bayoneting. The rebels were held in check by our few men long enough to allow the 10th Conn. to escape being surrounded and captured, for which we received the highest praise from all parties who knew of it. This performance on our part earned for us the reputation of a fighting regiment.

Our loss in killed, wounded and missing was forty-five. That night we took, according to our officers, one of the hardest marches on record, through woods and marsh. The rebels we defeated and drove back in the morning. They, however, were reinforced by 14,000 men, we having only half a dozen regiments. So it was necessary for us to escape.

I cannot write in full, expecting every moment to be called into another fight. Suffice it to say we are now on Morris Island. Saturday night we made the most desperate charge of the war on Fort Wagner, losing in killed, wounded and missing in the assault, three hundred of our men. The splendid 54th is cut to pieces. All our officers, with the exception of eight, were either killed or wounded. Col. Shaw is a prisoner and wounded. Major Hallowell is wounded in three places, Adj't James in two places. Serg't Simmons is killed, Nat. Hurley (from Rochester) is missing, and a host of others.

I had my sword sheath blown away while on the parapet of the Fort. The grape and cannister, shell and minnies swept us down like chaff, still our men went on and on, and if we had been properly supported, we would have held the Fort, but the white troops could not be made to come up. The consequence was we had to fall back, dodging shells and other missiles.

If I have another opportunity, I will write more fully. Goodbye to all. If I die tonight I will not die a coward. Goodbye.

LEWIS

Douglass' Monthly (Rochester, N.Y.), August 1863; *BAP*, 5:241.

Morris Island, S[outh] C[arolina]
Aug[ust] 1, 1864

Mr. Editor:

Two or three months ago, it was announced that Congress had passed a law equalizing the pay of colored troops. This was at the closing period of the session. The colored troops, which had been enlisted under the law of 1862, were unpaid. This was known, of course, at Washington. The noble Major Stearns was compelled to resign, because the pledges he had been authorized by Sec. Stanton to make to the colored man were broken by the War Department, who refused to pay soldiers who had black skins more than seven dollars per month.

Thus free men were reduced to servitude. No matter what services he might render—no matter how nobly he might acquit himself—he must carry with him the degradation of not being considered a man, but a thing. The foreigner, the alien, of whatever color, or race, or country, are enrolled and paid like native Americans; but the latest refinement of cruelty has been brought to bear on us.

In the Revolutionary War, and in the War of 1812, colored men fought, and were enrolled, and paid, the same as the whites; and not only this, were drilled and enlisted indiscriminately in the same companies and regiments. Little did our forefathers think that they were forging chains for the limbs of their own race. Look how nobly Forten, Bowers, and Cassey, and those colored patriots of the last war, rallied to the defence of Philadelphia; yet how were the colored people repaid? By stripping them in '36 of their right of franchise. Now the plan is to inveigle the black man into the service by false pretences, and then make him take half pay. If he doesn't take half pay and behave himself, as a vender of religious tracts down here said, "Shoot 'em." Why, sir, the rebels have not reached the daring extreme of reducing free men to slaves. Does the Lincoln despotism think it can succeed? There are those who say, you should not talk so—"you hurt yourself." Let me say to those men, we cannot be injured more. There is no insult—there is no cruelty—there is no wrong, which we have not suffered. Torture, massacre, mobs and slavery. Do you think that we will tamely submit like spaniels to every indignity?

I shall speak hereafter my wrongs, and nothing shall prevent me but double irons or a pistol ball that shall take me out of the hell I am now suffering: nearly eighteen months of service—of labor—of humiliation—

of danger, and not one dollar. An estimable wife reduced to beggary, and dependent upon another man—what can wipe out the wrong and insult this Lincoln despotism has put upon us? Loyal men everywhere hurl it from power—dismember it—grind it to atoms! Who would have believed that all the newspaper talk of the pay of colored soldiers having been settled by Congress was a base falsehood? There is not the least sign of pay, and there are hints from those in authority that we will not get paid, and will be held to service by the terrors of our own bullets. Seventeen months and upwards! Suppose we had been white? Massachusetts would have inaugurated a rebellion in the East, and we would have been paid. But—Oh, how insulting!—because I am black, they tamper with my rights. How dare I be offered half the pay of any man, be he white or red.

This matter of pay seems to some of those having slaveholding tendencies a small thing, but it belongs to that system which has stripped the country of the flower of its youth. It has rendered every hamlet and fireside in this wide country desolate, and brought the country itself to bankruptcy and shame. It is a concomitant of the system. Like as the foaming waves point the mariner to the hidden rocks on which his storm-driven ship will soon be lost, this gross injustice reveals to us the hidden insidious principles on which the best hopes of the true patriot will be dashed.

G. E. S.

Weekly Anglo-African (New York, N.Y.), 27 August 1864; *BAP,* 5:296–98.

THE MOVEMENT GOES SOUTH

Black abolitionists carried their message of freedom and equality into the heart of the rebellion as military scouts, teachers, missionaries, relief workers, and political organizers. Scores of northern blacks went South to help the newly freed slaves. Some, former slaves themselves, used their knowledge of regional customs and terrain to serve the Union army or aid thousands of slaves to escape the plantation. After the war, black abolitionists assumed the leadership of freedmen's education to attack white domination and the vestiges of slavery. The northern black press repeatedly urged African Americans to help instruct the freedmen and work for their enfranchisement. Failure to act, African American papers warned, meant a "dark day for the friends of freedom."

83 A WOMAN'S WAR

Harriet Tubman, famous for her underground railroad "expeditions," went to South Carolina in May 1862 to help free slaves and work with the freedmen. Tubman's letter, dictated to friends in Boston, describes her work as a Union scout.

Beaufort, S[outh] C[arolina]
June 30, 1863

* * * Last fall, when the people here became very much alarmed for fear of an invasion from the rebels, all my clothes were packed and sent with others to Hilton Head, and lost; and I have never been able to get any trace of them since. I was sick at the time, and unable to look after them myself. I want, among the rest, a *bloomer* dress, made of some coarse, strong material, to wear on *expeditions*. In our late expedition up the Combahee river, in coming on board the boat, I was carrying *two pigs* for a sick woman, who had a child to carry, and the order "double quick" was given, and I started to run, stepped on my dress, it being rather long, and fell and tore it almost off, so that when I got on board the boat there was hardly anything left of it but shreds. I made up my mind then, I would never wear a long dress on another expedition of the kind, but would have a *bloomer* as soon as I could get it. So please make this known to the ladies, if you will, for I expect to have use for it very soon, probably before they can get it to me.

You have, without doubt, seen a full account of the expedition I refer to. Don't you think we colored people are entitled to some credit for that exploit, under the lead of the brave Colonel Montgomery? We weakened the rebels somewhat on the Combahee river by taking and bringing away *seven hundred and fifty-six* head of their most valuable livestock, known up in your region as "contrabands," and this, too, without the loss of a single life on our part, though we have good reason to believe that a number of rebels bit the dust. Of these seven hundred and fifty-six contrabands, nearly or quite all the able-bodied men have joined the colored regiments here.

I have now been absent two years almost, and have just got letters from my friends in Auburn, urging me to come home. My father and mother are old and in feeble health, and need my care and attention. I hope the good people there will not allow them to suffer, and I do not believe they will. But I do not see how I am to leave at present the very important work to be done here. Among other duties which I have is that of looking after the hospital here for contrabands. Most of those coming from the mainland are very destitute, almost naked. I am trying to find places for those able to work, and provide for them as best I can, so as to lighten the burden on the Government as much as possible, while at the same time they learn to respect themselves by earning their own living.

Remember me very kindly to Mrs. ——— and her daughters; also, if you will, to my Boston friends, Mrs. C., Miss H., and especially to Mr. and Mrs. George L. Stearns, to whom I am under great obligations for their many kindnesses. I shall be sure to come and see you all if I live to go North. If you write me, please direct your letter to the care of E. G. Dudley, Beaufort, S.C. Faithfully and sincerely your friend,

H A R R I E T   T U B M A N

Commonwealth (Boston, Mass.), 17 July 1863; *BAP*, 5:220–21.

84 REV. J. W. LOGUEN HOME AGAIN

Jermain W. Loguen, renowned abolitionist leader from Syracuse, New York, traveled to the Tennessee plantation from which he had escaped thirty-two years earlier. His letter describes the condition of the freedmen and his anxieties over the status of African Americans in the postwar South.

Syracuse, [New York]
July 25th, 1865

Mr. Editor:

I am once more at my "Salt City" home, after an absence of nearly two months. I have been away down in my fatherland, where in days gone by I have often seen the slaveholder's merciless whip fall upon the backs of my poor brothers and sisters until the warm blood would flow therefrom and drop to the ground. I visited Columbia and while there looked in vain for the whipping-post and auction-block; those silent proclaimers of barbarism in man were removed from sight. The slave-pens, thank God, have changed their inmates. In place of the poor, innocent and almost heart-broken slaves, who have year after weary year been placed there to wait for the negro trader to make up his gang, and then driven in chains to the sugar or cotton fields, there to drag out a miserable existence away from friends and all that is dear; in place of the young slave mother begging for her only babe, with no mercy shown her, are some of the very fiends in human shape who committed those diabolical outrages. "Their sins have found them out," and I was constrained to give God the glory, for He has done a great work for our people.

I preached twice in Columbia in hearing of the old slave-pen. Colored and white came to hear me. They had all heard of Jarm's running away over thirty-two years ago, and had not a little curiosity to see and hear him. The Lord was with me and gave me great liberty on that occasion, as we Methodist preachers sometimes say. My old mother, though very feeble, rode ten miles that she might hear her long-lost son. On the old plantation all had changed. The home of my childhood was like a strange land.

It is almost impossible for a person to realize the changes brought about by this war without visiting the South. In place of slave-pens, you will see churches and schoolrooms filled with happy souls. In place of auctioneers there are missionaries who preach a full, free Gospel to the eager listening ones. They are anxious to learn to read and write, and the privilege to do so makes them appear happier than any other people in that part of the country.

God in His goodness has opened wide the door for the schoolteacher and missionary. Hundreds are needed to labor for the freedmen in Tennessee as well as in other States. There are many noble men and women in the cities of Nashville and Knoxville who stand ready to assist all who may go to labor. As in those two places, so in many others throughout the State, there are noble specimens of gentlemen and ladies among the colored people, and those are they that stand ready to help in the great work of elevation.

I found some whites there from the free States who were very kind, others who were very mean. Many of the copperheads from the North, who are in military power, are meaner than the Southerners; yes, meaner than the rebels themselves. We must work while it is day. If the military is withdrawn ere the colored man has his God-given rights granted and guaranteed to him, it will be a dark day for the friends of freedom all over the land. The black man *must* have equal rights before the law, or I fear this is a ruined Nation after all that has been done. The country so far has been greatly aided by the black man, and it still needs, in fact, and must have his support, if it would survive. The loyal representatives in Tennessee, Alabama, and Kentucky, are the colored soldiers; God bless them! Wherever they are there is safety for the colored people. I never spoke to a more noble set of men in my life than the colored soldiers at Chattanooga. Many of the white soldiers were drunken, and loafing about abusing colored people. The only trouble I had was with some of the white soldiers. Quite different with the black soldiers; they all *acted*, as well as *looked like men*. You can see in their every action that a great work is to be performed by them, and with dignity and manliness are they preparing themselves for the work.

> He is a hero, truly brave,
> That wars for freedom, not a throne.

It is necessary that we urge every strong man and woman, preacher and teacher, who can leave for a time their Northern laboring fields, to go and spend all the time they can in the South. Let them stay two, three, or more months, just as they can afford. The work must be done, and it is for us to do who have had the advantages of a free North and free schools. I am willing and ready to go again just as soon as I recover my health. Let us go and see our brethren and talk with them; they seem *glad* to see us. Why, my friend, I think you did more for God and humanity the months you spent in the South, than you could have done in so many years at the North.

We cannot all go South to live, but let all go who can and get acquainted with the freedmen. It does a Northern heart good to witness the meeting of husbands and wives, parents and children, brothers and sisters, and old friends long lost to each other. The whites are pressing in among them, some to do good, many to make money only; the latter class do more harm than good.

To show the patriotism and loyalty among the Southern people, I will say, that in Nashville, the capital of Tennessee, the colored people alone celebrated the Fourth of July. The celebration was a success, and it was with a feeling of pleasure that your humble servant delivered the oration.

I have many things to tell you, when we meet, of the old plantation, my mother, and old mistress. Yours, for the work,

J. W. LOGUEN

Weekly Anglo-African (New York, N.Y.), 5 August 1865; *BAP*, 5:353–55.

85 THE SOUTHERN FIELD AND THE PROPER AGENTS

Robert Hamilton, with typical perspicacity, warned that unless the idea of racial equality guided freedmen's education, slavery would endure for another generation.

We notice an increasing solicitude among the whites as to the influence likely to be exerted upon their freed brethren by those talented colored men who are now going South. This is quite natural. The whites are conscious of the fact that, heretofore, they have had the field all to them-

Freedmen's school. From Harper's Weekly, *15 December 1866.*

selves; that for patronage and perquisites they have taught what and how they pleased. It is natural and proper that colored men should feel that it is their mission now to enter this field, and educate and elevate their freed brethren. The field is appropriately ours—it is the only fair scope we ever had for usefulness before. Moreover, the race to be educated and elevated is ours, therefore we are deeply interested in the kind of education it receives.

1. There is a type of education which, if introduced at the South, will train our race in *mental subserviency* for fifty years to come. This would be a disaster. It would be exchanging physical for intellectual bondage. We object to teaching from the pulpit, the schooldesk, or from the platform that which will train the freed people to regard themselves as an inferior race. We claim no *superiority* over the whites, and we admit of no *inferiority*. We reject the patronizing style of some who would have us believe that the colored people are a race of Uncle Toms, or that they are calculated to be better Christians than whites. We do not need any such flattering. It will not stand the test of our Christian philosophy. We hold that nature

has made all men alike, and that by means of the Gospel and civilization they can be educated and elevated alike. This is the true standard. Anything lower than this is degrading. So far from aiming to develop the whole man, it tends to suppress the man.

2. No teacher or preacher, be they white or colored, should be entrusted with the education of freed people or their children, who is not prepared to teach and vindicate this doctrine. Unfortunately for them and for us, the great mass of the whites do not believe in the equality of the races. The influence of slavery, selfish interests, and a long course of training have established the whites in this opinion. That opinion they are free to exercise among themselves; but have they a right to impose that opinion upon us? Is it fair that they should use their influence to infuse or insinuate it among us to our degradation? We think not; and upon this point we are solicitous. We are deeply concerned about the fact that there are many whites now teaching among the freed people, and occupying other positions where they can mould their minds, who do not accord with us upon the subject under consideration. They have kindness of heart enough to regard the freed people as "poor unfortunate creatures," for whom something must be done; but on the main question of the manhood of the black man, they are not sound. They hold to the opinion of the inferiority of our race. Such persons should not seek or desire to be teachers among us—they cannot do us good. There are, we are happy to say, noble exceptions. Some of the whites now engaged in the work of teaching among us are as true as steel. Their hearts are in the right place and in the right state. Such we welcome to the field, and to our fellowship in the great work in which we are engaged. They help us; they do not hinder us. They elevate us; they do not degrade us. We do not feel ill at ease with them as co-workers; we do not feel inferior to them, and we do not wish them to feel inferior to us; we are not jealous of their influence among our people, and we do not wish them to be jealous of ours.

We think this is the way to evince the consistency of our principles; we welcome the whites to a fair mental and moral competition on our own ground, provided they are sound on this point.

In reference to the question of education at the South, we cannot speak about "reconstruction," for the colored people never had any system of education, but we can speak of construction, or organization. The educational system must be constructed or organized upon our basis—the equality of the race. Those who have not faith enough to undertake to assist in educating the race up to this standard should not enter the field as educators, for they will do more harm than good. As to the old system of preaching submission to slavery to these people, that must be utterly and forever abolished; it must be buried in the same grave with slavery. We do not see how men who have preached such doctrines can presume to stand up before the freed people.

3. In what we have written, we are not to be suspected of aiming to create any jealousy, or as fostering a feeling of bitterness toward any class of our fellow citizens, however misguided they may be; but the sacred obligations of patriotism impel us to state these views. We love our country, and we love our race; we wish to make the latter more valuable to the former. This can only be done by bringing the race up to the standard we have set. We must be true to our position, but we shall cultivate a spirit of kindness to all. Those with whom we cannot agree, we shall differ from, with firmness mingled with kindness, hoping that they may yet be brought to a right state of mind, and see that ours is the true principle of political economy. If we can succeed in bringing up the millions of our race to an equal standard of manhood with the same number of whites—as we believe we can—will it not, in that proportion, add to the strength and vital manhood of the population of the Republic for any State emergency? Why should the Republic be deprived of half the manhood of those millions, as will be the fact if they are to be educated only up to the halfway standard, against which we are objecting? We suppose it to be a sound principle of political economy that a State increases the productiveness of its population by providing that the masses not only be educated, but that they be educated to the highest possible capacity. The emergency of the late war has brought from among the race hundreds of thousands of ablebodied men for military service. Why should it be doubted that the same race may produce equally able-*minded* men? How shall we know unless we *aim* to educate up to a first-class standard? We take it that there is power in the *hearts* and *brains* of those sable sons of the South, as well as in their right arms, that will yet command the respect of the nation.

Weekly Anglo-African (New York, N.Y.), 9 September 1865; *BAP*, 5:366–68.

RECONSTRUCTION

African Americans expected that Reconstruction would destroy every vestige of southern slavery and northern discrimination. They saw Reconstruction as a historic opportunity to remake American society, yet one that threatened to pass unfulfilled. After thirty-five years of abolitionist labors and five years of national sacrifice and war, black leaders were unwilling to see democracy deferred again. Throughout the war, African Americans warned against acceptance of an incomplete freedom and were the first to understand the disastrous nature of federal policies calculated to return power to southern whites. Without land, economic opportunity, protection of their civil rights, and the vote, African Americans would endure a victory without peace.

86   THE PERILS BY THE WAY

Robert Hamilton used his editorial platform to urge blacks to organize and demand their full rights. Without the vote, he cautioned, the coming freedom would be "a partial emancipation unworthy of the name."

The first and greatest difficulty in the way of emancipation is that there are no settled principles, no adequate organization, arranged to compass it. The very discussions on the matter are desultory and do not seem to reach the pith of the question. By that strange pertinacity with which old ideas cling to the public mind, it is what to do with the whites, in the reconstruction of the rebel States, that principally occupies the attention of writers, the disposition of their black fellow-citizens seeming a matter of secondary, if of any, importance.

It would naturally be supposed that the Abolitionists, pure and simple, were the proper parties to lay out, at least in principles, the method of emancipation and affranchisement, for we include both these ideas in the kind of emancipation now under discussion, emancipation without affranchisement being a partial emancipation unworthy of the name. But for this thing the Abolitionists are not prepared, and it is no blame to them that they are not. Their mission was aggressive, destructive, mighty to tear down the strongholds of slavery and overwhelm its abettors with the debris of their ruined structures. That was a special mission, requiring its especial gifts of reckless daring and fiery energy such as has illustrated their pathway during the last generation of men. A very different mission, requiring also peculiar gifts, gifts of construction, tempered with calm thought, and sweetened with a deep love of all mankind, and a profound faith in humanity, is required to consummate emancipation at the South. It was, doubtless, a profound view of these truths which led J. M. McKim of Philadelphia to offer his resignation of office in the Abolition organization—his work as such *was done*. President Lincoln would seem to hold the same views, in appointing distinguished humanitarians rather than distinguished Abolitionists to form a commission to report well-known facts in regard to modern emancipation.

If it be true then that emancipation is perilled for the want of settled principles and adequate organizations to bring it about, this peril may be easily overcome. Organizations should be immediately formed, and the principles widely and continuously published to enlighten and convince the public mind. The duty of such organizations falls especially upon the free blacks (so called) of the free States; they know more on these subjects than all the world besides. To show how little the ablest and most philanthropic white men know on this matter, we need only quote the reiterated opinion of Horace Greeley, that "by enlisting in the army *now*, black men can save their race in this country, and the opportunity is rapidly passing away," etc., etc. Why, dear old *Tribune*! we enlisted freely, fought determinedly, not to say heroically, in '76 and '12, and you gave us chains and slavery, fugitive slave laws, and would have dehumanized us entirely if God had let you! There are our Irish brethren, have they not crimsoned every British battlefield with their blood, and have they not for their reward the scornful slur they "are aliens in blood, aliens in religion?" Nay, further, did not New York and Connecticut and Pennsylvania and Virginia and North Carolina grant citizenship to the extent of voting at the polls to black men for their soldierly deeds in the Revolutionary war, and then gradually took back the well-earned right? And why? Because of the second great peril in the way of emancipation today; to wit:

Gradual Emancipation. It cannot be expected that the condition which shall be fixed on the freedmen in the rebel States will be in advance of the general public sentiment of the land. And the highest point which such sentiment has attained is to grant gradual emancipation; by gradual emancipation, we do not mean the farcical programme recently gone through with in Missouri; we mean the process which the blacks have been undergoing in the so-called free States for the last fifty years. Until this war's necessities knocked the last vestige of prejudice—the military caste—from the usages of old Massachusetts, God bless her! there was not a free black man in all these United States. With the name, and some of the privileges of freemen, we have been, and are still undergoing, the oscillating process of gradual emancipation—today decked with laurels for the well-won victory, and tomorrow, hung at the lamppost because we are not white. Today we are "citizens of the United States," with Secretary [of State William H.] Seward who needs us to conquer back the South—tomorrow, when Jeff. Davis *et genus omne* accept Mr. Seward's cordial invitation to return to their vacant seats in Congress, what will we be, with that serene, bland, euphuistic Secretary Seward? Let us hear what a foreign black gentleman says of this gradual emancipation, as partially experienced by him in the noble State of New York ten years ago:

> You perhaps have read the narratives of African (African American) sufferings, but painfully intense as they are, they are only the outside—they are only the visible. There are a thousand little evils which can never be expressed. There is a sorrow of the heart, with which the stranger cannot intermeddle. There are secret agonies known only to God, which are far more acute than any external tortures. Oh! it is not the smiting of the back, until the earth is crimsoned with streams of blood; it is not the amputation of the limbs; it is not even the killing of the body; it is not these that are the keenest sufferings that a people can undergo. Oh! no; these affect only the outward man, and may leave untouched the majestic mind. But those inflictions which tend to contract and destroy the mind, those cruelties which benumb the sensibilities of the soul, these influences which chill and arrest the currency of the heart's affections—these are the awful instruments of suffering and degradation, and these have been made to operate upon the Afric-American.—*Rev. Edward Blyden in "Africa's Offering."*

Now we affirm that the highest grade of emancipation which the public mind assigns to the slaves in the rebel States, is this gradual emancipation, such as they see *enjoyed* by the free black of the free States, and which they think quite good enough for the colored man. Is there a man among us who is not shocked at the possibility of our brethren being obliged to pass through this process of gradual emancipation? this mockery of freedom? How then is this great peril of gradual emancipation to be overcome? By forming organizations and spreading the doctrines of IMMEDIATE EMANCIPATION with affranchisement. We who know and have felt the pain, the penalties, the soul-cutting degradations of gradual emancipation; we who have for years yearned for and struggled for the rights and privileges of free citizens, are of all men the first called upon to form these organizations and to preach these doctrines. It is here that we can serve our people and save our country; here that the Lord has mercifully appointed us to labor; here that we can labor with the greatest hope of success. Immediate emancipation is the New Evangel which alone can save our land and its glorious institutions; one period, one lustrum of our national history has gone down in darkness and fire and blood; if we would give a different and more glorious character to the new period on which we are about entering, then we must save the nation from the curse of gradual emancipation, or any other experiment for the indefinite perpetuation of slavery. "All free, or all slave," said Abraham Lincoln. Free now, liberty now, liberty henceforth, liberty forever! Could there be, will there be in all time a more glorious cause to struggle for? Would that we could convey to others a portion of what we feel on this subject; would that we could touch the hearts and the lips of our young men with the holy flame which this theme inspires, for this is our work, brethren! There is no use in our standing by marvelling at the doings of Providence, rejoicing over the noble sayings of our noble President, or expecting that emancipation is coming somehow or other— Providence has done all it can do, Abraham Lincoln has done much more than we ever dreamed he would do—it is our turn now to wheel into the ranks and shout the glad chorus of Immediate and Universal Emancipation!

Weekly Anglo-African (New York, N. Y.), 26 September 1863; *BAP*, 5 : 256–59.

8 7   CAPITAL VERSUS LABOR

James McCune Smith explained in this perceptive essay how land and labor policies could keep African Americans in bondage. Smith employed contemporary socialist critiques of capitalism to show that emancipation would be successful only if the government assured blacks of land ownership and fair conditions for labor.

Mr. Editor:

We have endeavored to show that there is neither in the political, nor religious, nor philanthropic worlds of the American people, any agency at work which can compass the entire abolishment of slavery. In spite of such proof, there are many who will persist in prophesying the certain downfall of slavery, as an outgrowth of this war. The reasons for this belief are too numerous to be examined in detail. They may be classified under two general statements: 1st. The Providence of God. 2d. The destruction of slavery by the removal of its support—by a sort of natural death.

In regard to the first ground of belief, we have nothing to say, for we believe that the age of "miracles is past." And, we fail to see in the history or character of the American people any special attraction for a special providence.

Hence we confine our examination to those influences, which, as an outgrowth of this war, will tend to abolish or maintain slavery. We have failed, in a former article, to discover any adequate force for the abolishment of slavery. In confirmation of this view, we call attention to a letter copied into another column from the Norfolk, Va., correspondent of the *Independent*.

The main support of slavery before the war, a support which will be strengthened rather than weakened at the end of the war, is that it is a condition of society in which *"capital owns labor."* The thousands of colossal fortunes which this war has already created will find no better investment than buying up the lands of the rebel States. And, owning the land, the ownership of labor also will speedily accrue to them. What defence can the landless, penniless, outlawed *emancipado* make against the land-monopolizing, monied, lawmaking capitalist—who says to him, work for this pittance or get you gone and starve! In free society, there is a perpetual conflict between labor and capital; the more nearly they are balanced, the more free the state of society, but when either gets the upper hand there is more or less of slave society introduced. Generally, capital is predominant, because capital can wait, while labor cannot. It is only in the instance where labor is scarce, and society exigent, that labor is in the ascendant—as today, in the north.

* * * In slave society, there is *no conflict* between capital and labor; labor lies prostrate, and capital dictates its own terms, which are perpetual subjugation; in other words, perpetual slavery. So far from this war diminishing the wish or the power of capital to own labor, it will increase both. Colossal monopolies are parceling out even the free States for their ownership. The slave in the South will have namesakes in fact, if not in title, North of Mason and Dixon's line. Capital invested in a single article, alcohol, actually bought up a working majority of last Congress; how much more easily could it subsidize any of the one-horse legislatures of a reconstructed rebel State, so as to make things right about the freedmen. The word *slavery* will, of course, be wiped from the statute book—by the bye, slavery is a *legal* institution in none of the slave States, being nowhere ordained by statute—but the "ancient relation" can be just as well maintained by cunningly devised laws. In fact, the word "slave" was already dying out of the Southern vocabulary; it was "my servant" and "my people."

The special manner in which capital will seize upon and own labor in the reconstructed States requires no foretelling. The white man, owning the land, the capital and the lawmaking, already owns labor. In deference to the world's opinion, capital may for a few years, after the war ends, deck its victim with the garlands of freedom—only to make the sacrifice more complete in the end. We need not even wait until the end of the war to see things drifting in this direction. * * *

On the coast of South Carolina, after a year of experimenting on the willingness of the freedmen to work and their ability to support themselves, a plan was begun of cutting up the large estates into twenty and forty acre plots, to be sold to the freedmen at government prices for government lands, and government terms of payment. This plan was eminently fair and just; it was also a radical abolishment of slavery. It made the freedman owner of his own labor, and also an owner of a fair share of the land. It promised success also; for at the first sale of these lands, the freedmen came up promptly and bought largely, showing the thrift and shrewdness of men worthy of citizenship. Capital, however, took the alarm. Capital went to Washington; capital hocus-pocuss'd and bought up the rest of the land, or at least placed it beyond the reach of the freedmen.

In 1860 we fell in with a youth about twenty years old, five feet four in height, of great energy of character, who was clerking it in one of our large wholesale houses, at eight hundred or a thousand dollars a year. In 1862, we heard of him as married, and putting up at the ——— Hotel (the most expensive in the city). "How so?" said we to a mutual acquaintance. "Cotton," was the reply. In the Spring of this year, we again fell in with our acquaintance of 1860. He had just returned from New Orleans, near which he had hired one or more plantations of a thousand acres, also about eight hundred and fifty freedmen, whom he paid eight dollars a month; and they were so fond of him, it was really painful for him to tear himself away. He had been always a violent hater of Abolitionists, but now they might set him down as a thoroughgoing Abolitionist; and he expected to clear about a million and a half dollars by his first year's operation. Wasn't he a first-rate Abolitionist?

And so capital, aided by the government (which is, in wartime, the minion of capital), pursues its ownership of labor, and whatever the condition of the freedman today under the biting necessities of war, that condition will not be bettered after peace; under the harrow, a nation is nearest to doing justice by its own downtrodden. It is no reply to these statements that government has recently raised the wages of all able-bodied freedmen to eighteen dollars a month. An able-bodied freedman on a cotton plantation today earns four thousand dollars per year when government raises his wages to $216 a year, add for his support another hundred, and there is a fair profit to capital of one hundred and eighty four dollars. And government will aid capital to cheat the freedman out of three thousand five hundred dollars per year!

It may be objected to all this that free labor will go down South, in the shape of emigrants from abroad or disbanded soldiers from our armies. Capital will outstrip the first in getting possession of the most fertile lands. As to our soldiers, how many able-bodied men will be left of them when this "cruel war" is over? "Our losses were only four thousand," is the weekly, and our "losses are small, only a thousand," the daily report of the newspapers. A thousand! one-fourth killed, one-fourth maimed for life, and one-fourth taken to Libby Prison or Belle Isle to be starved to death. How many soldiers will we have left from a war which costs us a thousand men per diem?

For these reasons, we do not see that American slavery will go out of existence as an issue or result of the present war.

s.

Weekly Anglo-African (New York, N.Y.), 27 August 1864; *BAP*, 5:299–302.

88 A BRIEF REVIEW

Philip Bell denounced Presidential Reconstruction as a failure and criticized Andrew Johnson for ignoring the calls for black suffrage while liberally "but injudicious[ly] pardoning" former Confederates.

The telegraph works spasmodically. Considerable news has come over the wires lately, but not much of general import. We give a brief abstract under the proper head.

The war does not appear to us to be ended, nor rebellion suppressed. They have commenced reconstruction on disloyal principles. If rebel soldiers are allowed to mumble through oaths of allegiance, and vote [Robert E.] Lee's officers into important offices, and if Legislatures, elected by such voters, are allowed to define the provisions of the Amnesty Proclamation, then were our conquests vain, and we may soon expect the reestablishment of slavery in its most hideous forms, to be followed by the worst of all wars—a servile insurrection—preceded, perhaps, by another rebellion—but not of the South this time; the North will rise and demand their rights as conquerors—the right of submitting terms to the conquered. Instead of pursuing a system of "liberal, but judicious hanging," as recommended by General Scott, the Government appears to have adopted a system of liberal but injudicious pardoning. Already we see the fruits of this failure on the part of Government to mete out full justice to the loyal blacks, and retribution to disloyal whites.

During the whole four long years of the war, we heard of no insurrection among the slaves; they escaped when they could to the Union ranks, often to be repulsed and driven back, but those anticipated horrors of slave rising, murdering, ravaging, pillaging, destroying plantations, and the "barbarities of St. Domingo," were never realized. The slaves waited long and patiently; they believed in the mercy of God and the justice of "Massa Linkum." Ours is a race proverbial for their faith, and the day at last came when they supposed their faith was to receive its reward and its full fruition. What is now the result? They are declared free, but they are turned over to the tender mercies of their former oppressors, full of hatred and rebellion as ever, and burning for revenge on somebody. Can we wonder at the daily accounts received of "Troubles with the negroes," "Mutiny among the black soldiers," and the like?

Everywhere throughout the country, men of true Union principles declare in favor of granting blacks the elective franchise. Gen. Banks, who of late has not appeared to be overburdened with negro sympathy, but who has witnessed in his own State of Massachusetts the salutary effects of negro suffrage, in a Fourth of July oration in New Orleans, asserted "the justice, right and necessity of conferring the elective franchise on the colored people of the South."

The rebels and traitors of the Southern States are doubtless willing negro suffrage should prevail at the North, but they wish to govern their own institutions. Just so here; doe-faced Northern political hybrids, semi-Union men, say there is no necessity of giving the blacks the elective franchise here, *we* (they) can do without their votes. The *Morning Call* is playing this tune on its one-stringed fiddle, and it makes most abominable discord, which it mistakes for harmony. We tell them the Union wants Union voters everywhere. "Liberty and Union" can never become "one and inseparable" until every Union vote is polled, and every traitor disfranchised. Then, and not till then, will the glorious old flag wave in triumph over a free land and a free people.

> Where'er a wind is blowing,
> Where'er a wave is flowing,

the banner of the Republic will be recognized as emblematic of Loyalty and Freedom.

Elevator (San Francisco, Calif.), 28 July 1865; *BAP*, 5:357–58.

89 THE PROSPECT SEEMS GLOOMY

No one better understood the consequences of Presidential Recon-
struction than the freedmen. Samuel Childress, a former slave from
Nashville, Tennessee, provided a discouraging assessment of federal
policies and gave voice to the lingering bitterness of a people betrayed.

Nashville, Tenn[essee]
Nov[ember] 29, 1865

Mr. Editor:

You desire to know our opinions respecting the policy of the President concerning the colored race. We are not acquainted with the whole of
it—we do not feel confident to advise the President, nevertheless we cannot
avoid having impressions of some sort respecting some things which have
been done, and some things which have been left undone. To us the prospect seems gloomy. We have no permanent homes, and we see no prospect
of getting any.

Most of us are accustomed to farm labor, and whatever skill we possess
is chiefly in that direction. Land is dear, and few of us are able to buy it.
We can hire out to our former masters, it may be said. It is true that we can
do so to a considerable extent; but it is well known that the temper of our
former masters has not greatly improved toward us.

Is it the intention of the Government to drive us to our worst enemies to
ask for work, and that too upon the very soil which has been forfeited by
the treason of the pretended owner? Our race has tilled this land for ages;
whatever wealth has been accumulated South has been acquired mainly by
our labor. The profits of it have gone to increase the pride and wickedness
of our old masters, while we have been left in ignorance and degradation;
all this oppression and wrong were committed under the United States Government, which stood ready with loaded guns and fixed bayonets to strike
us down if we resisted our masters.

The small oppressor was the State; the great oppressor was the United
States. When the nation conquered the rebels, the property of the latter was
forfeited to the Government. Accordingly Gen. Sherman says! "Soldiers,
when we marched through, and conquered the country of these rebels we

became owners of all they had, and I don't want you to be troubled in your consciences for taking, while on our great march, the property of conquered rebels. They forfeited their right to it, and I being agent for the Government to which it belonged, gave you authority to keep all the Quarter-masters couldn't take possession of, or didn't want."

It cannot be denied that the colored race earned nearly all this property. The United States, as High Sheriff of the Court of Heaven, held it in its hand, and could do with it what it pleased. Justice required that it should be paid over to the colored race who had been robbed of it. But what did it do with it? Let the Proclamations and pardons of the Government answer. It has gone back again to the very men whose hands are dripping with the blood of murdered prisoners, and whose cruelties cry to heaven for vengeance.

It would seem that it was regarded as a greater crime to be black than to be a rebel. If this is the ethics which is to prevail, then we have more judgments in store for the nation.

We think the Government ought in justice to the race to provide for their obtaining farms at such prices, and on such terms as would enable our people in a reasonable time to have a home of their own, on which they might hope to earn a living, and educate their children. Yours truly,

SAMUEL CHILDRESS

Weekly Anglo-African (New York, N.Y.), 29 November 1865; *BAP*, 5:404–5.

GLOSSARY

Adams, John Quincy (1767–1848), sixth president of the United States, also served in the U.S. Congress from 1831 to 1848, where he became an outspoken critic of slavery. Adams's work in defense of the mutineers on the slave ship *Amistad* helped advance the antislavery cause.

Allen, William G. (1820–?), a free black educator and author, taught at Central College in McGrawville, New York, from 1850 to 1852, after which he continued his antislavery activities and teaching career in the British Isles.

American and Foreign Anti-Slavery Society (AFASS) was founded in May 1840 by disaffected members of the American Anti-Slavery Society who repudiated the broad radical program of Garrison and his allies. Although several black leaders joined the new organization, most abandoned it by the mid-1850s.

American Anti-Slavery Society (AASS) was founded in 1833 by a coalition of black and white abolitionists and soon became the center of radical antislavery sentiment in the North. It had auxiliaries in virtually every northern state; its publications, especially the *National Anti-Slavery Standard*, reflected the society's commitment to immediate emancipation and radical reform. The split in 1840 solidified Garrisonian control of the organization, but it divided again in 1865 over what role abolitionists should play in Reconstruction.

American Colonization Society (ACS) was founded to promote the settlement of free black Americans in Africa. From its beginning in 1816 until the early 1830s, the society, a mix of northern philanthropists, clergymen, prominent national politicians, and southern slaveholders, presented itself as a benevolent reform organization that would uplift blacks, Christianize Africa, and eventually end slavery. Northern black leaders opposed the movement, denouncing it as a threat to their liberty and a bulwark of slavery.

American Home Missionary Society (AHMS) was organized in 1826 by northern Presbyterian and Congregational leaders to assist poor churches. Its reluctance to condemn slavery alienated its abolitionist members who withdrew to establish the American Missionary Association.

American Moral Reform Society (AMRS) was organized at the 1835 black national convention and established auxiliaries in several northern states. Its commitment to education, temperance, personal virtue, and economic uplift reflected blacks' early commitment to white reform principles. The organization promoted abolitionism but never developed a specific antislavery program. Its demise in 1841 reflected the growing militancy among blacks.

Amistad, a Spanish slave ship bound for Cuba in 1839, was commandeered by its cargo of captured Africans in a bloody revolt led by Joseph Cinqué. The vessel was later seized by the U.S. Navy, and the trial of the mutineers became an international diplomatic incident. They were freed by the U.S. Supreme Court in 1841 and returned to West Africa through abolitionist efforts.

Anglo-African Magazine (New York, N.Y.), a monthly literary journal, was published by Thomas Hamilton from January to December 1859. Hamilton's magazine featured a variety of works by noted black writers, including poetry, fiction, and essays on science, current events, and black culture.

Antislavery fairs were organized by women across the North and in Britain as an annual fund-raising event from the 1830s through the 1860s. Women abolitionists sold a variety of items and provided refreshments and entertainment at these social events. The money raised helped support antislavery lecturers and the reform press.

Appeal . . . to the Coloured Citizens of the World (1830), an antislavery and anticolonization tract written by David Walker, was one of the earliest expressions of black militancy and separatism. In the *Appeal*, Walker called on blacks to resist white oppression and take control of their own destiny.

Atlee, Edwin P. (1799–1836), a Quaker abolitionist, was secretary of the Pennsylvania Abolition Society during the 1820s and helped found the American Anti-Slavery Society in 1833. Philadelphia blacks considered him a great friend.

Bell, Philip A. (1808–1889), a pioneer in African American journalism, coedited the *Colored American* in New York City from 1837 to 1839. He moved to San Francisco in the 1850s, where he edited the *Pacific Appeal* during the Civil War and founded the *Elevator* in 1865.

Bibb, Henry (1815–1854), a Kentucky fugitive slave, was active in the Liberty party in Michigan during the 1840s. He published his slave narrative in 1849, founded the *Voice of the Fugitive* in 1851 in Windsor, Ontario, and helped organize the Refugee Home Society to assist fugitive slaves in Canada.

Black laws were a matrix of state legislation that denied blacks equal civil and political rights in the antebellum North. Among the more oppressive laws were those that denied blacks the right to vote, hold public office, testify in court, and attend white schools.

Black Republican (New Orleans, La.), published by Dr. S. W. Rogers from April to August 1865, focused on Reconstruction issues from a moderate freedman's perspective.

Brown, Henry "Box" (ca. 1815–?), escaped from Virginia slavery by having himself crated and shipped to Philadelphia. He published his narrative and toured England with an antislavery panorama in the early 1850s.

Brown, John (1800–1859), loathed the institution of slavery and committed himself to its violent overthrow. He led free-state guerrilla forces in Kansas during the late 1850s and sought the cooperation of northern blacks for his plan to incite a slave rebellion at Harpers Ferry, Virginia, in October 1859. The raid failed but contributed to the coming of the Civil War and the demise of slavery.

Brown, William Wells (ca. 1814–1884), a Kentucky fugitive slave, was a prominent black author, historian, and antislavery lecturer. He worked with the underground railroad in New York in the 1840s and lectured in England in the early 1850s. His publications include a narrative (1847); the first African American novel, *Clotel* (1852); *St. Domingo* (1855); *The Rising Son* (1874); and *My Southern Home* (1880).

Buchanan, James (1791–1868), fifteenth president of the United States, was a fiercely partisan Democrat whose acquiescence to proslavery interests greatly contributed to sectional tensions.

Buxton, a village in Ontario, was the site of the Elgin settlement, a model black agricultural community founded in 1849 by philanthropist William King.

Cary, Mary Ann Shadd (1823–1893), an outspoken journalist, educator, and women's rights advocate, left her Delaware home for Canada West in the early 1850s. She cofounded the *Provincial Freeman* in 1853, thereby becoming the first black woman editor in North America. Cary recruited black soldiers for the Union army during the Civil War and later earned a law degree from Howard University.

Clarke, Lewis G. (1815–1897), and *Milton Clarke*, Kentucky fugitive slaves, published their narrative in 1846 and were involved in antislavery activities in New England, Ohio, and Canada in the 1850s.

Colonization, a movement whose advocates believed that whites and blacks could not live together on terms of equality in the United States, attempted to settle free blacks and manumitted slaves in Liberia.

Colored American (New York, N.Y.), the longest-running, most influential black newspaper of the 1830s, was founded by Philip A. Bell in January 1837 as the *Weekly Advocate*. Samuel E. Cornish renamed it the *Colored American* when he assumed the editorship two months later. After several managerial changes, Charles B. Ray took control of the paper in 1839 and published it through 1841.

Contrabands were slaves who fled to Union lines during the Civil War. Defined as "contraband of war" by the federal government, they were confiscated from their southern masters as a way to deprive the Confederacy of its labor supply.

Cornish, Samuel E. (1796–1858), a Presbyterian clergyman, teacher, and founder of African American journalism, organized the First Colored (Shiloh) Presbyterian Church in New York City in the early 1820s. He coedited the first black newspaper, *Freedom's Journal*, published the *Rights of All* and the *Colored American* in the 1830s, and helped organize the American and Foreign Anti-Slavery Society in 1840 and the Union Missionary Society in 1841.

Craft, Ellen (1826–1890), and *William Craft* (1824–1900) were Georgia slaves whose daring escape to freedom in 1848 brought them international attention. During their nineteen years in England, they lectured on slavery, promoted the free produce movement, and published their narrative, *Running a Thousand Miles for Freedom* (1860).

Creole, an American brig, was commandeered by slaves who were being transported from Virginia to Louisiana in 1841. The slaves were later freed by British authorities in the Bahamas, straining relations between the two nations for more than a decade.

Davis, Jefferson (1808–1889), president of the Confederacy, also previously served in both houses of the U.S. Congress and as secretary of war.

Delany, Martin R. (1812–1885), a physician, editor, and author, founded the Pittsburgh *Mystery* in 1843 and coedited Frederick Douglass's *North Star*. His treatise, *The Condition, Elevation, Emigration and Destiny of the Colored People of the United States* (1852), was a landmark in black nationalist and emigrationist thought. He led the Niger Valley Exploring Party to West Africa in 1859, served as a major in the Union army during the Civil War, and afterward worked with the Freedmen's Bureau in South Carolina.

Douglas, H. Ford (1831–1865), a Virginia fugitive slave, was active in the black emigration movement in the 1850s and coedited the *Provincial Freeman* in Canada West. His light skin enabled him to enlist in a white Union regiment, the Illinois Ninety-fifth, in July 1862. The following year, he received an officer's commission and organized the Kansas Independent Colored Battery.

Douglass, Frederick (1817–1895), the most renowned and influential black leader of his time, escaped from slavery in Maryland in 1838. He lectured for the Massachusetts Anti-Slavery Society, published the first of three autobiographies in 1845, and founded the *North Star* (later renamed *Frederick Douglass' Paper*) in 1847. His intellect, compelling oratory, and personal charisma brought him international prominence. After the Civil War, he was active in Republican party politics and served as consul general to Haiti.

Dred Scott *v.* Sanford was a decision of the U.S. Supreme Court in 1857 that limited the authority of a free state to exclude slavery within its borders and allowed the spread of the institution into the territories. Writing for a majority of the justices, Chief Justice Roger B. Taney also denied black claims to American citizenship.

Emigration was a movement supported by many prominent African Americans that called for black resettlement outside of the United States. A variety of emigration programs promoted black settlement in Canada, West Africa, Central America, and the Caribbean, especially in the 1850s.

Faneuil Hall, a meeting place in Boston, became a symbol of liberty as the site of reform gatherings.

Fillmore, Millard (1800–1874), thirteenth president of the United States, earned the enmity of the antislavery community for signing the Compromise of 1850 that included the Fugitive Slave Law. In 1856, he ran as the American or Know Nothing party's presidential candidate.

Forten, James E. (1766–1842), a revolutionary war veteran and wealthy Philadelphia businessman, provided crucial financial support for William Lloyd Garrison's *Liberator* and served on the board of managers of the American Anti-Slavery Society in the 1830s. His *Letters From a Man of Color* (1813) was one of the earliest published protests against proscriptive black laws.

Forten, Sarah L. (1814–?), the youngest daughter of James E. and Charlotte Forten, was a founding member of the Philadelphia Female Anti-Slavery Society and helped organize antislavery fairs and other fund-raising benefits for Philadelphia's black community.

Fox, George (1624–1691), founded the Society of Friends, popularly known as Quakers.

Frederick Douglass' Paper (Rochester, N.Y.) was founded as the *North Star* in December 1847 and renamed by Frederick Douglass after a merger with John Thomas's *Liberty Party Paper* (Syracuse, N.Y.) in June 1851. Douglass's paper, published until July 1860, circulated widely among reformers in the United States and Britain.

Freedom's Journal (New York, N.Y.), the first African American newspaper, was founded in March 1827 by Samuel E. Cornish and John B. Russwurm. The newspaper became a forceful voice for anticolonization when Cornish assumed complete control in 1828 until its demise in March 1829.

Free Soil party was founded in August 1848 by a coalition of antislavery Whigs, radical Democrats, and abolitionists. Although abolitionists hoped the party would adopt their principles, it failed to venture beyond opposition to the extension of slavery.

French Revolution of 1848 ended monarchical rule in France and established a republican government based on universal manhood suffrage.

Fugitive Slave Law of 1850 was enacted by Congress to assist southern slave owners in the capture and return of fugitive slaves. The law created a body of federal officials to issue warrants and decide claims against blacks accused of being fugitives. Enforcement of the law threatened the freedom of free blacks as well as escaped slaves and deepened sectional divisions over the issue of slavery.

Garnet, Henry Highland (1815–1882), a Presbyterian minister, established his reputation as a militant abolitionist with his call for slave violence at the 1843 black national convention. In the 1850s, he promoted the free produce movement in England, carried out mission work in Jamaica, and served as pastor of the Shiloh Presbyterian Church in New York City. He founded the African Civilization Society in 1858 to encourage missions and black settlement in Africa. After the Civil War, he served as president of Avery College in Pittsburgh and later was appointed U.S. minister to Liberia.

Garnet, Julia Ward (1811–1870), married to Henry Highland Garnet, was a teacher and businesswoman, active in antislavery fairs, the free produce movement, and freedmen's education.

Garrison, William Lloyd (1805–1879), founded the radical antislavery movement and edited the *Liberator*, the most important reform newspaper of the Civil War era. His comprehensive approach to social reform, which encompassed a call for the immediate end of slavery, nonresistance, women's rights, and racial equality, split the antislavery community in 1840. Northern blacks respected his contribution to African American freedom but rejected his strategy that ignored the broader interests of blacks.

Gradual abolition was the antislavery philosophy prevalent among reformers prior to the 1830s. Gradualists believed that human progress, the advancement of Christian ideals, and enlightened government policies would result in the slow but inevitable demise of slavery.

Greeley, Horace (1811–1872), established and edited the *New York Tribune*, one of the country's most influential papers. He advocated a variety of reforms and opposed slavery.

Hamilton, Thomas (1823–1865), and *Robert Hamilton* (1819?–), sons of the noted New York City abolitionist William G. Hamilton, contributed substantially to the development of the antebellum black press. Thomas Hamilton worked with several reform newspapers before establishing his own weekly, the *People's Press*, in 1841. Robert Hamilton, a music teacher and political abolitionist, collaborated with his brother. In 1859 Thomas Hamilton founded the most influential black newspaper of its time, the *Weekly Anglo-African*, and also published a literary periodical, the *Anglo-African Magazine*.

Hamlin, Hannibal (1809–1891), Abraham Lincoln's first vice-president, also previously represented Maine in both houses of Congress and after the Civil War served as U.S. minister to Spain.

Harper, Frances Ellen Watkins (1825–1911), a Maryland free black, was one of the leading African American poets of the nineteenth century. She lectured on antislavery, temperance, and education. Her publications include *Poems on Miscellaneous Subjects* (1854) and *Iola Leroy* (1892), a novel.

Harpers Ferry, Virginia, was the site of a raid in 1859 by abolitionist John Brown and a twenty-one-man force that attacked the federal armory, hoping to incite a slave insurrection. When the effort failed, Brown and many of his companions were tried and hanged. The incident pushed the North and South toward violent confrontation over slavery.

Holly, James T. (1829–1911), an Episcopalian clergyman, was the leading black advocate of Haitian immigration. He coedited the *Voice of the Fugitive* with Henry Bibb and participated in the black emigration conventions in the 1850s. He promoted Haitian immigration in *Vindication of the Capacity of the Negro Race* (1857) and other essays and established a settlement and mission in Haiti in the early 1860s.

Immediate abolition was adopted by Anglo-American abolitionists beginning in the 1820s after they rejected gradual approaches to ending slavery. Immediatists denounced black bondage as a sin and proclaimed that it must be immediately abandoned without compensation to slave owners.

Impartial Citizen (Syracuse, N. Y.), a bimonthly antislavery and reform newspaper, was founded in February 1849 as the result of a merger between Samuel Ringgold Ward's *True American* (Cortland, N. Y.) and Stephen A. Myers's *Northern Star and Freeman's Advocate* (Albany, N. Y.). Ward made the *Impartial Citizen* a Liberty party organ in the summer of 1849 and published it until the fall of 1850.

Jim Crow is a term used to indicate discrimination based on race (for example, Jim Crow laws).

Johnson, Andrew (1808–1875), Lincoln's second vice-president, became the seventeenth president of the United States upon Lincoln's death. His desire to restore white rule in the South and his obstruction of congressional Reconstruction led to his impeachment.

Jones, Thomas H. (1806–?), a North Carolina fugitive slave, escaped in 1849 and worked as an itinerant preacher and antislavery lecturer in New England until the threat of reenslavement by the Fugitive Slave Law forced him to take temporary refuge in Canada. He published his narrative, *The Experience of Tom Jones*, in 1854.

Kansas-Nebraska Act was enacted by Congress in 1854 to organize the vast new territories of Kansas and Nebraska. It included a provision for "popular sovereignty," which permitted the question of slavery to be determined by the inhabitants of the territories. The act angered many in the North who felt it was a proslavery tactic and prompted the formation of the Republican party.

Kidnapping of fugitive slaves and free blacks was common during the antebellum period. Thousands were seized clandestinely in the North and sold into slavery in the South.

Liberator (Boston, Mass.), the premier American antislavery weekly, was founded by William Lloyd Garrison in January 1831. Garrison published the *Liberator* until December 1865 as an uncompromising voice for immediate emancipation, anticolonization, disunionism, nonresistance, and women's rights.

Liberty party, founded in 1839, was the nation's first antislavery political party. The Liberty party's commitment to racial equality and its willingness to promote African Americans for office attracted many black leaders. But the party never developed much strength beyond enclaves in New York and Massachusetts and dissolved during the 1850s.

Locofocos, the radical wing of the northern Democratic party, opposed banks, corporations, monopolies, tariffs, usury laws, and imprisonment for debt. Although hostile to slavery, Locofocos were not active abolitionists.

Loguen, Jermain Wesley (1813–1872), a Tennessee fugitive slave, was an African Methodist Episcopal Zion clergyman, a noted antislavery lecturer, and an underground railroad manager in Syracuse, New York. He participated in the fugitive slave rescue of William "Jerry" McHenry in 1851, published his autobiography, *The Rev. J. W. Loguen, As a Slave and As a Freeman* (1859), and during Reconstruction carried out AMEZ mission work in the South.

McKim, James Miller (1810–1874), was corresponding secretary for the Pennsylvania Anti-Slavery Society for twenty-five years. During the 1860s he worked for several freedmen's aid societies. After the Civil War, he supported black suffrage and helped to abolish Philadelphia's segregated transportation system.

Maine Liquor Law was passed by the state legislature in 1851. It prohibited the sale and manufacture of alcoholic beverages except for medical or industrial use. Twelve other northern states enacted similar legislation within four years.

Martin, J. Sella (1832–1876), a Presbyterian clergyman, escaped from slavery in 1856 while working on the Mississippi River and served as pastor for several congregations in New York and Massachusetts. Regarded as a dynamic orator, he carried out several lecture tours in England in the 1860s to promote the Union cause and freedmen's aid. After the war, he coedited the *New National Era* with Frederick Douglass.

Mason-Dixon line was the popular name given to the boundary dividing the slave and free states.

Massachusetts Fifty-fourth Regiment, one of the first northern black regiments to serve in the Civil War, was organized during the early months of 1863. Blacks endowed it with tremendous symbolism, believing that its valiant conduct would sustain their right to citizenship and full civil rights. Its heroic assault on Fort Wagner, South Carolina, on 18 July 1863 helped diminish northern opposition to accepting blacks in the army.

Mexican War, fought between 1846 and 1848, settled a protracted dispute between the United States and Mexico for control of the American Southwest. By the Treaty of Guadalupe Hidalgo, which ended the conflict, Mexico ceded its northern provinces of California and New Mexico to the United States, prompting a long struggle between antislavery and proslavery forces over the expansion of slavery into these new western territories.

Moral reform, a social philosophy adopted by most black abolitionists of the 1830s, promoted mutual aid, hard work, thrift, learning, piety, and sobriety as the keys to advancement. Moral reformers believed that white bigotry stemmed from the condition of blacks and argued that as blacks improved their social, intellectual, and economic situation, racism would gradually disappear.

Moral suasion relied upon appeals to individual conscience to end a broad spectrum of social evils, including war, intemperance, and slavery. Reformers believed that the pulpit, the press, and the power of persuasion were sufficient to transform society.

Myers, Stephen A. (1800–?), an Albany, New York, journalist and temperance advocate, founded his first newspaper, the *Northern Star and Freeman's Advocate,* in 1842. He lobbied state legislators on black issues, operated a temperance hotel, and supervised activities of the local vigilance committee and underground railroad.

National Anti-Slavery Standard (New York, N.Y.), the official organ of the American Anti-Slavery Society, began publication in June 1840. The Garrisonian weekly continued until 1871 under several editors, including Nathaniel P. Rogers, Lydia Maria Child, David Lee Child, Sydney Howard Gay, and Oliver Johnson.

Nell, William C. (1816–1874), an antislavery lecturer and historian, was a longtime supporter of William Lloyd Garrison and the *Liberator*. He led the campaign for school integration in Boston in the 1840s and later became involved in political antislavery. His *Colored Patriots of the American Revolution* (1855) was pioneering scholarship in African American history.

Nonresistance was advanced by Garrisonian abolitionists and antebellum peace advocates. This extreme form of pacifism opposed all war and all forms of force or compulsion, including the use of self-defense and participating in electoral politics.

Northern Star and Freeman's Advocate (Albany, N.Y.) was an antislavery and temperance newspaper founded by Stephen A. Myers in 1842. The paper merged in 1849 with Samuel R. Ward's *True American* (Cortland, N.Y.) to become the *Impartial Citizen* (Syracuse, N.Y.).

Northup, Solomon, a New York free black, was kidnapped in 1841 and sold into slavery. With the aid of northern abolitionists, he eventually regained his freedom. His narrative, *Twelve Years a Slave* (1853), created a public sensation and sold twenty-seven thousand copies in its first two years.

North Star. See *Frederick Douglass' Paper.*

Pacific Appeal (San Francisco, Calif.), a weekly newspaper founded by Peter Anderson and Philip A. Bell in April 1862, served the black community in California and the western territories. After Bell left the paper to start the *Elevator* in 1865, Anderson continued to publish the *Appeal*, with the assistance of William H. Carter, until 1880.

Patrols were organized bands known as "slave patrols" or "patter rollers" that regulated slave conduct in the plantation South. Patrols watched the roads at night, detained blacks who were without passes, checked slave quarters for arms and stolen goods, and broke up unauthorized slave assemblies.

Pennington, J. W. C. (1807–1870), a Presbyterian clergyman, escaped from slavery in Maryland in 1828. He founded the Union Missionary Society in 1841, made several antislavery lecture tours in Europe, and received an honorary doctorate from the University of Heidelberg. He wrote one of the earliest African American histories, *A Textbook of the Origin and History of the Colored People* (1841), and published his narrative, *The Fugitive Blacksmith* (1850).

Pennsylvania Freeman (Philadelphia, Pa.) was first published in August 1836 as the *National Enquirer and Constitutional Advocate of Universal Liberty*.

John G. Whittier renamed it after he replaced Benjamin Lundy as editor in March 1838. The Garrisonian weekly continued until June 1854, with an interruption from December 1841 to January 1844, under several editors, including C. C. Burleigh, James Miller McKim, Mary Grew, Oliver Johnson, and Cyrus M. Burleigh.

Phillips, Wendell (1811–1884), son of a patrician Boston family, became the North's most eloquent antislavery advocate. His unwavering commitment to racial equality earned him the admiration of northern blacks.

Political abolition was a movement that attracted many abolitionists after 1840 who believed that the formation of antislavery political parties and the support of antislavery candidates for office represented far more effective means of combating slavery than simple appeals to conscience.

Purvis, Robert (1810–1898), a Philadelphia businessman and the son-in-law of James E. Forten, was one of the leading advocates of black civil rights in Pennsylvania. He helped found the American Anti-Slavery Society in 1833 and the state auxiliary society in 1837.

Quaker religious thought, which stressed the dignity and worth of humanity, propelled many members of this religious group into the forefront of the antislavery movement. Quakers joined Garrisonian antislavery societies and played a major role in the underground railroad. John Woolman and Anthony Benezet established the founding principles of Quaker abolitionism.

Ray, Charles B. (1807–1886), a New York City journalist and Congregational clergyman, was a member of the local vigilance committee and the American Anti-Slavery Society in the 1830s. As editor of the *Colored American* from 1839 to 1841, he promoted political antislavery, temperance, and antiemigration. He served as secretary of the Union Missionary Society and carried out mission work in New York City.

Remond, Charles Lenox (1810–1873), a Massachusetts antislavery lecturer, was a founding member of the American Anti-Slavery Society. He organized antislavery societies throughout New England and in 1838 was hired as a full-time lecturer for the Massachusetts Anti-Slavery Society. He addressed the World's Anti-Slavery Convention in London in 1840 and lectured throughout England.

Republican party was organized in the wake of the bitterly contested Kansas-Nebraska Act of 1854. The party drew together disparate elements of northern political life to halt the spread of slavery and end the perceived domination of southern interests over the federal government.

Its moderate antislavery stance, which opposed only the extension of slavery, repelled most abolitionists and attracted tepid black support in 1860. But wartime policies, especially emancipation, and the realities of Reconstruction politics drew an overwhelming number of northern blacks and former slaves into the party.

Roberts, Benjamin F., a Boston printer, founded two short-lived newspapers. His unsuccessful suit to integrate Boston's public schools in the 1840s set an important legal precedent for subsequent court rulings upholding racial segregation.

Seward, William H. (1801–1872), New York's most powerful Republican senator, won the respect of state blacks for his defense of their rights. But his moderate antislavery principles caused southern whites to detest him and northern abolitionists to distrust him. Seward served as both Abraham Lincoln's and Andrew Johnson's secretary of state.

Shipley, Thomas (1786–1836), was a Philadelphia lawyer and Quaker abolitionist who risked his life to protect blacks during several urban race riots. Robert Purvis eulogized him in *A Tribute to the Memory of Thomas Shipley, Philanthropist* (1836).

Smith, Gerrit (1797–1874), was perhaps the black community's greatest benefactor and one of the most ardent defenders of racial equality. A friend and patron of many blacks, Smith donated vast tracts of land to black settlers and became the leading figure in the antislavery Liberty party.

Smith, James McCune (1813–1865), a New York City physician, was involved in antislavery activities in Scotland while earning his medical degree from Glasgow University in the 1830s. An outspoken political abolitionist and antiemigrationist, he served as interim editor of *Frederick Douglass' Paper* and published essays on a variety of scientific and historical topics. His professional status, intellect, and civic leadership made him one of the most highly regarded and influential black abolitionists.

Stearns, George Luther (1809–1867), a Boston businessman and abolitionist, was named by the Lincoln administration to head its black recruitment effort for the army. Stearns directed a recruiting network throughout the North and upper South employing over twenty black agents.

Stephens, George E. (1832–1888), a Philadelphia Civil War correspondent and soldier, reported for the *Weekly Anglo-African* on the Union army campaigns in Maryland and Virginia. In 1863 he enlisted in the Massachusetts Fifty-fourth Regiment.

Stewart, Maria W. (1803–1879), a Boston lecturer and author, was active in women's antislavery organizations. In 1832 she became the first American woman to deliver a public lecture. She published her speeches and essays in 1879 as *Meditations from the Pen of Mrs. Maria W. Stewart*.

Still, William (1821–1901), Philadelphia vigilance committee director and underground railroad agent, assisted hundreds of fugitive slaves in their escape through Pennsylvania. His interviews with fugitives provided the basis for his work, *The Underground Railroad* (1872).

Tappan, Lewis (1788–1873), was a wealthy New York businessman and abolitionist who assumed a leading role in the antebellum evangelical and reform communities. Tappan helped found the black-dominated Union Missionary Society and its successor, the American Missionary Association.

Thoughts on African Colonization (1832), the most influential anticolonization publication, was written by William Lloyd Garrison based on information that he received from James E. Forten and other black abolitionists. The 238-page tract included reprints of several anticolonization protests drafted by northern blacks.

Truth, Sojourner (ca. 1797–1883), a New York fugitive slave, gained prominence in the North as an effective antislavery lecturer, evangelist, and women's rights advocate.

Tubman, Harriet (ca. 1821–1913), a Maryland fugitive slave, gained renown for her daring expeditions into the South to assist slaves in their escape. She served as a Union army guide and a nurse for contrabands during the Civil War.

Turner, Nat (1800–1831), a Virginia slave preacher, organized and led the bloodiest slave revolt in American history. Believing his mission to be divinely inspired, he and about forty slaves ravaged the Virginia countryside in August 1831, killing nearly sixty whites before the insurrection was finally crushed.

Uncle Tom's Cabin (1852), the most renowned and influential antislavery novel, was written by Harriet Beecher Stowe. Stowe's fictionalized account of slave life in the South sold 300,000 copies in the first year and helped turn northern public opinion against slavery.

Underground railroad was a loosely organized network of free blacks, Quakers, and other abolitionists who assisted fugitive slaves escaping through the North and the upper South, often on their way to Canada. The underground railroad hid runaways and supplied them with food, temporary shelter, transportation, and vital information.

Union Missionary Society (UMS) was organized in 1841 by black clergymen in response to the plight of the *Amistad* captives. During its brief existence, the UMS supported missionary work in Africa, New York City, the Hawaiian Islands, and Canada West. In 1846 it merged with other missionary societies to form the American Missionary Association.

Van Buren, Martin (1782–1862), eighth president of the United States, modernized American political parties. His political acumen, which helped the Democratic party dominate antebellum politics, also earned him a reputation as a cunning political opportunist.

Vesey, Denmark, a free black carpenter in Charleston, South Carolina, was arrested and executed for plotting a massive slave revolt in June 1822.

Vigilance committees sheltered fugitive slaves and protected free blacks from kidnappers. Most northern black communities organized these committees as local branches of the underground railroad.

Walker, David (1785–1830), a Boston clothes merchant and militant abolitionist, founded the Massachusetts General Colored Association in 1826. His *Appeal* (1829) was one the first published calls for militant resistance to white oppression.

Ward, Samuel Ringgold (1817–ca. 1866), a Congregational clergyman, temperance advocate, and journalist, was the son of Maryland fugitive slaves. He participated in Liberty party politics in the 1840s and founded several reform newspapers, including the *Impartial Citizen* and the *Provincial Freeman*. In 1851 he took part in the fugitive slave rescue of William "Jerry" McHenry in Syracuse, New York. Afterward, he traveled to Britain for an antislavery fund-raising tour and published *Autobiography of a Fugitive Negro* (1855) before settling in Jamaica.

Watkins, William J. (ca. 1826–?), a journalist and antislavery lecturer, was the son of William Watkins of Baltimore, Maryland. He participated in civil rights and political antislavery activities in Boston and New York, coedited *Frederick Douglass' Paper* in the 1850s, and worked as a recruiting agent for the Haytian Emigration Bureau in the early 1860s.

Weekly Anglo-African (New York, N.Y.), a newspaper founded by Thomas Hamilton in July 1859, promoted black culture and published reports from black communities throughout the North. George Lawrence, Jr., assumed editorial control of the paper in March 1861, renamed it the *Pine and Palm,* and made it an organ for Haitian immigration. In August, Robert Hamilton and James McCune Smith re-created the *Weekly Anglo-African* as an antiemigrationist weekly. Published through December 1865, the paper provided a militant voice for black Americans during the Civil War.

Whig party was organized in the late 1830s. The Whigs were strongest in the industrializing North and generally promoted federally sponsored internal improvements and protective tariffs. Many blacks allied with such Whigs as New York's William Henry Seward to advance their own interests and thwart the proslavery Democratic party.

Whipper, William (ca. 1804–1876), a Pennsylvania businessman, was the leading advocate of moral reform in the 1830s. He participated in the black national convention movement in the 1830s and helped found the American Moral Reform Society in 1835 to promote temperance, education, and the free produce movement.

BIBLIOGRAPHICAL ESSAY

PRIMARY SOURCES

The largest, most important collection of antebellum black documents is *The Black Abolitionist Papers, 1830–1865* (Ann Arbor, Mich., 1979), 17 microfilm reels. Selected documents from the microfilm edition appear in C. Peter Ripley et al., eds., *The Black Abolitionist Papers*, 5 vols. (Chapel Hill, N.C., 1985–92) (abbreviated throughout as *BAP*). For the Civil War and Reconstruction, see Ira Berlin et al., eds., *Freedom: A Documentary History of Emancipation, 1861–1867*, 4 vols. to date (Cambridge, Mass., 1982–). The correspondence of many black abolitionists who had ties with the American Missionary Association is on microfilm and accessible through the Amistad Research Center's helpful guide, *Author and Added Entry Catalog of the American Missionary Association*, 3 vols. (Westport, Conn., 1970). Frederick Douglass's speeches and writings appear in John W. Blassingame, ed., *The Frederick Douglass Papers*, 3 vols. to date (New Haven, Conn., 1979–), and Philip S. Foner, ed., *The Life and Writings of Frederick Douglass*, 5 vols. (New York, N.Y., 1950–75).

The pioneering African American historian Carter G. Woodson has edited two anthologies of African American documents: *Negro Orators and Their Orations* (New York, N.Y., 1925) and *The Mind of the Negro* (Washington, D.C., 1926). Other collections of African American writings include Dorothy Porter, ed., *Early Negro Writing, 1760–1837* (Boston, Mass., 1971) and *Negro Protest Pamphlets* (New York, N.Y., 1969), and Herbert Aptheker, *A Documentary History of the Negro People in the United States* (New York, N.Y., 1951). The writings and speeches of several African American women are highlighted in Dorothy Sterling, ed., *We Are Your Sisters: Black Women in the Nineteenth Century* (New York, N.Y., 1984). Recent editions of Frances Ellen Watkins Harper's works include Maryemma Graham, ed., *Complete Poems of Frances Ellen Watkins Harper* (New York, N.Y., 1988), and Frances Smith Foster, ed., *A Brighter Day Coming: A Frances Ellen Watkins Harper Reader* (New York, N.Y., 1990).

Biographical sketches and other information can be gleaned from the works of two African American abolitionists: William C. Nell, *Colored Patriots of the American Revolution* (Boston, Mass., 1855), and Martin R. Delany, *The Condition, Elevation, Emigration and Destiny of the Colored People of the United*

States (New York, N.Y., 1852). Willard B. Gatewood, Jr., ed., *Free Man of Color: The Autobiography of Willis Augustus Hodges* (Knoxville, Tenn., 1982), and Jermain Wesley Loguen, *The Rev. J. W. Loguen, As a Slave and As a Freeman* (New York, N.Y., 1859), also provide interesting firsthand observations on antebellum African American life and culture.

The black convention movement is documented in Howard H. Bell, ed., *Minutes of the Proceedings of the National Negro Conventions, 1840–1864* (New York, N.Y., 1969), and Philip S. Foner and George E. Walker, eds., *Proceedings of the Black State Conventions, 1830–1865*, 2 vols. (New York, N.Y., 1979–80).

Antebellum black newspapers and periodicals represent a major source of research material. The following are available on microfilm: *Freedom's Journal, The Rights of All, Colored American, Impartial Citizen, North Star, Frederick Douglass' Paper, Douglass' Monthly, Voice of the Fugitive, Provincial Freeman, Weekly Anglo-African, Anglo-African Magazine, Pacific Appeal,* and *Elevator.* Donald Jacobs, ed., *Antebellum Black Newspapers* (Westport, Conn., 1976), provides an extensive name and subject index for the first three newspapers cited above. Several antebellum reform newspapers on microfilm also document African American life and culture. The most valuable are the *Liberator, Pennsylvania Freeman, National Anti-Slavery Standard,* and *Pine and Palm.*

SECONDARY SOURCES

Among the biographies of black abolitionists, the most useful include Joel Schor, *Henry Highland Garnet: A Voice of Black Radicalism in the Nineteenth Century* (Westport, Conn., 1977); William Cheek and Aimee Lee Cheek, *John Mercer Langston and the Fight for Black Freedom, 1829–1865* (Urbana, Ill., 1989); William Edward Farrison, *William Wells Brown: Author and Reformer* (Chicago, Ill., 1969); Victor Ullman, *Martin R. Delany: The Beginnings of Black Nationalism* (Boston, Mass., 1971); and Wilson J. Moses, *Alexander Crummell: A Study in Civilization and Discontent* (New York, N.Y., 1989).

Two of the best biographies of Frederick Douglass are Benjamin Quarles, *Frederick Douglass* (Washington, D.C., 1948), and William F. McFeely, *Frederick Douglass* (New York, N.Y., 1990). Biographical essays on black abolitionists appear in R. J. M. Blackett, *Beating against the Barriers: Biographical Essays in Nineteenth-Century Afro-American History* (Baton Rouge, La., 1986), and David Swift, *Black Prophets of Justice: Activist Clergy before the Civil War* (Baton Rouge, La., 1989).

For additional biographical information, see Rayford W. Logan and Michael F. Winston, eds., *Dictionary of American Negro Biography* (New York, N.Y., 1982), and Edward T. James, ed., *Notable American Women, 1607–1950: A Biographical Dictionary*, 3 vols. (Cambridge, Mass., 1971).

The study of black abolitionism should begin with the two most perceptive interpretations: Jane H. Pease and William H. Pease, *They Who Would Be Free: Blacks' Search for Freedom, 1830–1861* (New York, N.Y., 1974), and Benjamin Quarles, *Black Abolitionists* (London, 1969). Robert C. Dick, *Black Protest: Issues and Tactics* (Westport, Conn., 1974), focuses on the problems of strategy and methods in the movement. Benjamin Quarles, *The Negro in the Civil War*, 2d ed. (Boston, Mass., 1969), carries black abolitionism into the Civil War years.

Studies of northern free black communities that provide the context for black abolitionism include Gary B. Nash, *Forging Freedom: The Formation of Philadelphia's Black Community, 1720–1840* (Cambridge, Mass., 1988); Julie Winch, *Philadelphia's Black Elite: Activism, Accommodation, and the Struggle for Autonomy, 1787–1848* (Philadelphia, Pa., 1988); James Oliver Horton and Lois E. Horton, *Black Bostonians: Family Life and Community Struggle in the Antebellum North* (New York, N.Y., 1979); Rhoda G. Freeman, "The Free Negro in New York City in the Era before the Civil War" (Ph.D. diss., Columbia University, 1966); David Katzman, *Before the Ghetto: Black Detroit in the Nineteenth Century* (Urbana, Ill., 1973), chapter 1; and Rudolph M. Lapp, *Blacks in Gold Rush California* (New Haven, Conn., 1977). For more generalized studies of African American life, see Leonard P. Curry, *The Free Black in Urban America, 1800–1850: The Shadow of the Dream* (Chicago, Ill., 1981), and Ira Berlin, *Slaves without Masters: The Free Negro in the Antebellum South* (New York, N.Y., 1974).

For an introduction to slave life and culture, see John W. Blassingame, ed., *Slave Testimony* (Baton Rouge, La., 1977), and Eugene D. Genovese, *Roll, Jordan, Roll: The World the Slaves Made* (New York, N.Y., 1972).

The best interpretative studies of the antislavery movement include Lawrence J. Friedman, *Gregarious Saints: Self and Community in American Abolitionism, 1830–1870* (Cambridge, Mass., 1982); James Brewer Stewart, *Holy Warriors: The Abolitionists and American Slavery* (New York, N.Y., 1976); Leonard L. Richards, *"Gentlemen of Property and Standing": Anti-Abolition Mobs in Jacksonian America* (New York, N.Y., 1970); and Russell B. Nye, *Fettered Freedom: Civil Liberties and the Slavery Controversy, 1830–1860* (East Lansing, Mich., 1949). David Brion Davis offers three landmark studies: *The Slave Power Conspiracy and the Paranoid Style* (Baton Rouge, La., 1969), *The*

Problem of Slavery in the Age of Revolution, 1770–1823 (Ithaca, N.Y., 1975), and *Slavery and Human Progress* (New York, N.Y., 1984). Robert William Fogel, *Without Consent or Contract: The Rise and Fall of American Slavery* (New York, N.Y., 1989), offers new insights and a synthesis of current literature on abolitionism.

For the antislavery movement during the Civil War, see James M. McPherson, *The Struggle for Equality: Abolitionists and the Negro in the Civil War and Reconstruction* (Princeton, N.J., 1964), and Eric Foner, *Reconstruction: America's Unfinished Revolution, 1863–1877* (New York, N.Y., 1988).

THE RISE OF BLACK ABOLITIONISM

The history of the colonization movement is told in P. J. Staudenraus, *The African Colonization Movement, 1816–1865* (New York, N.Y., 1961). Penelope Campbell, *Maryland in Africa: The Maryland State Colonization Society, 1831–1857* (Urbana, Ill., 1971), examines the most important state colonization society. For an abolitionist critique of colonization that includes various documents on African American opposition to the movement, see William Lloyd Garrison, *Thoughts on African Colonization* (Boston, Mass., 1832; reprint, New York, N.Y., 1969). *Freedom's Journal* and the *Liberator* give generous coverage to the early African American protest against colonization.

Opposition to colonization contributed greatly to the rise of black abolitionism in the 1820s. Evidence of this link can be found in David Walker, *David Walker's Appeal, in Four Articles; together with a Preamble to the Coloured Citizens of the World*, 3d ed. (Boston, Mass., 1830; reprint, New York, N.Y., 1965), and Dick, *Black Protest*, chapter 1. Reports of the early black national conventions in Bell, *National Negro Conventions*, reflect African American anxiety over colonization. For the colonization debate and the development of black abolitionism in two northern African American communities, see Winch, *Philadelphia's Black Elite*, chapter 2, and Horton and Horton, *Black Bostonians*, chapter 7.

Any study of immediate abolitionism should begin with the pamphlet that inspired the movement, Elizabeth Heyrick, *Immediate, Not Gradual Emancipation* (London, 1824). Among the most perceptive examinations of immediatism are David Brion Davis, "The Emergence of Immediatism in British and American Antislavery Thought," *Mississippi Valley Historical Review* 49:209–30 (September 1962), and *Slavery and Human Progress*, part 3; Aileen S. Kraditor,

Means and Ends in American Abolitionism: Garrison and His Critics on Strategy and Tactics, 1834–1850 (New York, N.Y., 1969); and Stewart, *Holy Warriors*, chapter 2. John L. Thomas, *The Liberator: William Lloyd Garrison* (Boston, Mass., 1963), and Bertram Wyatt-Brown, *Lewis Tappan and the Evangelical War against Slavery* (Cleveland, Ohio, 1969), offer biographies of two leading immediatists. Chapter 2 of Pease and Pease, *They Who Would Be Free*, and Quarles, *Black Abolitionists*, chapter 2, highlight the African American contribution to the early development of immediatism.

The principles that shaped antebellum reform thought are examined in John L. Thomas, "Romantic Reform in America, 1815–1865," *American Quarterly* 17:656–81 (Winter 1965). Ronald G. Walters, *American Reformers, 1815–1860* (New York, N.Y., 1978), surveys the reform issues, and David Brion Davis, ed., *Ante-Bellum Reform* (New York, N.Y., 1967), provides several penetrating essays on the subject.

Black moral reform has received little scholarly attention, with the notable exceptions of Frederick Cooper, "Elevating the Race: The Social Thought of Black Leaders, 1827–1850," *American Quarterly* 24:604–25 (December 1972), and Monroe Fordham, *Major Themes in Northern Black Religious Thought, 1800–1860* (Hicksville, N.Y., 1975), chapter 2. Chapter 6 of Winch, *Philadelphia's Black Elite*, focuses on the contributions of moral reformers in one African American community. For an interpretation of temperance in the context of black abolitionism, see Donald Yacovone, "The Transformation of the Black Temperance Movement, 1827–1854," *Journal of the Early Republic* 8:281–97 (Fall 1988). *Freedom's Journal* and the *Colored American* publicized moral reform activities and frequently editorialized on moral reform issues.

The best overview of racial prejudice and legal discrimination against free blacks in the North is Leon F. Litwack, *North of Slavery: The Negro in the Free States, 1790–1860* (Chicago, Ill., 1961). Harriet Wilson, *Our Nig*, ed. Henry Louis Gates, Jr. (New York, N.Y., 1983), provides a fictional portrait of racial bigotry in the North. Stanley Schultz, *Culture Factory: Boston Public Schools, 1789–1860* (New York, N.Y., 1973), touches on segregation and discrimination in public education.

BLACK ABOLITIONISTS AND THE
ANTISLAVERY MOVEMENT

The substantial contribution of African American lecturers to the anti-slavery movement is highlighted in Quarles, *Black Abolitionists*, and Pease and Pease, *They Who Would Be Free*. For a more focused study on fugitive slave lecturers, see Larry Gara, "The Professional Fugitive in the Abolition Movement," *Wisconsin Magazine of History* 26:196–204 (Spring 1965). Black lecturers in Britain receive extended treatment in R. J. M. Blackett, *Building an Antislavery Wall: Black Americans in the Atlantic Abolitionist Movement, 1830–1860* (Baton Rouge, La., 1983).

Among the important studies of the slave narrative, the most useful are William L. Andrews, *To Tell a Free Story: The First Century of Afro-American Autobiography, 1760–1865* (Urbana, Ill., 1986); Frances Smith Foster, *Witnessing Slavery: The Development of the Ante-Bellum Slave Narratives* (Westport, Conn., 1979); and Charles T. Davis and Henry Louis Gates, Jr., eds., *The Slave's Narrative* (Oxford, Eng., 1985).

Many slave narratives are readily accessible in modern editions, including Frederick Douglass's landmark autobiographies, *Narrative of the Life of Frederick Douglass* (Boston, Mass., 1845) and *My Bondage and My Freedom* (London, 1854). Blassingame, *Slave Testimony*, provides an excellent anthology of brief narratives. For a narrative that focuses on the ordeals of slave women, see Harriet A. Jacobs, *Incidents in the Life of a Slave Girl, Written by Herself*, ed. Jean Fagan Yellin (Cambridge, Mass., 1987). Among the best narratives with detailed accounts of slave escapes is William Craft and Ellen Craft, *Running a Thousand Miles for Freedom* (London, 1860). Interesting narratives by William Wells Brown, Henry Bibb, and Solomon Northup have been reprinted in Gilbert Osofsky, ed., *Puttin' on Ole Massa* (New York, N.Y., 1969).

The role of African American women in the antislavery movement is treated in Shirley J. Yee, *Black Women Abolitionists: A Study in Activism, 1828–1860* (Knoxville, Tenn., 1992); Sterling, *We Are Your Sisters*, chapters 8–13; and Jean Fagan Yellin, *Women and Sisters: The Antislavery Feminists in American Culture* (New Haven, Conn., 1989), chapters 2–4. Recent biographical studies include Marilyn Richardson, ed., *Maria W. Stewart, America's First Black Woman Political Writer: Essays and Speeches* (Bloomington, Ind., 1987).

The influence of abolitionism on the African American community and its institutions is an underlying theme in Winch, *Philadelphia's Black Elite*; Horton and Horton, *Black Bostonians*; and Freeman, "Free Negro in New York City."

Studies directed more specifically at abolitionism and the African American church include Emma Lapsansky, " 'Since They Got Those Separate Churches': Afro-Americans and Racism in Jacksonian Philadelphia," *American Quarterly* 32:54–78 (Spring 1980), and Carol V. R. George "Widening the Circle: The Black Church and the Abolitionist Crusade, 1830–1860," in *Antislavery Reconsidered: New Perspectives on the Abolitionists*, ed. Lewis Perry and Michael Fellman (Baton Rouge, La., 1979).

For the problem of racial prejudice in the antislavery movement, see Quarles, *Black Abolitionists*, chapter 3; Pease and Pease, *They Who Would Be Free*, chapter 5; and Carlton Mabee, *Black Freedom: The Nonviolent Abolitionists from 1830 through the Civil War* (London, 1970), chapter 7. Chapter 2 of Kraditor, *Means and Ends in American Abolitionism*, offers a thorough assessment of the antislavery schism.

BLACK INDEPENDENCE AND THE ANTISLAVERY MOVEMENT

The theme of independence is developed in Sterling Stuckey, *Slave Culture: Nationalist Theory and the Foundation of Black America* (New York, N.Y., 1987). For evidence of independence in the black convention movement of the 1840s, see Bell, *National Negro Conventions*. Schor, *Henry Highland Garnet*; Cheek, *John Mercer Langston*; and Ullman, *Martin R. Delany*, offer biographies of three leading exponents of African American independence.

For the character and function of the antebellum black press, the African American newspapers themselves offer the best source of information. I. Garland Penn, *The Afro-American Press in the Nineteenth Century* (Springfield, Mass., 1891), is an older but still useful reference. Bella Gross, *"Freedom's Journal* and the *Rights of All,"* *Journal of Negro History* 17:241–86 (July 1932), introduces the first African American newspaper. Penelope Bullock, *The Afro-American Periodical Press, 1838–1909* (Baton Rouge, La., 1981), treats the black literary and religious journals.

Much of the local black abolitionist activity centered around vigilance committees and the underground railroad. Black response to the threat of kidnapping is examined in Julie Winch, "Philadelphia and the Other Underground Railroad," *Pennsylvania Magazine of History and Biography* 61:3–25 (January 1987). Chapter 7 of Quarles, *Black Abolitionists*, deals specifically with the African American contribution to the underground railroad, as does Katherine

Dupré Lumpkin, "The General Plan Was Freedom: A Negro Secret Order on the Underground Railroad," *Phylon* 28:63–76 (Spring 1967). William Still, *Underground Railroad* (Philadelphia, Pa., 1872; reprint, Chicago, Ill., 1970), provides an important source of fugitive slave interviews collected by a leading black abolitionist. Charles Blockson, ed., *The Underground Railroad* (New York, N.Y., 1987), presents an interesting anthology on the network created to assist escaping slaves, and Larry Gara "demythologizes" the underground railroad in *The Liberty Line: The Legend of the Underground Railroad* (Lexington, Ky., 1961).

For the emergence of antislavery politics, see Gerald Sorin, *Abolitionism: A New Perspective* (New York, N.Y., 1972), chapters 5 and 6. Richard H. Sewell, *Ballots for Freedom: Antislavery Politics in the United States, 1837–1860* (New York, N.Y., 1976), examines the Liberty and Free Soil parties. The black suffrage campaign in New York is treated in Phyllis F. Field, *The Politics of Race: The Struggle for Black Suffrage in the Civil War Era* (Ithaca, N.Y., 1982). Chapter 8 in Quarles, *Black Abolitionists*, and Pease and Pease, *They Who Would Be Free*, chapter 9, discuss African American participation in political antislavery.

Northern blacks challenged discrimination and segregation in the 1840s. Chapter 6 of Horton and Horton, *Black Bostonians*, recounts the local campaign against segregated schools. Leonard W. Levy and Harlan B. Phillips, "The *Roberts* Case: Source of the 'Separate but Equal' Doctrine," *American Historical Review* 56:510–18 (April 1951), focuses on the related court case, *Roberts v. Boston*. Specific discrimination issues are the subject of Louis Ruchames, "Race, Marriage, and Abolition in Massachusetts," *Journal of Negro History* 40:250–73 (July 1955), and "Jim Crow Railroads in Massachusetts," *American Quarterly* 8:61–75 (Spring 1956), and Ronald Formisano, "Edge of Caste: Colored Suffrage in Michigan, 1827–1861," *Michigan History* 56:19–40 (Spring 1972). Chapters 7–11 of Mabee, *Black Freedom*, offer a more general discussion. For the problem of violence as an antislavery tactic, see Dick, *Black Protest*, chapter 4, and Pease and Pease, *They Who Would Be Free*, chapter 11.

BLACK ABOLITIONISTS, THE SLAVE POWER,
AND THE FEDERAL GOVERNMENT

The national struggle over slavery in the 1850s is the subject of David M. Potter, *The Impending Crisis, 1848–1861* (New York, N.Y., 1976). For an overview of black abolitionism during this decade, see Pease and Pease, *They*

Who Would Be Free, chapters 11 and 12, and commentary by black abolitionists in *Frederick Douglass' Paper*. The proslavery policies of the federal government convinced many northerners of the existence of a slave power conspiracy, a subject treated in Davis, *Slave Power Conspiracy*.

Passage of the Fugitive Slave Law of 1850 placed all blacks at risk. Stanley W. Campbell, *The Slave Catchers: Enforcement of the Fugitive Slave Law, 1850–1860* (Chapel Hill, N.C., 1968), surveys the law and its enforcement. Chapter 8 of Horton and Horton, *Black Bostonians*, discusses resistance to the law in one important community. For specific incidents of violent opposition to the law, see Thomas P. Slaughter, *Bloody Dawn: The Christiana Riot and Racial Violence in the Antebellum North* (New York, N.Y., 1991); Jane H. Pease and William H. Pease, *The Fugitive Slave Law and Anthony Burns: A Problem in Law Enforcement* (New York, N.Y., 1975); and Nat Brandt, *The Town That Started the Civil War* (Syracuse, N.Y., 1990), a history of the Oberlin-Wellington rescue and its impact.

The crisis of the 1850s prompted thousands of blacks to abandon their American homeland for Canada, West Africa, Central America, and the Caribbean. The best study of the black emigration movement is Floyd J. Miller, *The Search for a Black Nationality: Black Emigration and Colonization, 1787–1863* (Urbana, Ill., 1975). Martin Delany, the major theorist of the movement, presents his rationale in *Condition, Elevation, Emigration and Destiny of the Colored People*. The *Pine and Palm* served as the organ for the Haitian immigration movement. Most black emigrants went to Canada, and two black Canadian newspapers chronicled their experiences: *Voice of the Fugitive* and *Provincial Freeman*. Robin W. Winks, *The Blacks in Canada: A History* (New Haven, Conn., 1971); William H. Pease and Jane H. Pease, *Black Utopia: Negro Communal Experiments in America* (Madison, Wis., 1963); Jason Silverman, *Unwelcome Guests: Canada West's Response to American Fugitive Slaves, 1800–1865* (Millwood, N.Y., 1985); and Michael F. Hembree, "The Question of 'Begging': Fugitive Slave Relief in Canada, 1830–1865," *Civil War History* 37:314–27 (December 1991), treat major themes of black life in Canada. Benjamin Drew, *A North-Side View of Slavery* (Boston, Mass., 1856; reprint, New York, N.Y., 1968), contains revealing interviews with fugitive slaves who fled to Canada.

The story of John Brown and the Harpers Ferry raid is told in Stephen B. Oates, *To Purge This Land with Blood: A Biography of John Brown* (New York, N.Y., 1970). Brown's white conspirators are the subject of Jeffery Rossbach, *Ambivalent Conspirators: John Brown, the Secret Six, and a Theory of Slave Violence* (Philadelphia, Pa., 1982). Benjamin Quarles, *Allies for Freedom: Blacks and John Brown* (New York, N.Y., 1974), examines African American support for Brown. Quarles has compiled the essential documents on this relationship in *Blacks on John Brown* (Urbana, Ill., 1972).

BLACKS AND THE CIVIL WAR

For an overview of African American life and thought during the Civil War, see Quarles, *Negro in the Civil War*, and the chronicle provided by the *Weekly Anglo-African*. From the time the first shot was fired on Fort Sumter, blacks debated their involvement in the conflict. A sampling of these discussions, as well as others tracing the course of African American opinion throughout the war, appears in James M. McPherson, *The Negro's Civil War* (New York, N.Y., 1965). The full text of the debate between Alfred M. Green and "R. H. V." is in Green, *Letters and Discussions on the Formation of Colored Regiments* (Philadelphia, Pa., 1862; reprint, Wilmington, Del., 1970). David W. Blight, *Frederick Douglass' Civil War: Keeping Faith in Jubilee* (Baton Rouge, La., 1989), examines the meaning of the war for a leading black abolitionist.

Abraham Lincoln's Emancipation Proclamation made the war a struggle for African American freedom. John Hope Franklin, *The Emancipation Proclamation* (New York, N.Y., 1965), is the best source on the making and meaning of that decree. The transition to freedom in two key southern states is traced in C. Peter Ripley, *Slaves and Freedmen in Civil War Louisiana* (Baton Rouge, La., 1976), and Clarence L. Mohr, *On the Threshold of Freedom: Masters and Slaves in Civil War Georgia* (Athens, Ga., 1986). Benjamin Quarles, *Lincoln and the Negro* (New York, N.Y., 1962), sketches the shifting relationship between blacks and Lincoln.

Once blacks were permitted to fight for the Union, they enlisted in large numbers. The story of these black troops is told in Dudley Taylor Cornish, *The Sable Arm: Negro Troops in the Union Army, 1861–1865* (New York, N.Y., 1966). Joseph Glaathaar, *Forged in Battle: The Civil War Alliance of Black Soldiers and White Officers* (New York, N.Y., 1990), analyzes the racial interaction in black Union regiments. Luis F. Emilio, *History of the Fifty-Fourth Regiment of Massachusetts Volunteer Infantry, 1863–1865*, 2d ed. (Boston, Mass., 1894; reprint, New York, N.Y., 1968), is a history of the most famous African American unit written by one of its officers.

Hundreds of black abolitionists went South as teachers, missionaries, and relief workers among the freedmen during and after the war. Joe M. Richardson,

Christian Reconstruction: The American Missionary Association and Southern Blacks, 1861–1890 (Athens, Ga., 1986), and Clarence E. Walker, *A Rock in a Weary Land: The African Methodist Episcopal Church during the Civil War and Reconstruction* (Baton Rouge, La., 1982), recount aspects of this experience. African American women who worked with the freedmen tell their story in Sterling, *We Are Your Sisters*, chapters 15–16, and Brenda Stevenson, ed., *The Journals of Charlotte Forten Grimké* (New York, N.Y., 1988). Elizabeth Keckley, *Behind the Scenes: Thirty Years a Slave and Four Years in the White House* (New York, N.Y., 1868; reprint, New York, N.Y., 1968), offers an insider's account of contraband relief efforts.

Black abolitionists played a central role in the drama of Reconstruction, a fact first recognized by W. E. B. Du Bois in his monumental volume, *Black Reconstruction in America* (New York, N.Y., 1935). The best and most comprehensive account is Eric Foner, *Reconstruction: America's Unfinished Revolution, 1863–1877* (New York, N.Y., 1988). The promise and failure of federal efforts for the freedmen is the subject of Carl T. Osthaus, *Freedmen, Philanthropy, and Fraud: A History of the Freedman's Savings Bank* (Urbana, Ill., 1976), and William S. McFeely, *Yankee Stepfather: General O. O. Howard and the Freedmen* (New York, N.Y., 1968), which provides the best history of the Freedmen's Bureau. Howard N. Rabinowitz, ed., *Southern Black Leaders of the Reconstruction Era* (Urbana, Ill., 1982); Thomas Holt, *Black over White: Negro Political Leadership in South Carolina during Reconstruction* (Urbana, Ill., 1977); and Loren Schweninger, *James T. Rapier and Reconstruction* (Chicago, Ill., 1978), explore African American politics at the national, state, and local levels during the period.

INDEX

Aaron, Samuel: Liberty party and, 145
Abolitionism: black churches and, 10, 26;
    black community and, 107–13; free
    blacks affected by, 106–7; gradual
    emancipationists criticize, 73; C. B.
    Ray discusses, 106–7; Republican
    party and, 16. *See also* Abolitionists;
    Antislavery movement; Black aboli-
    tionism; Black abolitionists; Garrison-
    ian abolitionists; Gradual abolition;
    Immediate emancipation
Abolitionists: black criticism of, 11–12,
    121–23; black women as, 12–13,
    60–61, 89–93, 96–105, 112–13, 203–4,
    244–45; Civil War and, 22; coloniza-
    tion supported by, 2; S. E. Cornish dis-
    cusses, 114–16; emancipation and,
    252–55; gradual abolition abandoned
    by, 4–5; R. Hamilton discusses,
    252–55; hiring practices of, 118–20;
    immediate emancipation accepted by,
    5; J. W. Lewis discusses, 121–23; S. A.
    Myers discusses, 118–20; philosophy
    of, 65; prejudice among, 11–12, 114–
    20; B. F. Roberts discusses, 131–32;
    S. R. Ward discusses, 116–17. *See also*
    Abolitionism; Antislavery movement;
    Black abolitionism; Black abolitionists;
    Garrisonian abolitionists; Gradual abo-
    lition; Immediate emancipation
Adams, John Quincy, 171, 263
"Address to the Colored People of the
    United States" (F. Douglass), 127–28
"Address to the Slaves of the United
    States of America" (H. H. Garnet), 17,
    165–69
Adelphi Hall (Philadelphia, Pa.), 1
Africa, 32, 42, 47; black immigration to,
    20; missions in, 2, 108–9

African Clarkson Association, 152
"Africano" (pseud.): on election of 1864,
    232–33; J. C. Frémont supported
    by, 232–33; letter by, 232–33; on
    A. Lincoln, 232–33
Africa's Offering (E. Blyden), 254
Akron, Ohio: women's rights convention
    in, 101
Allen, Emily, 105
Allen, William G., 194, 263
Altee, Edwin P., 100
Amalgamation, 73
American and Foreign Anti-Slavery
    Society (AFASS), 11, 263
American Anti-Slavery Society (AASS),
    263; abolitionists join, 4; annual meet-
    ing of (1857), 175; black involvement
    in, 11; colonization rejected by, 1; Dec-
    laration of Sentiments of, 1; founding
    of, 1, 4; R. Purvis addresses, 175–78;
    C. B. Ray discusses, 106–7; C. L.
    Remond as lecturer for, 8, 71; schism
    in, 11
American churches: colonization sup-
    ported by, 2; prejudice in, 58–59; seg-
    regation in, 117; T. S. Wright criticizes,
    58–59
American Colonization Society (ACS),
    50, 192, 263; black emigration encour-
    aged by, 33; black opposition to, 1–4,
    25, 29–37; Board of Managers of, 36;
    founding of, 2, 29; Liberian colony
    of, 29; racism encouraged by, 33; sup-
    port for, 2–3. *See also* Colonization;
    Liberia
American Home Missionary Society
    (AHMS), 263; antislavery and,
    110–12; black abolitionists and,
    110–12; H. H. Garnet and, 111–12;

U.S. Supreme Court: black citizenship
denied by, 19; personal liberty laws
invalidated by, 17. See also *Dred Scott
v. Sanford*

Van Buren, Martin, 229, 277
Vandyne, Robert H., 211
Vashon, George B.: *Colored American*
supported by, 108; letter by, 108; Pittsburgh Juvenile Anti-Slavery Society
and, 107–8
Vermont: Free Soil party in, 145
Vesey, Denmark, 168, 199, 210, 277
Vigilance committees, 277; antislavery
and, 106; black abolitionists and, 12,
15, 135–40; creation of, 15, 135; fugitive slaves and, 15, 135–40; in New
York City, 15, 135–37; D. Ruggles
discusses, 135–37. See also Fugitive
slaves; Underground railroad
Violence: as antislavery tactic, 17; black
abolitionists and, 17, 162–69, 179–84;
F. Douglass defends, 184; Fugitive
Slave Law provokes, 179–84; H. H.
Garnet defends, 165–69; A. W. Hanson
discusses, 162–65; G. Lawrence, Jr.
defends, 210; W. J. Watkins defends,
182–83. See also Brown, John; Harpers
Ferry raid; Racial violence; Slave
violence
Virginia: slave escapes from, 15

Walker, David, 1, 277; black abolitionists
and, 38–42; colonization rejected by,
2–3, 40–42; essay by, 42–46; on free
black conditions, 38–48; on kidnapping, 41; slave violence advocated by,
44–46; on slavery, 41–42; speech by,
38–42
War of 1812: blacks in, 242, 253
Ward, Samuel Ringgold, 277; abolitionism and, 110–11; abolitionists criticized by, 10–11, 116–17; AHMS and,
110–12; on antislavery, 10; antislavery

activities of, 9, 13, 69; on antislavery in
churches, 110; black suffrage and,
143–46; *Impartial Citizen* published
by, 112; letters by, 110–11, 116–17,
143–46; on Liberty party, 143–46;
politics and, 16; on racial prejudice,
116–17; segregation in churches criticized by, 116
Washington, George, 183
Washington, Madison, 168
Washington, D.C.: fugitive slave rescues
in, 15; slave trade in, 76; underground
railroad in, 15
Washington County, Me., 71
Waterloo (battle of), 225
Watkins, William J., 121, 277; activities
of, 148; anticolonization of, 3; on black
independence, 2, 4; on A. Burns rescue,
182–83; on Democratic party, 149; editorial by, 182–83; lecture tours of, 150;
letter by, 148–51; on Republican party,
148–51; slavery described by, 182–83;
violence defended by, 182–83
Webster, Daniel, 2
Weekly Anglo-African (New York, N.Y.),
129, 211, 277–78; black participation in
Civil War discussed in, 22–23; correspondence to, 211–15, 232–33, 235–43,
246–48, 256–59, 261–62; editorials in,
208–10, 225–27, 248–55; on Emancipation Proclamation, 25
Wellington, Duke of, 22
West Africa: black immigration to, 185
West Indies: black immigration to, 191,
197; slavery in, 199
Western Pennsylvania Antislavery Society, 110
Whig party, 278; black abolitionists and,
16, 141
Whipper, William, 278; H. H. Garnet
criticizes, 123–26
White, Jacob C., Jr.: essay by, 55–56;
temperance advocated by, 55–56
Whittier, Elizabeth H.: letter to, 96–101